D0206316

Between Marriage and the Market

Comparative Studies on Muslim Societies
General Editor, Barbara D. Metcalf

Between Marriage and the Market

Intimate Politics and Survival in Cairo

Homa Hoodfar

UNIVERSITY OF CALIFORNIA PRESS

Berkeley / Los Angeles / London

A portion of this book is adapted in part from "Household Budget-ing and Financial Management in a Lower-Income Cairo Neighbor-hood," by Homa Hoodfar, in *A Home Divided: Women and Income in the Third World,* edited by Daisy Dwyer and Judith Bruce, repro-duced with the permission of the publishers, Stanford University Press. © 1988 by the Board of Trustees of the Leland Stanford Uni-versity.

University of California Press
Berkeley and Los Angeles, California

University of California Press
London, England

Copyright © 1997 by The Regents of the University of California

Library of Congress Cataloging-in-Publication Data

Hoodfar, Homa.
    Between marriage and the market : intimate politics and survival in Cairo / Homa Hoodfar.
        p.   cm. — (Comparative studies on Muslim societies ; 24)
    Includes bibliographical references and index.
    ISBN 978-0-520-20825-4 (pbk. : alk. paper)
        1. Households—Economic aspects—Egypt—Cairo Region.
2. Home economics—Egypt—Cairo Region.   3. Poor—Egypt—Cairo Region.   4. Sex role—Egypt—Cairo Region.   I. Title.
II. Series.
HC830.Z7C343   1997
339.2'2—dc21   96-37296
                                                                                CIP

Printed in the United States of America
        4 5 6 7 8 9

The paper used in this publication meets the minimum requirements of American National Standard for Information Sciences—Permanence of Paper for Printed Library Materials,
ANSI Z39.48-1984 ⊖

To my mother, who taught me to appreciate the resourcefulness of women. To Leila el-Kilani, who made me a better anthropologist and a better person by teaching me the value of the unspoken word. To Frederic Shorter, extraordinary mentor of so many students and scholars of the Middle East. And above all, to the women of the neighborhoods, who so generously shared their thoughts and daily lives with me.

Contents

Acknowledgments

In January 1983, I arrived in Cairo, lonely, anxious, and poor. By 1984, my friends and neighbors, particularly in the neighborhoods, had helped me to regard Egypt as home, and even twelve years later I often find myself homesick and longing for Cairo. There, I experienced more kindness and generosity than I could possibly acknowledge. My friends' and neighbors' names have been changed in this account for the usual reasons of anthropological anonymity, but I wish to express to them my deepest gratitude and appreciation, for adopting me as their daughter and sister and for generously sharing with me their joy and sorrow, their thoughts and criticisms, and their food and homes. I have learned from them not just about their lives but about myself and my culture, as well as the British university culture in which I was being trained as an anthropologist. I would like them to know that despite the difficult political and financial situation, the early years of my fieldwork remain the happiest and most meaningful time of my life.

This study would not have materialized without the support of several scholars, advisers, friends, and family during the years of the research. Special thanks and gratitude go to Professor Paul Stirling, whose door was always open for advice and encouragement. Dr. Barbara Ibrahim, whom I met for the first time shortly after my arrival in Cairo, has been instrumental through her advice, encouragement, and continuous support in the success of my research. Dr. Cynthia Myntti's advice, encouragement, and sharing, among other things, of her field experiences gave me confidence at just those hard moments when it was most needed. Dr. Cynthia Nelson, my adviser while in Cairo, and Dr. Nanneke Redclift, my supervisor at Kent University, were a source of encouragement and intellectual challenge. Professor Teodor Shanin, despite his apprehension about the focus of my research, remained a constant source of intellectual support and encouragement even after I left Manchester University. I owe much to Dr. Richard Lobban, who provided critical structural and methodological advice at the outset of the research in Cairo and has continued to provide encouragement and intellectual support.

I am among the lucky students who were adopted by Dr. Frederic Shorter in Cairo. He patiently and generously lent me his ear and guided me to see that the dividing line between biology and economy is but an artificial boundary and one not always useful in understanding the complexity of everyday life. His dedication to his adopted students and his generous and gracious support for their research are truly remarkable. I am also indebted to Professor Peter Worsley not only for encouraging me at the planning stage to take up my research on women and households but also for his insightful comments on the finished thesis, as my external examiner. Professor B. Baviskar, who was visiting McGill University during the year I taught there, became a source of support and inspiration. I am also grateful to Dr. David Howes who read the entire manuscript and offered many insightful comments. Christine Eickelman, Douglas Abrams Arava, my editor at the University of California Press, and two anonymous reviewers have been most encouraging and have made many constructive comments that have improved the manuscript. I would also like to thank Sheila Berg at the University of California Press, whose copyediting was sensitive and thorough.

Throughout this research I have benefited greatly from the advice, comments, and encouragement of Arlene MacLeod, Mona Anis, Sima Motamen, Rosemary Kent, Steve Jordan, Fatma Khafagy, Hania Sholkamy, Samira el-Kilani, Mahmoud and Shohrat al-Alem, and Karen Glasgow. Diane Singerman, whom I met in Cairo, not only has been a constant source of intellectual and emotional support but also over the years has shared patiently many moments of my frustration. Carolyn Makinson, with her unending energy, optimism, intellectual inquisitiveness, and logical approach to problem solving, has become a role model for me, and I am grateful to her for her generous intellectual support and constant encouragement.

Mark Grimshaw read much of the early drafts and patiently took time to edit them; he was a source of much-needed encouragement in the austere city of Canterbury. I am also thankful to Professor John Davis for organizing the pasta seminars that brightened socially and intellectually the lonely life of many graduate students in Canterbury. Patricia Kelly has shared with me her insightful knowledge of the Muslim discourse on many topics and has read and edited several drafts of this book. She has been an encouraging force behind the completion of the manuscript. Heather Howard and Marlene Caplan read and edited and provided helpful comments to improve the manuscript. Jody Staveley patiently printed and reprinted each chapter several times, and with such goodwill. I am also indebted to my husband, who found himself married not only to me but to the "Cairo project" as well, and sometimes he objected to the co-wife he did not choose. I am also indebted to him for reading and editing part of this work and changing it from my Persian-English to English and for crossing out hundreds of "a"s and "the"s where they were not needed and inserting them where they were missing.

I am deeply indebted to Leyla el-Kilani who opened her home and her heart to me soon after my arrival in Cairo and has treated me as her daughter ever since. My parents and brothers, at times despite their early apprehensions about anthropology, have been a constant source of encouragement. I shall be forever indebted to my sister, Katayoon Hoodfar. We were two "foreign" students in the United Kingdom, hoping to complete our graduate studies and return home, when we found ourselves in the middle of a political upheaval and revolution, followed by the senseless Iran-Iraq war, and the at least initially worsening situation for women in Iran. Judging our disciplines unessential, the Iranian government canceled our parents' permit to send us funds shortly after the revolution. As Iranians we were disqualified from applying to most sources of scholarship and grants, and it became evident that we could not both afford to pay the high cost of education for "foreign" students in the U.K. However, my sister generously gave up her own plans for doing her doctorate, took a job teaching in the U.K., and supported me until I finished my studies. Her generosity presented a reversal of roles, since according to our tradition and cultural norms, it should have been me, the elder sister, who provided support for her. This of course made me even more sensitive to the value of familial support, interdependence, and the resources of poverty.

I would also like to express my gratitude to the Department of Sociology and Anthropology of the American University in Cairo where

I was affiliated as a research fellow during the first year of my field research. A small expense allowance in summer 1983 from the Ford Foundation was probably the most significant grant I have ever received. However modest, it covered my field expenses, and without it I could not have renewed my visa and would have had to leave without completing the research. The Population Council in Cairo provided me with research funds in 1985 and enabled a return to Cairo to look at the impact of international migration on families and the role of women left behind. Later, the Population Council in New York awarded me a fellowship that enabled me to complete my doctoral dissertation. The Social Science and Humanities Council of Canada provided me with a three-year grant (1992–1994) to return to Cairo on several occasions to carry out follow-up studies. I am also indebted to my colleagues, especially Dr. Susan Hoecker-Drysdale who accommodated my teaching schedule to enable me to complete the fieldwork and finish the manuscript.

Glossary

Arabic singular and plural noun forms are separated by a comma.

afrangi European-style, Westernized
agnabi foreign (non-Arab), usually refers to white Europeans or North
    Americans
babbur portable kerosene stove
baladi adj. relating to traditional urban practices
dallala, dallalat woman petty trader
daya midwife
fallahi adj. relating to the village or villagers
fallahin villagers, peasants
fatiha the first chapter of the Qur'an
fino refined white rolls
ful a popular dish made with beans
gallabiya a loose, long shirtlike garment, the common dress of traditional
    Egyptians
gamᶜiya, gamᶜiyat literally "association"; often refers to a savings club or ro-
    tating credit association to which each member contributes a fixed sum at
    regular intervals and from which each member will receive the collected
    kitty once during the term of the club; also a cooperative store that sells
    subsidized goods
ghalbanin defeated or hopeless
girgir watercress
hadith a saying traced back to the Prophet Muhammad
hakim a traditionally trained health practitioner
halal legitimate and permitted according to Islamic laws
hamdullah "Thanks to God," a frequently used expression indicating grati-
    tude or resignation

haya sha͑biya popular (traditional) neighborhood
infitah Egypt's liberal economic policy introduced in 1974
khal maternal uncle
khala maternal aunt
khalti my mother's sister
kushari a dish of cooked rice and lentils
magmu͑a study group, private lessons given to a group of students
mahr an amount of cash or tangible property pledged to be paid by the
    groom to the bride
malik king
muakhkhara second and last payment of bride wealth
muhaggaba, muhaggabat a woman who wears an Islamic scarf
mulukhiya a popular dish made with mallow, a green leafy vegetable
muqaddama first payment of mahr
muwazzafa, muwazzafat female government employee, usually white-collar
naqqash painter
nasib destiny; fate; literally "share" or "portion"
sa͑idi Upper Egyptian, from the Upper Nile River area in the south of
    Egypt
sha͑b the people, the nation
sha͑bi grassroots or popular
shari͑a Islamic law based on the Qur'an, sayings of the Prophet, consensus
    of the community, and local custom
sitt al-bayt, sittat al-bayt homemaker; literally "lady of the house"
suq market
ta͑a obedience
tahur act of purification; circumcision
tam͑iya a popular dish made with beans
tamsiliya soap opera
tamwin grocery store
ulad kalb dog's children, an insult
͑ulama religious scholars
wagib duty
yawm al-ghasil wash day
zagheh-neshin shantytown

Introduction

My Early Lessons in Household Economy

The fieldwork for this book started in 1983, and my last visit to Cairo was in February 1994. But my interest in the cultural contexts of household economy, particularly women's roles in it, goes back to my childhood in Tehran, Iran, where I was born and raised. Despite my mother's young age, her social class and access to information meant that, in the tradition of her hometown of Hamedan, she was the matriarch of a large network of women who frequently sought her help and advice on financial and domestic problems. I was eight years old when Aunt Ashraf, a relative whom I especially liked, came to visit my mother to discuss her decision to quit her job in a tobacco company in Tehran. My siblings and I were also in the room, although since we were children, we were ignored apart from the occasional call to fetch tea and water. So I overheard the conversation of the women as I usually did, but this time the subject of their discussion had such an impact on me that I can still recall it in minute detail.

Aunt Ashraf's husband was a second cousin of my mother and at least eighteen years older than my aunt. In the rapid social and economic changes occurring in Iran in the 1950s, he had lost both his money and his social position. He spent most of his meager income on himself, leaving the family destitute and living in a single room where they shared washroom facilities with several other households. After her second child was born, Aunt Ashraf tired of arguments over money and decided to look for a job. Through friends and family she managed to find one at a large tobacco company. I heard her say many times that if she had only had the chance to finish primary school, she would have found a much less demanding and better-paying job. Invariably, after complaining, she would thank God so as not to be ungrateful for all she did have—her health, her two beautiful daughters, and a husband who, though not ideal, was not as bad as many others. He never physically abused her and was kind to their daughters. Aunt Ashraf's mother, widowed very young, helped with child care. However, a few months before this visit to my house, Aunt Ashraf's mother had died, leaving her without any support.

Aunt Ashraf had decided to leave her job, which was a difficult decision since it meant a loss of income and the security of her old-age pension. She valued the pension greatly, as widowhood seemed inevitable and she did not have a son to rely on. She explained to my mother that with her daughters getting older, she could not leave them at home unsupervised, particularly since several of the neighbors had grown sons. Even if the situation was not actually threatening their virtue, it might damage their reputations and reduce their chances of finding good husbands. My mother, looking at me and my sister, commented, "When you have daughters you have to think of so many things. It would have been different if they were sons." I was old enough to know that daughters have to uphold their own and their family's honor and reputation, but the difference between me and my brothers was still not clear to me.

If Aunt Ashraf quit her job and stayed home, by shopping wisely and doing even more penny-pinching, she might be able to reduce her family's expenses. Moreover, if she did not go to work she could do much more knitting, something she did in the evenings to supplement her income. A few months after her resignation, the company would give her all her pension money, which she thought would be 500 tumans (then $120). With this, she could buy a sewing machine and set up a small carpet-weaving frame. She could sew for friends and neighbors, and when she did not have any sewing or knitting, she could weave carpets, an art most girls of her traditional background learned as children. She also explained to my mother that this kind of work would enable her to hide her earnings from her husband and she might be able to persuade him to give her more money, particularly since, like all men, he was very concerned with his honor in the neighborhood and liked the idea of her staying home to supervise their daughters. If things worked out well maybe she could even save some money for her daughters' trousseaus and, perhaps within a few years, the girls would find suitors and marry. After a couple of hours of visiting and chatting, assessing her various options, she and my mother came to the conclusion that, given the situation, her plan was a good one. However, my mother advised her to wait a little before she submitted her resignation since there might be some aspects they had not considered. "You can always resign but you cannot get a job every day, particularly not one with an old-age pension," my mother advised before Aunt Ashraf left our house.

In the end, she did resign, her plan worked well, and her daughters were married off. Then her husband got sick and was unable to work. For years, they had to rely on her meager income. Finally, when he died, she was frail and no longer able to work long hours. Though her daughters offered to have her move in with them, Aunt Ashraf refused as they were both housewives and did not have cash incomes of their own, and she feared it might cause friction between her daughters and their husbands. Traditionally sons are expected to look after their parents, especially their elderly mothers, but she had no sons. Friends and relatives continued to give her work, enabling her to survive, but she always regretted having given up the security of her old-age pension, which would have allowed her to live a dignified life in her old age.

In my early teenage years, under social pressure from a society obsessed with modernization, we moved from our old-style home in an old quarter to a modern suburban middle-class neighborhood of Tehran. Soon I discovered a sizable shantytown (*zagheh-neshin*) in the immediate vicinity of our new residence. There I became familiar with many families whose lives were ridden with the problems of poverty.[1] I became preoccupied with the coping strategies they adopted to improve their lives. When I finally went to do research in Cairo, it was to

1. Many shantytowners were employed in our neighborhood and others nearby, so I became acquainted with some of the women who worked in our street. My window opened directly onto the shantytown, and I had ample chance to observe daily life there. I admired the resourceful and clever ways some of them used to improve their lives, although the adults of our middle-class neighborhood considered that these women were lazy and not so ambitious. Moreover, I was fascinated by the strong, well-organized resistance that women and children demonstrated when the government, pressured by our neighborhood association, tried to rehouse them in a different part of Tehran. The battle lasted three years, and finally they were rehoused. For more details and a comparative approach to my fieldwork in Iran and Cairo, see Hoodfar 1994.

investigate the ways in which the economic and cultural constraints of the wider society shape the coping and survival strategies of the poor, and how their choices may, in turn, affect the socioeconomic structure of the wider society.

Other aspects of my own experience also helped determine my research questions, particularly regarding the nonegalitarian nature of the household and family and the definitions of economic activity. My family was comfortably middle class, and we were proud of our cultural heritage and traditions. My mother was a homemaker of traditional upbringing who despite little formal education was very capable, realistic, and down to earth. My father, in contrast, was highly educated, a poet, a nationalist with a strong secularist streak, and a thoroughly "modern" man. Friends and relatives had much respect for him and considered him quite enlightened for his time. They often sought his advice on various matters, particularly about their children's education. My parents gave us a happy and harmonious home, and my mother's marriage was considered by herself and most of our relatives to be successful. Nonetheless, on many occasions I heard my father say that it was hard for him to single-handedly support a family of seven, that if families wanted to improve themselves and educate their children well, the women would have to work too.

My father usually went to work at 6:30 in the morning and came home around 2:00 in the afternoon. My mother would serve his lunch and tea, and he would take a nap. Then his friends would come to discuss politics, read poetry, and play backgammon. If they did not come, my mother felt obliged to have a game of backgammon with him. She got up an hour before he did, worked all day, rarely had a chance for a short rest in the afternoon, and went to sleep long after the rest of us. But rarely did my father or others credit her for her long hours of work running our household; only my father's income, which my mother managed, was considered an essential contribution. Traditionally, as the eldest daughter I was designated to help my mother, and soon I learned the real value of her contribution to our domestic economy. By the time I was sixteen, believing nobody should take my hard work for granted, I had decided I would not be a housewife, a decision my mother (and father) wholeheartedly supported.[2] This decision, however, did not ex-

---

2. This was not because I considered housework degrading. On the contrary, I still gain prestige in the eyes of my husband, friends, and colleagues from having the ability to single-handedly organize big dinner parties and perform domestic work. I am grateful

empt me from helping my mother around the house, and this training made me very aware of the role of nonmonetary as well as cash contributions to the well-being of the family.[3]

As a young and somewhat politicized teenager, I was convinced that women were mostly to blame for their lot. I believed all it took to change the world was conviction and determination, and I often repeated an old Iranian proverb that says if people refuse to be oppressed, there can exist no oppressors.[4] My mother's attempts to make me understand the structural and cultural constraints of our life failed miserably. It was not until some years after my short-lived and disastrous first marriage at the age of twenty-three that I finally understood what my mother had been trying to teach me.[5] Under great disapproval from my father and kin, I filed for divorce and only then learned that the law treated me differently from my husband. Though we were supposed to be equal, society expected me to be forgiving and readily offer sacrifices of all kinds to save my marriage. My husband, however, was to be constantly forgiven for his mistakes and treated like a king, especially since he was highly educated and held a respected social position.

Thus the constraints of society and law brought me to understand my mother's lesson and to appreciate how difficult it is to challenge the world from a powerless and subjugated position. I understood why so many women try to manipulate their circumstances from *within* a culture and a legal system, and why breaking all the cultural norms can be very painful and not necessarily advantageous. Running and waiting,

---

to my mother for help in having made me learn these tasks when I was young. Moreover, as a foreign student in England, I was eligible for few scholarships and I had to manage on an extremely tight budget that represented all of my life savings and my parents' contributions. My domestic skills, especially my limited sewing, proved to be a great asset and also won me many friends when I went to the field in Egypt.

3. This made me very critical of the formal definition of economic activity and the calculation of gross national product when I was training in economics and business studies in the early 1970s in the United Kingdom and later in Iran. Appropriately, this definition has finally been broadened to include at least some of the subsistence activities of the informal economy. Eventually, after many ups and downs, I trained in development studies and social anthropology—disciplines that recognize alternative ways and approaches, albeit in a limited manner.

4. Now I view this saying, which at the time appeared to me to be a call to resistance, as an unwarranted statement that blames victims for their sufferings.

5. I had married in England, at the recommendation of my father who gained some comfort from the idea that I was no longer quite alone. I had broken all the family rules by traveling by myself to England, where I had no friends and initially did not know the language. It was the first time a young woman in my kin group had traveled on her own.

month after month, in the corridors of the family court in prerevolutionary Iran—when women supposedly enjoyed many more rights than currently—talking and exchanging stories with other women and men, I also learned that men as well as women can be victims and losers. I realized that the key to social change lies beyond legislation. And so, when I began my fieldwork I carried with me, besides my economic and anthropological training, the life experiences of a Middle Eastern woman put to many tests. This I believe has helped me relate to my research community and understand their ambitions and life choices.

Theoretical Framework

Massive peasant migration to urban centers and suburbs of the developing world and the resultant growth of shantytowns, informal housing areas, and even the use of tombs as shelters for the living (Watson 1992) have attracted political and scholarly attention (Moser 1981; Lobo 1982; ILO 1989; Gilbert 1992; Angotti 1993).[6] Interest in the lives of the poor and the causes of poverty during times of rapid social change is not new (Lewis 1959; Mayhew 1965; Perlman 1976; Lloyd 1979). However, attention to gender-specific forms of poverty and the differential impact of development processes on women and men is a recent dimension (Buvinic, Lycette, and McGreevey 1983; Youssef and Hetler 1983; Sharma 1986; World Bank 1991; Beneria and Feldman 1992; Mencher and Okongwu 1993; Thorbek 1994). As a graduate student preparing to do field research on coping strategies of the poor and the changing role of women in household economies (which was how I phrased my research topic at the time), I plowed my way through a considerable body of literature.

One of the early theories that attempted to explain the increasingly visible inequalities in the distribution of wealth was the culture of poverty approach, which maintained that a set of cultural traits and practices among the poor was perpetuated across generations through socialization, making it impossible to break from the "cycle of poverty" (Lewis 1959, 1961, 1966). In effect, since the perpetuation of poverty

6. I use the term "developing" as a convenient label because it is essential to differentiate between the historical experience of this group of countries and that of "advanced" industrialized countries. However, I am conscious of its limitations and that of other terms such as "Third World," "less-developed," or "underdeveloped."

was attributed to behavioral patterns rather than to the structures of socioeconomic development, the poor were blamed for their own condition. Since then, more sophisticated studies on marginality and the informal sector have explicitly recognized the active and resourceful role played by the poor in earning livelihoods despite lack of access to well-paying jobs or social services (Perlman 1976; Moser 1981; Lobo 1982; Schmink 1984; Beneria and Feldman 1992; Gonzalez de la Rocha 1994). These studies demonstrated that the so-called marginal population was marginal only in terms of benefiting from the formal economic sector, whose structural constraints curbed their participation.

Detailed empirical studies on marginality and the informal economy gave rise to the concept of survival strategies, which specifically recognized the poor's active role in combating their situation by making conscious decisions and choices between various options (Chant 1991; Gonzalez de la Rocha 1994).[7] Studies of survival strategies, including migration, have drawn attention to the elaborate means households have developed to assess how best to match their resources (available labor, capital, information, social networks, skills) to opportunities in the labor market (Wood 1981; Chant 1991; Gonzalez de la Rocha 1994; Safa 1995; Hoodfar 1996a). Where conditions are not to their advantage, the poor may divert their resources into other subsistence activities (Redclift and Mingione 1985; Cigno 1991; Singerman 1995; Hoodfar 1996b). These findings, along with detailed documentation concerning women and development, resulted in dissatisfaction with the formal definition of what constitutes economic activity.

Studies further demonstrated that a household's control over domestic resources and the choice of one alternative over others are shaped, if not directed, by the external socioeconomic environment. In other words, an understanding of the behavior of the domestic unit requires an examination of domestic factors, such as age structure, gender composition, and availability of material and nonmaterial resources, along with external factors, such as labor market conditions, distribution of wealth, and the socially accepted minimum standard of living. These studies have paved the way for a long overdue micro/macro approach to economic issues. In this study, I am particularly interested in the way macro social and economic policy is reflected in the domestic unit and how, in turn, the choices made at the household level influence and reshape the socioeconomic structure of the wider society.

7. The concept was first used by Duque and Pastrana (1973) in a study of poor families in a peripheral area of Santiago (quoted in Schmink 1984: 88).

HOUSEHOLD

Detailed studies of survival strategies, informal economies, and migration patterns have drawn attention to the fact that most
people, particularly in the developing world, go through life interacting
with the greater society as members of a household rather than as au-
tonomous individuals (Netting, Wilk, and Arnould 1984; Sharma 1986;
Chant 1991; Cigno 1991; Booth 1993; Gonzalez de la Rocha 1994). This
is especially true in Egypt, where individuals rarely live in a single-person household and where the interdependence of family and household
members is emphasized (Rugh 1984; Shorter and Zurayk 1988; Weyland
1993; Singerman 1995). An individual's choices and decisions are therefore affected by the roles the wider society ascribes to her or him as a
member of a household—an institution that has proven resilient in the
face of social change and economic development (Wilk 1984; Booth
1993; Anderson, Bechhofer, and Gershuny 1994; Singerman and Hoodfar 1996). It has also been argued that the domestic unit acts as a buffer
to protect the individual from the shock of state policies and rapid social
changes (Sayigh 1981; Booth 1993; Singerman and Hoodfar 1996). In
an uncertain world where the labor market is susceptible to sudden
changes and the state machinery is continuously threatened by instability, membership in household or kin-based groups is a person's chief
means of access to resources and security (Lomnitz 1977; Wellman and
Wortley 1989; Cole 1991; Aramaki 1994; Gonzalez de la Rocha 1994;
Singerman 1995). In other words, their lack of resources and security
ties the members of a household together. For these reasons, we need
to look at individual economic behavior in the context of the household.

The study of women and development during the last two decades
has improved our understanding of survival strategies (Moser and
Young 1981; Buvinic, Lycette, and McGreevey 1983; Beneria and Roldan
1987; Tinker 1990; Beneria and Feldman 1992; Mencher and Okongwu
1993; Thomas 1994; Thomas-Emeagwali 1995). This literature under-
scores the role of household structure and family relations—including
the sexual division of labor—in determining how different members of
a household participate in economic activity or benefit from it. These
debates have broadened the focus of research on economic behavior to
include the household and gender ideology as well as the labor market.
The need to adopt the household/domestic group as a unit of analysis
is particularly significant if the focus of attention is women's economic
behavior as, almost universally, women tend to invest more time in activities that have remained outside the cash economy. Through these

activities women make important economic contributions to the domestic unit (and the national economy). Consequently, in assessing the viability of entering the labor market, women weigh the importance of these so-called extra economic contributions to the household against the utility that their wages can bring. Because of women's roles and responsibilities within the household, the supply of female labor cannot be explained solely in terms of individual strategies for economic participation (Beneria and Roldan 1987; Chant 1991; Cole 1991; Booth 1993; Gonzalez de la Rocha 1994; Hoodfar 1996b).

The household, like other social institutions, is not transhistorical but is subject to modifications in its internal structure, organization, and economic role, as a result of external pressures such as economic change. Therefore, it must be treated as part of the complex of institutional structures of a given society (Wallerstein 1984: 17; Chant 1991; Cole 1991; Booth 1993; Singerman and Hoodfar 1996). Furthermore, the household unit is always in flux and should therefore be studied diachronically to capture the dynamics of its evolutionary nature.[8] The effects of the cycle of family life—expansion, consolidation, and dispersion—on the economic organization of the household have long been recognized by those researchers who have relied primarily on empirical studies rather than on their sociological imaginations.[9] The return of the household as a unit of analysis is more a revival of a scholarly tradition than a groundbreaking perspective.

THE HOUSEHOLD AS A NONEGALITARIAN UNIT

Household-focused studies resulted in a wealth of detailed information about the ways in which households divert resources to domains that yield maximum return while accounting for risk factors.

8. Studies document that even fertility, a biological aspect of the household/family/domestic unit, is influenced to a considerable degree by external factors (Leibenstein 1981; Kagitcibasi 1982; Hoodfar 1994; Obermeyer 1994).

9. Chaianov (1966), writing about Russian peasant households in the nineteenth century, took the household as his unit of analysis and used a definition of the household that is still relevant: "The family interests us as an economic phenomenon, not a biological one. We, therefore, . . . must express its internal composition as a function of consumption and working units in the different phases of the family cycle. . . . Each family, then, depending on its age, constitutes in each of its different phases a completely distinct work apparatus, according to its labour force, the intensity of demand exerted by its needs, the consumer-worker ratio, and the possibility of application of the principles of complex cooperation" (pp. 54–56).

By the late 1970s, the scope of these studies had expanded to include not just cash but also other forms of utility produced in various ways. However, in many of these studies the household itself was assumed, often implicitly, to be an egalitarian unit or the domain of a "moral economy" where individuals selflessly contributed to the welfare of one another (Sahlins 1972: 189–196; Standing 1984, 1989, 1991; Deere 1990). Hence the premise "rational man" was replaced by that of "rational household."[10] Historical and cultural/structural diversities that exist in the way household responsibilities are divided according to age and gender hierarchies were not taken into account.

The emergence of a new feminist literature on women and development, gender ideology, and intrahousehold relations, based on a wide range of cross-cultural documentation, effectively questioned these assumptions of egalitarianism (Folbre 1986a, 1988; Beneria and Roldan 1987; Roldan 1988; Chant 1991; Gonzalez de la Rocha 1994). However, just as gross national product or income per capita measurements alone do not tell us about the distribution of wealth and the welfare of a nation, documentation of household practices and survival strategies that indicate a rise in the standard of living for the unit does not tell us how individual members are benefiting. Many studies show that often a slight improvement in the standard of living of a household may come at a considerable and uneven cost to individual members (Mies 1982; Beneria and Roldan 1987; Stolcke 1988; Sen 1990; Cole 1991; Jelin 1991; MacLeod 1991; Singerman and Hoodfar 1996). In many societies a woman's contribution to her household often exceeds that of her male partner, but her share of benefits is less (Folbre 1984; Papanek 1990; Thomas 1991; Beneria and Feldman 1992). While neoclassical theory has convincingly argued that the division between women's participation in nonmarket activities and men's in market activities is based on efficiency and the maximization of utility, one partner contributing more and receiving less has not been justified.[11]

---

10. The concept "rational man" is a central premise of neoclassical economic theory. It refers to the idea that individuals make choices that yield the highest benefits.

11. The introduction of psychic utility or emotional rewards that neoclassical theorists often use as justification does not solve the problem, as introducing nonmaterial variables into the model forfeit the viability of empirical research of household and intrahousehold economic behavior. A method to measure psychic utility efficiently has not yet been developed (Becker 1981). Further, as Folbre (1984) points out, the argument that child care (which accounts for much of the discrepancy between the contributions of men and women) is its own reward is self-defeating, for if this were true why would men choose to deprive themselves of such pleasures? Incompatibility with their productive activities

Moreover, the expanding literature on domestic violence (Homer, Leonard, and Taylor 1985; Johnson 1985; Viano 1992; Baumgartner 1993; Toch 1993) invalidates the classic argument of altruism—used at times to rationalize unequal gender relations in domestic economy.[12] Inegalitarian relationships, then, are more likely explained in terms of the constraints imposed on individuals as a result of race, ethnicity, sex, or position in gender or age hierarchies (Folbre 1984, 1988; Beneria and Roldan 1987; Tinker 1990; MacLeod 1991; Beneria and Feldman 1992). Data from many societies suggest that women are less likely to have marketable skills, their wages in the labor market are less than those of men, they tend to be concentrated in the least secure occupations, their property rights may be limited, and their marriage and divorce rights may be at the discretion of others; and, regardless of the degree of their investment in the welfare of their children, women may lose parenting rights in the event of divorce or on leaving the household. In short, they lack effective power to promote their own interests within the household (Young, Wolkowitz, and McCullagh 1981; Beneria and Roldan 1987; Sen 1990; Thomas 1991; Gonzalez de la Rocha 1994). Therefore, the processes of development and social change should be understood in conjunction with preexisting economic, cultural, and ideological aspects that influence and, in turn, are influenced by such change. Factors affecting the individual's position within his or her domestic unit and intrahousehold relations continuously evolve in response to social changes. However, while it is important to take into account the structural and cultural/ideological constraints, it must not be assumed that individuals are passive recipients of change and victims of cultural/economic forces that they have no part in generating. Men and women are social agents who actively resist, struggle, and reform their environment, including their own domestic relationships.

---

cannot explain men's lack of participation in child care either. Using survey data from the Philippines, Folbre demonstrates that men's participation in child care does not significantly increase when they are engaged in economic activities compatible with the task, or even when they are unemployed. Morris (1984) reports similar findings in her study of unemployment in Wales.

12. After all, altruism is supposed to take the form of a voluntary contribution. Within a model based on the premise of rational man, how can we argue that there is not necessarily a direct relationship between access to the household's resources and the actual and potential contribution? Why should a partner who is seeking to maximize her or his utility in wider society choose to remain in a unit where she or he is at a disadvantage? If the premise of the rational man is to hold true for women too, we must seek other explanations.

The household is an institution characterized by what Amartya Sen (1990) has termed "cooperative conflict." He points out that while members of a household face outside forces as a unit and harmonize their activities, this does not exclude them from having internal conflicts of interest regarding the distribution of the fruits of their activities. Moreover, a prevailing atmosphere of cohesion and integration in a household may go hand in hand with many legitimized inequalities. The strategic choices that yield the highest return for all members of the household may be unfavorable to a particular member who may not have the power to change her or his circumstances (see also Beneria and Roldan 1987; Dwyer and Bruce 1988; Beneria and Feldman 1992).[13]

WHAT CONSTITUTES "ECONOMIC CONTRIBUTION"

Theoretically, economic activities are all those activities that satisfy human needs through the production of goods and services, regardless of whether they are channeled through the cash market or other forms of exchange. Ideological prejudices and historical practices of national accounting systems have, however, during the last century, given priority to the market-oriented sector, hindering the incorporation of other forms of economic activity into national accounts (Goldschmidt-Clermont 1990; Folbre and Wagman 1993).[14] In her survey of empirical research on both industrialized and developing countries, commissioned by the International Labour Office (ILO), Luisella Goldschmidt-Clermont (1982, 1987) demonstrates that unpaid household work and other subsistence activities in many countries form as

13. The inclusion of structural gender and age role differences and conflicting interests of different members in the study of household survival strategies has introduced a new level of complexity. The major constraint arises from the difficulty of defining "perception of interest," particularly in cross-cultural studies or studies in which the results must be analyzed using terms and concepts evolved with reference to societies and cultures other than the one under study (Asad 1986). Perceptions of self-interest, legitimacy, and achievement are socially constructed and deeply influenced by prevailing norms and practices of the community (Sen 1990).

14. These prejudices are often subsumed under the rubric "problems of measurement" (Waring 1988; Beneria 1992). The situation has become exasperating. While under pressure to produce internationally compatible statistical information, many developing nations have little experience with modern national accounting and lack resources to develop their own systems. Thus they tend to adopt models from the developed world that are often themselves outdated. Consequently, national accounting procedures are persistently inadequate.

much as 40 percent of the estimated national economy.[15] Therefore, national accounting figures are only a rough estimate of actual national economies.

Including more subsistence activities in the assessment of national economies is among the improvements recommended by the United Nations (UN) since 1968, but few governments have fully implemented these changes (Waring 1988; Beneria 1992).[16] At least partly because governments are generally more concerned with activity they can monitor and tax, they have shown very little interest in devising accounting techniques for nonmonetary economic activities and transactions that would not easily lend themselves to the application of taxes. In any case, even the improved UN definition of what should be formally considered "economy" excludes a substantial share of own-account production, much of which is women's work (Beneria 1981, 1992; Recchini de Lattes and Wainerman 1986; Waring 1988).[17] The fact remains that whether or not these economic activities appear on the national balance, they represent real value to the people who produce and consume them.

This arbitrary definition of economic and productive activity works to women's disadvantage. There is no good reason why cooking and food processing should be considered less productive than growing food, especially when cooking for one's employer is an economic activity but cooking the same food for one's own household is not (Waring 1988). Or, as Nancy Folbre (1986a) asks, why is caring for children considered less productive than caring for livestock? What women do is categorized as domestic and taken for granted, but what men do is work.[18]

---

15. Goldschmidt-Clermont compiled a report in 1982 based on a survey of seventy-five research studies on unpaid labor carried out in the "developed" world. These studies estimated that the value of unpaid work accounts for between 25 and 40 percent of measured national income. Her second report in 1987 of forty studies of unpaid work in the developing countries estimated that unpaid work forms about half the labor expended for meeting human needs and between 25 and 50 percent of total consumption.

16. India is an exception in its development and implementation, prior to the UN's report, of a national accounting system incorporating many subsistence activities.

17. Goldschmidt-Clermont (1987: 8) in her ILO-commissioned study has categorized these items as goods and services (meals, washed clothes, care of children and of the ill), which are the product of domestic activities; processing for own consumption of primary commodities by those who do not produce them; own-account production of commodities consumed in households and not sold on the market; and the upkeep and repair of dwellings and other buildings.

18. An important debate that has implications for women is what constitutes "work" as opposed to leisure. In an attempt to solve the problem for empirical work, Gronau (1977:

According to the UN Convention "all persons of either sex who furnish the supply of labor for the production of economic goods and services" should have been included in labor force statistics during the last two decades (ILO 1976: 32, quoted in Beneria 1981: 21). Adoption of such a definition by national governments would give visibility to women and children in national figures. These debates are not motivated by a new form of statistical fetishism. These figures, used for social and economic planning, can be misleading and possibly lead to a faulty diagnosis of development problems. For instance, social planners who operate with a mythical image of actual labor force participation may overestimate the extent of availability of human resources. This can lead to the implementation of policies that stretch the long working hours of an already overworked population (Rogers 1980; Waring 1988). Without meaningful data, peasant poverty might be attributed to a lack of motivation for a better material life. However, studies of peasant responses to inflation or migration for higher wages document that what appeared to have been a lack of motivation was in fact the lack of a reasonable return after all the economic factors and the cost and benefits for all the members of a peasant household were considered. Similarly, as I discuss in chapter 4, women's low response to the formal labor market is more often the result of a rational economic assessment of the opportunity-cost ratio than the consequence of purely cultural factors.

Statistically invisible groups of the economically active population are categorized as consumers as opposed to producers. They falsely appear to be a burden to their households and the national economy. These assumptions become embodied in the ideology of the nation, to the disadvantage of invisible groups, the largest of which is women (Waring 1988). Although many women contribute more hours of work to support their households than their husbands do, they are often heard to declare "I do not work" or "I am only a housewife," because

----

1104) has suggested that "work" is what one would rather have someone else do, while it is almost impossible to enjoy leisure through a surrogate. This distinction, however, is derived from the assumption that one would not enjoy work. While the increasingly alienating nature of work in modern industrialized societies may render some truth to this definition, for some groups or occupational categories work remains a source of pleasure and satisfaction. While I accept Gronau's definition of leisure, his definition of "work" is best rephrased as those activities that someone else can perform, yielding the same result. In other words, activities for which there can be a market substitute (Reid 1934).

their labor is not remunerated (chap. 4). These assumptions have significant implications for the status and position of women in their households and in society.

In much the same way as national income is measured, household income and standard-of-living measures are often based on the household's monetary earnings. While the level of household living is a reflection of cash income, subsistence contributions such as housework, repairs, construction, and the utilization of public goods and services are omitted, leaving us with an incomplete picture. Furthermore, empirical studies have demonstrated that networking and access to information are crucial to assessing the labor market or maximizing other forms of economic activity (Lomnitz 1977; Lomnitz and Perez-Liazur 1987; Wellman and Wortley 1989; Aramaki 1994). In light of all these factors, I have defined economic contribution simply as all those activities that bring direct or indirect material benefit to the household.

Objectives of the Study

As I continued to read about various aspects of the household economy, I was struck by the lack of empirical research and information about the Middle East, especially compared to the wealth of information from Latin America. What little existed focused primarily on gender ideology and the role of Islam in the lives of women and families, although more recently the focus has shifted to the return of veiling and fundamentalism. It was as though Muslims, and in particular Middle Eastern people, lived in the realm of ideology and religion while the rest of the world lived within the economic structure.[19] Such a division is of course artificial and a creation of the limited vision and skills of social scientists, since in reality people of all cultures live their lives with influences of ideology and economy simultaneously as they try to satisfy their emotional and material needs (Barnett and Silverman 1979; de Certeau 1984; Bourdieu 1990). However, the portraits of Middle Easterners primarily in the realm of ideology stemmed from

19. Although there were few micro studies of the economic lives of communities, many studies looked at social policies, political movements, or the impact of oil revenues on the economy. See, for instance, Abdel-Fadil 1980; al-Ahwany 1984; Richards and Waterbury 1990; Handoussa and Potter 1991; and Amin 1995.

more than a century of orientalist writings presenting them as driven by religion and the extreme male sexual appetite (Said 1978; Alloula 1986; Kabbani 1986; Mabro 1991; Lazreg 1994). This distortion that betrayed my personal experience and previous research in Iran convinced me that—despite the concern and apprehension expressed by some of my professors, who wanted me to take up a more "serious" topic—my research on household economy in the Middle East was vital.

So in January 1983 I went to Cairo to research the survival strategies of low-income households in newly urbanized neighborhoods.[20] Although the emotional and ideological aspects of everyday life are significant, I chose to focus on economic contributions and the distribution of material benefits within the household. This study accounts for patriarchal authority and Muslim mores and prescriptions only to the extent that they are manifested in family dynamics, decision making, and the legal and economic system that prevailed in Egypt. Similarly, I examined the structural forces of the society, such as the ideology of the state, industrialization, changing labor market conditions, and state policies toward public goods and services, in terms of their impact on the household as a whole and the changing position of individuals within the household. In the process I have brought together the somewhat disparate fields of political economy, development, gender studies, urban anthropology, and social change that reflected my interdisciplinary as well as cross-cultural education.

In trying to explain people's choices about their household economies and their survival strategies, I relied on a holistic approach that would make it possible to examine social (cultural and ideological) factors and economic rationales for income acquisition and distribution within the household without neglecting the influence of individuals. Although social scientists have been slow in adopting a multilayered framework, I found that many people in my research communities explained it eloquently. In fact, my favorite term for this framework, the "backgammon approach," came from an older Iranian informant.

Everyone's primary concern, he said, is to do as well as possible economically and socially. Hence, real-life decision making is a very delicate matter involving many factors, some of which are out of one's control.

---

20. The concept of strategy in sociological literature is discussed by Crow (1989). I have adopted Altorki's (1986: 149) definition of strategy as a rational calculation of behavior that an individual adopts to promote his or her interests.

Backgammon, like life, can be won only with both luck and strategy.[21] The roll of the dice and the constellation of pieces already played on the board determine the player's possible options. However, one must also be able to see what moves are possible in a given situation and have a good knowledge of the rules in order to manipulate them to one's advantage while preventing competitors from breaking or bending them to one's disadvantage. For instance, he explained, whether one is born rich or poor, male or female, in time of plenty and peace or war and revolution all affect one's life, yet one has little influence over these matters. By choosing the best possible option, the player can make the most of good or bad luck.

The study of household survival strategies and economic behavior is basically the study of how households best match their own resources, such as capital and labor, with opportunities in the formal and informal labor market and with the production of utility in other economic domains while accounting for factors such as risk, security, and time span.[22] Opportunities and constraints of the wider society (macro conditions), whether they are artifacts of markets, political situations, or cultural and gender ideologies, are as important to the study of survival strategies as the micro (the household and its internal dynamics) factors.

To look beyond an approach that treats household/family as a solely ideological unit, I have examined the economic as well as social forces that encourage individuals to remain within their household and unite and cooperate with other members despite the existence of conflicts of interest. This approach also makes it possible to examine whether socioeconomic change reproduces, exaggerates, or modifies existing inequalities within the household, particularly between husband and wife. Throughout this work, I have tried to incorporate a discussion of the aspects of Egyptian culture and economy that affect household economic strategies and resource accumulation and distribution, as well as the impact of economic and social change on gender relations.

21. Backgammon is played widely in the Middle East. Folk history has it that backgammon was developed in pre-Islamic Iran to counter chess, which had been introduced from India. Whereas backgammon combines skill and chance, chess relies solely on the player's expertise and alertness.

22. I have used "production of utility" to accommodate not only income in cash and in kind but also the material benefits resulting from domestic and "do-it-yourself" activities (such as building and repairing one's home) that usually lie beyond the sphere of cash-earning and subsistence activities.

In addition to this holistic approach, the study of survival strategies requires a meaningful working definition of a household's income. The standard of living of an urban household is a reflection not only of its cash income but also of its full income and resources. The full income of a household consists of several elements: (1) the economic activities directed toward the production of material utility, whether they are cash-generating activities in the formal or informal sectors or non-market activities such as housework, food processing, house repair, or subsistence production; (2) the extent to which a household draws on public services such as free schooling, medicine, or subsidized goods; (3) rent and other transfers such as gift exchanges. These categories embody the outcome of other activities such as networking and information gathering. Hence, in this work, income refers to material benefits that household members draw from all activities, whether these benefits are cash or other.

As this book is above all an anthropological account of daily life in the neighborhoods, I have in the following chapters provided a summary of major concerns and dilemmas that I faced in the field as an outsider, though not a European. I discuss how my gender and religion posed a major obstacle in my contacts with the male informants and resulted in the imbalances in the quality of the data I collected from men and women.

As it is not possible to understand individual and household economic and social choices without knowing the context in which these choices are made, I outline the development of the social and economic policies that have shaped Egypt's society, political structure, and labor market. Since the mid-1970s, Egypt's growing international debt forced the government to implement structural adjustment policies and effectively dismantle the state's role in providing social amenities, basic food subsidies, education, and health care. This change has had a major impact on how households allocate their resources.

The definition of who is considered a member of a household varies from culture to culture. In Egypt, households are almost universally based on blood and marriage kinship (Rugh 1984; Shorter 1989). Therefore, it is not surprising that the literature on the Middle East has often used the terms "family" and "household" interchangeably. Here, I use "family" rather than "household" only where the emphasis is on kinship rather than on a unit that is based on the pooling of resources. While blood kinship is a given—at least ideologically—marriage kinship is a domain where individuals have more room to choose whom they want to be related to. Therefore, who one marries and under what conditions are important life and survival decisions, though the sterile definition of economic life has meant that these elements are often omitted from economic studies. Marriage is particularly important since the nuclear family is the predominant domestic unit in Egypt (Shorter and Zurayk 1988) and specifically in my research communities. Moreover, as marriages are arranged by parents, especially in the case of daughters, emphasis is placed on how the future household/family will survive economically as well as socially. To this end, parents—particularly aware of the legal and cultural limitations on women—have adopted strategies to ensure marriages that from the outset secure their daughters' positions vis-à-vis their husbands. The involvement of parents in arranging the marriage of a daughter, though curtailing the freedom of young women, puts them in stronger positions as they enter marriage as compared with many of their counterparts in urban Latin America who enter into *compromiso* (common-law) unions. These issues are the essence of chapter 2, where I discuss the prevailing ideology regarding sex roles and marriage, as well as the legal and customary responsibilities of each partner within marriage. The main focus, however, is on the ways in which women and their parents have manipulated traditional practices to circumvent some of the customary and legal limitations placed on women. Drawing on my data, I argue that the success of these newly evolved strategies reinforces the positive role of parents' involvement in marriage arrangements for their daughters, even for those women who aspire to be associated with "modern" rather than "traditional" culture.

Traditional as well as modern ideologies designate men as household breadwinners, and thus men are under considerable pressure to maximize their cash income. In chapter 3 I outline different strategies that men employ to increase and diversify their cash income. Low-income earners are alert to market change and quick to respond to it. Working in several jobs and migrating to oil-producing countries are common strategies employed to raise cash. By decreasing the supply of labor, on the one hand, and by creating demand for goods and services, on the other, large-scale migration has improved the wage structure of the unskilled and semiskilled laborers considerably. Moreover, migration has been the single most important buffer against the shock of Egypt's structural adjustment policies for those who occupy the bottom echelons of the labor hierarchy.

In chapter 4, where I look at women's paid activities, I examine how modern labor laws, the sexual division of labor, and gender ideology stimulate women's responses to the labor market. I discuss how women's opportunity-cost considerations encourage uneducated or unskilled women to participate in informal rather than formal cash-earning activities. Educated women chose to work in the public sector despite its low wages because this is the only formal sector workplace that has made allowances for women's double burden as mothers and homemakers as well as employees. Women's low rate of labor market participation is often viewed as an indicator of their conservatism and traditional tendencies. However, my data indicate that where the terms of labor market are favorable, traditionalism or religiosity did not prevent women from seeking employment.

Cross-cultural studies have indicated that the welfare of the household is affected by who manages the cash, the man or the woman (Dwyer and Bruce 1988). However, access to and control over monetary resources are important indications of one's position in the household power structure. In chapter 5, I examine factors that influence household budgeting and money management, as well as the extent to which women's cash-earning activities lead to the expansion or contraction of women's access to household or husbands' monetary resources. Male migration also has an impact on women's access to husbands' income, and both men and women adopt strategies that safeguard and promote their influence in controlling cash resources.

In chapter 6, I examine nonmonetary contributions, which account for a large portion of a poorer household's total income. These include activities such as housework, childbearing, production of foodstuffs, and construction and repairs of the dwelling. Historically, the ability to make use of public goods and services, including subsidized goods, free medicine, and education, has had a significant impact on a Cairene household's standard of living. While the present government has suffered a loss of credibility because of its failure to deliver these goods and services, Islamic oppositional groups have filled this role in some neighborhoods, generating much legitimacy for themselves. The time, skill, and effort expended in channeling these resources to the household are important contributions that are often overlooked. Moreover, as the data indicate, efforts to take advantage of these public goods have caused changes in the actual, if not always ideological, gender division of labor.

Households need to reproduce themselves, both biologically and socially, in terms of the community or social group to which they belong or with whom they aspire to be associated. Consumption is an important aspect of this social reproduction. Material culture and consumption, such as the use of modern medicine, education, and food, are some of the ways households express membership in their changing communities and in the wider society. Poverty hinders people and households from participating in the consumption patterns of their community, so they have to devise strategies to improve their standard of living while simultaneously consolidating their membership in the rapidly changing society. In chapter 7, I examine the social and economic elements that influence consumption patterns and strategies in the research community and question the validity and usefulness of the arbitrary division between consumption and saving.

Chapter 8 is devoted to the significance of networking and informal associations for the welfare of low-income households. To minimize economic insecurity and discrimination against the poor by modern institutions such as banks, low-income earners have adapted old reciprocal relations to their "modernizing" realities. For instance, the revitalization and spread of the traditional practice of saving clubs (*gamᶜiyat*) and with it the role of women who historically have organized them is one strategy to combat the inaccessibility of the banks. Similarly, other horizontal and vertical networks, particularly those of women, help the household to secure other forms of support. Relationships with relatives have been shaped to minimize obligations while enhancing the kind of support that is more effective among cash-poor households.

Chapter 9 addresses the role of sexuality and fertility in the lives of men and women and their households. Women value their fertility and sexuality not only in terms of fulfilling a basic and instinctual need but also as a variable in their survival and economic security throughout their life cycles as adult women. Social and economic factors also mitigate against the adoption of new attitudes to customs such as female circumcision and son preference, both by women and by the community.

Chapter 10 brings together the major factors discussed in the preceding chapters and provides an overview of survival strategies. In addition, this chapter outlines the prominent cultural, economic, and ideological factors that influence relations between households, particularly between husbands and wives.

CHAPTER I

The Research and Its Social and Physical Setting

Arriving in Cairo

Near the end of January 1983, I obtained a visa, borrowed 400 pounds from friends and family, and bought a ticket to Cairo with funds provided by Kent University.[1] I left a few days later for a country where I knew no one and whose language I did not speak. My only precious property was a notebook that contained a few names and addresses given to me by friends and professors. I was less confident than I had been on previous fieldwork projects, since in addition to the normal difficulties, I also faced financial and political constraints.[2] I kept asking myself if this was a realistic endeavor. Would I be accepted by Egyptians? I wondered. Wouldn't the very people I wanted to meet and make friends with ask me what a young Muslim woman was doing traveling around the world by herself? I had not yet realized that the pursuit

1. As an Iranian I was disqualified from most grants, particularly since I had decided to carry out my fieldwork in a country other than my native land. Most Western-based agencies did not (and most still do not) encourage horizontal contacts among "Third World" scholars and students. Third World governments, particularly Middle Eastern ones, are not keen to provide financial assistance for social sciences, partly because they consider social sciences a nuisance that encourages democratic demands and social unrest.

2. At the time, the Egyptian government, like all other governments of the region, was worried about the possibility of Iranian visitors advocating an Iranian-style revolution. I imagined, and others warned me, that as a single, Iranian, Muslim woman who left England to live in a poor neighborhood of Cairo, I would arouse the suspicion of the national security office.

of education and knowledge of other Muslim cultures is as legitimate a reason for departing from the accepted norms as one may have.

Outside of my native Iran, I had never been in a developing society, and on arriving in Cairo I found myself making comparisons between Iran and Egypt, and occasionally Britain. I immediately registered for an Arabic course, and friends of friends helped me to find affordable lodging and academic affiliation. I also began the process of joining the Department of Anthropology at the American University in Cairo as a research fellow.[3] Next, with only a map and the advice of my Egyptian contacts, I began to explore the neighborhoods. During the first few weeks I felt strange; it was as though I was walking through my school history books and my grandfather's bewitching stories. Cairo has always been a significant center for Middle Eastern culture and art, and despite the diminution of its role in the twentieth century, it continues to have a special place in the minds and hearts of Middle Easterners.

Modern Cairo, like many major cities of the Third World, has grown far beyond its maximum capacity of about 2 million people. Current estimates of Greater Cairo's population vary from 12 million to 14 million. Given the state of available resources, it is a major challenge for the authorities to provide basic services such as water, sanitation, electricity, public transportation, medical care, schooling, employment, and, most of all, housing. Industrialization and the consequent waves of urban migration have caused the metropolis to expand in all directions, encompassing many of the surrounding villages that historically provided vegetables and fruit for Cairo.[4] These villages now house thousands of migrants and Cairenes who have been unable to find a residence in Cairo proper, forcing the villagers to urbanize as the city arrived at their doorsteps. The urban experience of the people of these villages differs markedly from that of other rural migrants (Oldham, el-Hadidi, and Tamaa 1987; Hoodfar 1989). Many of the formerly poor farmers with a meager parcel of land (sometimes as small as 40 square meters) were suddenly considered among the richer residents of the area, and many have become landlords who rent to poorer migrants. Furthermore, although

3. Originally I had hoped to join Cairo University or the prestigious Islamic university Al-Ahzar. However, an Egyptian contact warned me that since I was Iranian, the very political atmosphere of national universities might compromise my position. Thus I joined American University.

4. Abu-Lughod (1961) and others have shown that the bulk of Cairo migrants are of rural origin, with only a small percentage from other urban centers.

they are now integrated into the urban life of Cairo, the villagers have not had to give up membership in their community of origin.

For my research I had planned to locate a poor neighborhood, similar to the ones where I had worked in Tehran before and after the revolution.[5] Within a few weeks, I realized that most of my assumptions about the level of poverty in Egypt were wrong. Egypt, though poorer than Iran, had a much more equitable distribution of income (Abdel-Fadil 1980; Beattie 1994). Having been introduced to poverty by the mud hut neighborhoods that bordered some of Tehran's middle class suburbs, I quickly grasped the impact of public-oriented economic and social policies on the standard of living. Largely through subsidies, the Egyptian government had ensured affordable minimum basic food and clothing to the majority of its population.[6] In some amazement, after days of walking and riding buses around Cairo, I realized that although the city appeared to be run-down, its poorer neighborhoods were very different from Tehran's shantytowns. Rather, it had many large and growing informal housing areas; that is to say, most owners owned their land but had no permission to build on it.[7] Officially, many of these lots were zoned as agricultural, not residential, despite their current high population density.

Over the next two months, I identified three neighborhoods that were appropriate for my research and arranged to live with a family in one of them. The household included two parents, six of their eight children, and the grandmother, and it later also included me. The residence was a small two-room apartment, and the father was constructing a third room on the second floor in his free time.[8] The two daughters— one was finishing primary school teacher training and the other was

5. For a comparative approach to my fieldwork experiences in Cairo and Tehran, see Hoodfar 1994.

6. The situation was of course far from perfect. Many of the policies favored urban areas over rural (Waterbury 1978), and some have argued that the rich drew more benefits from the system than the poor. However, the fact remains that before Egypt adopted more aggressive structural adjustment policies toward the end of the 1980s (Sullivan 1992; Lofgren 1993a, 1993b; Parfitt 1993) the nation had very few cases of severe malnutrition (Khouri-Dagher 1986).

7. For a description of other informal neighborhoods, see Tekçe, Oldham, and Shorter 1994.

8. The father was an unskilled worker who had migrated to Libya for four years and had saved enough money to buy the piece of land on which he gradually built after his return. The construction of the second and third floors is now completed. One daughter is married and is living in the ground floor flat, where we all lived before. The third floor is occupied by the eldest son, whose marriage is eagerly anticipated by everyone except himself.

entering her last year of high school—took it upon themselves to help me with Arabic lessons and other necessary social skills. They delighted in having me repeat words with dubious meanings in front of their friends and in retelling all the social and linguistic mistakes I made. As one of the daughters aptly said, I provided them with their summer fun, and, in return, they taught me Arabic and the essentials of Egyptian *sha'bi* (grassroots) life. By October 1983, I felt confident enough to move on my own to my second research neighborhood where I lived until the end of April 1984, when I returned to Britain.

Contrary to my worries, I found that people readily accepted my reason for traveling alone, and they adopted me as their fictive sister, daughter, or aunt. If, at times, being Iranian rather than Egyptian (or at least a white European) was a drawback, in most situations being Muslim was an advantage, particularly after the women tested the extent of my Islamic knowledge. As a Middle Easterner, I knew the significance of being invited to share meals with families. Drawing on my earlier fieldwork experience, I announced that I was vegetarian, which my friends in the neighborhoods took with much amusement, since their reason for not eating much meat was financial, not ideological.[9] Moreover, my favorite foods were *ful* and *tam'iya* (two bean dishes) and *mulukhiya* (a green vegetable dish), which are the most common foods of low-income people. This meant that my neighbors could freely invite me to their homes, and indeed during the entire time that I lived on my own, I rarely cooked or ate alone. If I refused an invitation and stayed in my flat under the pretext of studying for my Arabic courses, invariably some food would be sent, along with someone to keep me company.

Indeed, I found it very difficult to stay in my flat except to sleep at night. The idea of living alone and being left alone is very unpleasant to Egyptians and they could not accept that I, their friend, should be left alone. Initially, many families, particularly those who did not have older sons, tried to convince me to move in with them; however, aware of the consequences that belonging to a particular household would have for my interactions with other members of the neighborhood, I resisted.[10] I explained that my father had allowed me to go to Egypt only on the promise that I would live in my own flat in a decent neigh-

9. Ideally, entertaining a guest involved big meals with a substantial amount of meat. Since the poor cannot afford meat, they often refrain from inviting people to meals. However, a guest who arrives at mealtime is always welcomed to join the family meal.

10. Initially I had thought their continued insistence was due to their eagerness to receive my rent. However, as I got to know people more, I was ashamed to realize that

borhood, and since he did not know them, naturally he would not agree. Culturally and religiously, respect for one's parents' wishes is a highly praised virtue, so my friends felt disarmed and settled for keeping me company as often as they could.

Their extreme generosity was sometimes an obstacle to writing up my field notes. Except for the two afternoons a week when I left the neighborhood for my Arabic lessons, I spent every day socializing and keeping company with the women, going vegetable shopping in the local *suq* (market), visiting neighbors, walking to the local hospital, discussing problems of budgeting, prices, children's education, soap operas, and marriage proposals, and assessing the virtues of potential grooms and my friends' dreams and aspirations for themselves and their families. I was eager to find time to write notes on these discussions and observations. This proved to be very problematic. Almost every morning, sometimes as early as 6:30, I was summoned by a child, who would knock on my door as a messenger or of her or his own accord to say that her or his mother wanted me as soon as possible; often the child would remain until I was dressed and ready to go. When I finally managed to return to my flat in the evening, if my light was on for more than fifteen or twenty minutes, I would hear a knock on my door and find a couple of women who had come to keep me company. When they saw that I was writing (or studying, as they said) they would say, "Don't worry, you continue studying and we'll just sit here on the bed so you won't be alone." Although I was deeply touched by their concern, in my long years of student life, away from home in Britain, I had become accustomed to reading and working alone and I often found it difficult to concentrate in the presence of others. Soon, however, I learned to use what was my major worldly possession at that time, a small cassette recorder. I would come home in the evening, light a candle, and lay down on my bed while I talked into my cassette recorder. I also made sparse notes while visiting and whenever I had a chance.[11] Later I discovered that some of my friends enjoyed hearing their voices on cassette tape, so I also recorded some of our informal discussions or interviews. Toward the end of my stay in 1984, I spent many evenings

---

it was their extreme generosity and genuine affection for me as a single young woman that was the basis of these repeated invitations.

11. I noted keywords to remind me of significant points and observations. This was not considered unusual since I used the same notebook to record the new Arabic words I encountered.

at the home of a friend who lived in another part of the city, trying to transcribe as many tapes as I could, organizing my data, and making sure I had all the information I needed to write my thesis.

After having lived in Cairo for fifteen months, my departure at the end of April 1984 was a sad one. Nothing in my training or my Middle Eastern upbringing had prepared me to say good-bye to people who had befriended me, protected me, and given me their shoulders to cry on when I was homesick, sad, and frustrated over the destructive and senseless war between Iran and Iraq. I left not knowing when, or if, I would ever see them again.[12] I was delighted when, quite unexpectedly, a research proposal I had submitted with an Egyptian friend to the Population Council to look at the impact of international male migration was funded. Originally, I planned to study households with couples present. However, as my research progressed and I saw the important role of migration among low-income communities, I realized that my research would benefit if I broadened my sample to include households whose male head had migrated to the Gulf. When I suggested this to a friend, she too was enthusiastic and we developed the proposal. Thus, a year later, in 1985, I returned to Cairo and the neighborhoods for another year of fieldwork on the impact of male migration on the role of wives and the well-being of children left behind, which had become a controversial subject in Egypt (Hoodfar 1996b). This time I did not live in the neighborhoods but commuted daily, though I frequently stayed overnight with friends in the research areas. This trip was followed by several other shorter visits to the neighborhoods and my friends in 1988, 1992, 1993, and 1994. In 1984, however, given the kind of constraints that I faced as an Iranian anthropologist, carrying out a longitudinal research project in Egypt appeared to be more wishful thinking than a real possibility.

Living in the research community proved to be extremely valuable, and provided me with the chance not just to familiarize myself with the values and attitudes of people in the neighborhoods but also to participate as a community member. Furthermore, I developed a better understanding of day-to-day problems, such as the lack of adequate and safe transportation, water, electricity (particularly in the heat of summer), and shortages of subsidized basic foods. More important, I

12. At that time my passport was about to expire and I had to explain to both Iranian and Egyptian authorities why I needed to be in Cairo. Neither official found my explanation of doing anthropological fieldwork convincing.

learned to appreciate the strategies that people devised to deal with these daily crises. For instance, had I not been living under the same conditions, I doubt I would have understood why women did their laundry in the middle of the night, or why they preferred to join the informal economy rather than work in a factory where the wages were higher (see chapters 4 and 6).

Although I felt somewhat bitter when I compared my situation with that of the well-funded North American and European researchers who enjoyed a support system for learning the language, getting visas, and making contacts with colleagues in the field, my poverty and powerlessness in the field were not without advantages. It was hard for neighborhood people to imagine that, having come from England, I was as poor as they were. Sometimes they gently teased me and called me "goldless princess," since I had no gold jewelry, which represented the economic status of neighborhood households. But I felt the poverty deeply, and particularly in the first nine months of my fieldwork I passed many nights worrying about how to raise yet another $100 to renew my visa, whether I had the money to buy an Arabic textbook, and whether I could pay my rent and still afford a gift of sweets and fruit for the families who fed me day after day. During this time I learned to budget.

A constant source of anxiety was not being able to afford suitable gifts for members of my very wide network when there was news of a wedding engagement, childbirth, or trip. The gift exchange is an important means of reaffirming one's membership in a network. Worst of all was that the gifts and their material worth became common knowledge, and depending on how the community had assessed my financial means, this would signify the value I gave to my friendships. This also meant that I would have to spend an equal amount on gifts for each household I visited. Early on in my fieldwork, however, an incident occurred which helped me to resolve the gift problem, to some extent at least.

One day, I heard that Amira, who helped me a great deal with my Arabic, had successfully passed her teacher training exams. I innocently bought a bunch of flowers for her. This created a great deal of laughter, and soon neighbors were called to come to see my gift. Amira explained to the others, "She has brought me this bunch of flowers, just like we see on TV! I never thought anyone would bring me flowers."[13] Then

---

13. *Baladi* women, if they could afford to buy flowers at all, bought them only for weddings. No one in these neighborhoods bought cut flowers for themselves or as hospitality gifts.

she turned back to me and said, "Among us we don't have money for flowers. We buy something useful. What can we do with flowers?" I realized my rather stupid mistake, but all the same, with a straight face, I told her that she could look at them and enjoy their delicacy and beauty. Their laughter made up for my mistake. The flowers sat in a plastic jar for months afterward and served as a running joke that resurfaced whenever they ran out of topics to tease me about.

Flowers were not very expensive in Cairo, certainly if one knew where to buy them and was prepared to bargain. As a strategy, I decided to act the naive foreigner and continued to buy flowers for all special occasions. The women continued to laugh at me for treating them like my *agnabi* friends (literally, "foreign," but usually reserved for white Europeans and North Americans). But I felt there was also a sense of pleasure and satisfaction in receiving equal treatment from me, despite their social-class differences. When the Ford Foundation granted me a small subsidy for field expenses, my situation eased a little and I managed to buy a camera with which I took color photographs that were much appreciated gifts.

Another question that tormented me was how to explain what I was doing. Social research, particularly anthropological fieldwork, is not a very widely understood concept in Egypt or the rest of the Middle East.[14] I tried my best to explain what I was doing there besides learning to speak Arabic, but I did not know whether my Egyptian friends understood me and my research. One day, to my amazement and delight, two of the women, introducing me to their friends, explained that I came from England but that my parents are Muslims from Iran.[15] Maryam and Najwa went on to explain that my father had sent me to Egypt to study Arabic and learn about Muslim people and Muslim

14. On one occasion when I went to see an official to inquire about whether I should obtain permission for the kind of research I intended to do, and, if so, what the legal procedure was, I tried to explain my thesis topic and that I would conduct my research by just meeting and observing people. He became cynical, and maybe also a little annoyed, since my study did not appear serious to him. I doubt that he believed that such work could be considered doctoral field research. He said, "If that is what you call research, then I suppose that every tourist in this country will need to come to my office." In the end, his only instruction was that as a non-national, I should report my place of residence to the local police, which I duly did.

15. I was always introduced as coming from England, which technically was true, but also could imply that I was English. I suppose it was more prestigious to have a friend from Europe, but at the same time they were very proud I was a Muslim. I became keenly aware that the two credentials have very positively affected the way the community perceived me and presented me to the others.

families, not just from books but by living with shaᶜbi people of Cairo; they added that he could not send me to Iran because of the war with Iraq. They told their friends that I was taking Arabic classes at American University in Cairo but that my accent might be difficult to understand; Maryam and Najwa would "translate" for them. In any case, they concluded I had made a lot of progress over a few months. After that, I accepted the women's definition of my mission in Cairo. As my Arabic improved, I explained that I was writing my thesis on shaᶜbi family life. They understood this to mean I was writing an exam for my professor at American University about shaᶜbi family life. I was often deeply touched by their patience in making sure I fully understood the issues in question, because they wanted me to get good marks on my exam so that my father would not regret sending me to Egypt.

As a Middle Easterner I was keenly aware of the importance of reciprocal relationships, so I took great care to return my friends' favors, kindness, and love in whatever way and to the extent I could. I helped with housework and food preparation, which meant cleaning mountains of vegetables. I watched babies, took children to the hospital, and, through my contacts outside the neighborhoods, located the best low-cost medical services. Young mothers often asked me about contraceptives and requested that I consult with my professor and my friends at the university.[16] I helped the children with their studies, particularly math and English. I also helped with Arabic dictations, which the younger children loved as it allowed them to correct my accent and laugh at my mispronunciations and made learning more pleasurable.

During my first period of fieldwork, I often wondered whether they were aware of the importance of the knowledge and training they were giving me, both for my studies and for my life. And I wondered what contributions I was making to their lives. The following episode convinced me that perhaps my relationships had more impact on the lives and thoughts of my friends than I had realized.

In January 1984, after I had lived in the neighborhoods for a year and had made many friends there, I decided to carry out some informal but more systematic interviews to see how women and men described their contributions to the household. I started with some of the younger mothers whom I knew very well. Having explained this to Umm Walid, she said I could interview her while we were cleaning some rice for dinner. I began by asking how many times a day she washed

16. University professors were held in high esteem, and people often thought my professors knew whatever there was to know.

her dishes, what her housework included, and so on. At first, she joked as she answered me. However, seeing me writing down her responses, she suddenly became quiet and looked at me in a puzzled way. Then, looking worried and distressed, she went to the balcony and called Nasser, a friend of her husband who had finally passed his high school exams after several attempts and was looking for a job. When Nasser walked in, Umm Walid explained to him that in a few months I would have to go back to England and write an exam for my professor. Would Nasser agree to answer some important questions for an hour or two? I tried to explain that it was not Nasser I wanted to interview, since he knew nothing about housework. Her expression grew even more worried and she said,

You stupid, you are going to fail your exam after all that money your father spent to send you here. Who cares what I do and how many times a day I wipe Walid's bottom? Nasser is educated. He knows about life and important things in Egypt and can tell you important things and you will get a good mark.

I was very touched by her concern, and at the same time angered that she reacted as if her work was insignificant, even though she had told me many times how important domestic work was for the family. Meanwhile, Nasser had taken a seat and asked her for a drink and was trying to convince me that he could answer any questions, as he knew it all. Finally, after an hour or so, Nasser left, but Umm Walid refused to answer my questions. She said I should show my questions to my professor. Only if he approved would she answer them. I had to agree. Some days later, after convincing her that my professor did not object, I carried out the interviews with her and other women, in the midst of much laughter and joking as they were not used to anyone taking their domestic work and ideas seriously, never mind as the subject of research.

My return to the neighborhood in 1985 was understood to mean that I had done well on my exam and had won a scholarship to do more courses, exams, and research about Egyptian sha°bi families. A couple of months after my return, I visited Umm Walid, who was in the middle of a dispute with her husband. He accused her of being a good-for-nothing woman who did nothing all day while he worked to support her. At this point, she angrily turned to her husband and said,

Tell me if I do nothing from morning to night, if looking after two boys, cooking and cleaning and running a home with the meager money you give is nothing, then why would American University send a student from England to ask me about my work? Why don't they send someone to ask you or Nasser what you do? Tell me!

Her husband looked first at her and then at me and, half in anger and half in amusement, told me, "See, you have made these women so big-headed we cannot even say a word to them." Then he demanded that his wife make tea for me and we went back to socializing.

In another incident, a young woman had found a job as a teacher in the Gulf, but her parents were reluctant to let her go since unmarried Muslim women should not travel and live on their own. She asked them what was wrong with traveling, pointing out that I, a Muslim woman, had come to Egypt where I did not even know the language. Hadn't I lived all by myself and wasn't I well behaved, she asked. Hadn't they on many occasions praised me as a symbol of the modern Muslim woman? Finally they agreed. She went to the Gulf and helped her family improve their financial situation, and later she married another Egyptian migrant and set up a home for herself.

The few incidents of this kind were among the more rewarding experiences for me. I realized that my interest in the details of everyday work of women as well as men helped many women gain a new consciousness that they could use to their advantage. To some degree, I believe I contributed to the evolution of their worldview and thoughts as they contributed to mine.

Methodology

As an anthropologist, my primary method of collecting and understanding data has been through participant observation. However, after I had been in the field for almost a year and had developed a better understanding of daily life in the community, I felt that since my sample was rather large for a study of this kind, the incorporation of detailed questionnaires and in-depth interviews would enhance the results of the research. I designed open-ended questionnaires on issues such as family and employment history of all working members of the households; housing arrangements and residential mobility in the city; and inventory of household goods, including the period of ownership and the manner in which the household goods were obtained. Another section was devoted to the division of labor within the household, and another asked for details and history of management of household financial affairs and consumption patterns of husbands and wives.[17]

After experiencing good progress in completing the questionnaires with the women of the households, I found that I would have to adopt another approach with the male heads of the households. Interviewing husbands in the presence of their wives always ended up in a major family dispute due to discrepancies in how each of them viewed the limits of husbands' responsibilities and rights. Because of lack of space and the limitations imposed on me by the prevailing ideology of sexual segregation I had to interview the men at home in the presence of their wives. Five interviews out of nine resulted in severe family disputes primarily because husbands and wives did not agree on the limits of men's financial responsibilities. Husbands and wives were very familiar with me and had no qualms about arguing in front of me; in fact, they often encouraged me to take sides, which did not help the situation. When I interviewed the ninth husband it ended up in such a fight that I dropped the idea of interviewing the men but continued to talk with them informally and ask their views on my topics of concern whenever the opportunity arose. However, the nine formal interviews that did take place proved to be very useful in helping me to understand the differences between husbands and wives. In the long years of my research I have met all the husbands of the households in my core sample except for two, though many of them migrated to the Gulf at some time during the research. Nonetheless, I have not had the opportunity to talk to all the husbands at great length. In these situations I have relied on the information given by their wives and children, neighbors and families.

I designed two other questionnaires for interviewing the children of the households who were, in 1984, aged thirteen or older. The questionnaire for young women concerned their future plans, education, occupation, family, views on marriage and the husband and wife relationship, and the credentials they seek in their ideal future husbands. The questionnaire ended by asking them how different they thought their marriage and family life would be from their mothers'. Now, when

17. These questionnaires were made up of more than one hundred mostly open-ended questions divided into several sections. I knew the questions by heart, and on each visit I would try to complete one or two sections so as not to make it too trying. I either made notes of these informal and semistructured interviews or taped them. Sometimes my friends would ask me to play back the tapes to them, in which case they often supplemented their replies with additional information.

I visit them years after these conversations, we often talk informally about the difference between what they expected and their actual lives and marital relationships. The young men's questionnaire was equally concerned with education and occupational plans, including their views on love and marriage, characteristics and credentials that they thought their wives should have, and the role and responsibilities of husbands and wives in marriage.

These interviews were intended to supplement the qualitative data I was collecting on the same households rather than replace it. These informal interviews were helpful in three major ways. First, they provided me with an efficient way of gathering family and employment history as well as household inventories for a sample that was relatively large for a study of this kind. Second, they gave me the opportunity to observe the gap between ideology and actual practice on issues such as the sexual division of labor and female employment. Finally, they provided me with a practical means of gathering comparable data.

It goes without saying that, as with most anthropological studies, I met my informants through my network and daily activities in the neighborhoods.[18] Throughout the text I have distinguished between informants and friends to convey the somewhat different relationship I have had with my contacts in the neighborhoods. With the exception of a few older and some younger men whom I came to know very well, I refer to the men as informants, because due to the gender ideology that I, a single Muslim woman, had to observe, my relationship with them remained limited and somewhat formal. My relationships with the women were quite varied, however. I came to know, like, and develop very warm relationships with many women in the neighborhoods. With others, particularly older women, I developed a close but semiformal, almost mother-daughter relationship characterized by respect. There were yet other women in my network whom I visited and chatted with, but my emotional attachment to them remained limited.

I made my notes (or tapes) in a mix of three languages: English,

18. The concept of neighborhood employed here differs from the more formal and geographic usage in the literature, where neighborhood usually implies definite social or physical boundaries. I have used "neighborhood" the way informants tended to use it, implying a sense of ego-centeredness and the dimensions of a local network. My informants generally considered their alleyway and those adjacent to it as their neighborhood, though at times it stretched farther to incorporate members of their network who lived locally but farther away. The alleyways may or may not fall into the same administrative subdistrict.

Arabic, and Farsi. Gradually, I reverted mostly to Arabic and Farsi because I found the two languages so compatible: many expressions and idioms were virtually word-for-word translations from one language to the other. This was often a great aid in recalling issues in the evening when I made my notes or tapes. I tried to make my notes in the form of direct quotations (he/she said, I said). I had deliberately chosen this model because with my limited Arabic it was easier and it had proved a more effective way of remaining true to the observations. Thus the "quotations" here are often essentially a recollection of my observations. The exceptions are those instances in which I had the opportunity to tape the conversations.

The very dense housing arrangements and the high degree of social interaction proved to be helpful in keeping constant contact with my large number of informants. My sample focused on younger households that were still in their family-building phases. Simultaneously, I aimed to include a variety of family forms: nuclear, extended, and de facto female-headed households as well as polygynous households. I also aimed to include a variety of occupational categories as well as a range in the length of time the households had been located in the urban setting.

The People

Although I came to know many households while living in the neighborhoods, the core sample for this study was sixty-two households. Over the years there has been considerable change in the number and composition of my core sample. Many of the migrants have returned, and residents have migrated. A few marriages have been dissolved one way or the other. Sadly, a few of my older informants have passed away. New children have been born. Many whom I interviewed as young men and women are now married or engaged. A large number have moved into the labor market, and some, both males and females, have migrated to the Gulf in the hope of improving their material situations. I present the data I collected on the families as of 1986 as a baseline, weaving in the new developments that occurred as the research progressed.

Nuclear families are the norm in Cairo, particularly among low-income social groups, and, as will be discussed in subsequent chapters, it is rare for people to form households outside marriage and kinship.

Table 1 *Distribution of Family Cycle*

Years of Marriage	Frequency
1–5	7
6–10	19
11–15	16
16–20	4
21–25	5
25 and more	11

Table 2 *Age Distribution of Wives and Husbands*

	Frequency	
Age Group	Wife	Husband*
15–20	2	0
21–25	17	0
26–30	12	6
31–35	12	15
36–40	6	12
41–45	8	7
46 and above	5	20
All	62	60

* Two of the husbands were deceased.

Eighty-seven percent of the households in the core sample were nuclear, 5 percent (n = 3) were actual female headed (not including the de facto female-headed households of migrants), and 8 percent (n = 5) were extended households. The years of marriage among the informants varied from two to forty-two (table 1). The age of the wives in the sample ranged from sixteen to fifty-six. The men typically were older (table 2). The number of children per family ranged from zero to eight. The majority of the children in the sample were under fourteen years old (table 3).

Illiteracy is widespread in the neighborhoods, particularly among women. Many women have never attended school. Many others have forgotten how to read and write after as many as five or six years of schooling, for unless they work in the formal sector they rarely use these skills except for reading bus numbers and prices, which almost all women were able to do whether or not they had received any formal

Table 3 *Number of Children*

Number of Children	Frequency
0	3
1	7
2	16
3	13
4	9
5	4
6	6
7	0
8	4
Total	202

Table 4 *Educational Level of Male and Female Heads of Household*

Level of Education	Male	Female
Illiterate	16	32
Partially literate	7	7
Primary school or equivalent	22	14
Above primary school	3	3
High school	9	6
Above high school/university	3	0
All	60	62

education. By contrast, many men who had never gone to school learned to read and write because the security of their employment depended on these skills. Table 4 summarizes the level of education among the male and female heads of households. It is noteworthy that all school age children (both male and female) who were under twelve were attending school. There were only a few teenage and unmarried daughters who had never attended school. All of these young women are now married and are strongly committed to sending their own daughters to school.

In the eyes of most people in the neighborhoods, however, housing and the general characteristics of a household's accommodations, not education, were the most important indications of a household's social standing in the community. Most buildings are privately owned by absentee landlords and landladies. The more recent constructions, which are the most common and popular accommodation, contain flats consisting of two small rooms with a corridor between them. There is a toilet, but rarely a kitchen. Many of the flats also have a very narrow balcony that overlooks the alley. This space may be used for cooking and hanging laundry, as well as for socializing with neighbors on adjacent or opposite balconies. Most flats are occupied by one household, although poorer people have to share. Older-style houses usually have many rooms that are occupied by different households who share toilet facilities. To acquire one's own home, however humble, was the most important aspiration of all households, and those who owned their residence had a feeling of achievement. Since the 1980s, remittances from migrants working in the Gulf have made it possible for many people to become home owners. Many buy small lots (often not more than 40 square meters) in the agricultural areas surrounding Cairo in the hope of gradually building a modest flat for themselves. "God willing," they say, they will add more floors to the house to accommodate their children as they marry.

Among my informants, three households had bought land and built their own homes after years of work in the Gulf countries by household members. Three other households had inherited some share of the building they lived in along with their other siblings. Two others had bought land twenty years ago and had gradually built their own homes themselves, with the help of kin.[19] Seven households lived in rented flats or rooms that belonged to their in-laws. The rest lived in either one- or two-room accommodations (see table 5). Most of the dwellings with two rooms were self-contained flats, with five exceptions. One household lived in a shack after the collapse of their rented dwelling. Those living in one-room dwellings rarely had a separate space to cook.

The Neighborhoods

The three neighborhoods in which I conducted my research are among the most densely populated and busy areas of Giza

---

19. Since 1986, two more households have managed to buy small pieces of land where they plan to build flats in the years to come. They hope that by this time Cairo will have extended even farther into the countryside since at present the lots are "in the middle of nowhere."

Table 5 *Size of Dwelling Units*

Number of Rooms	Frequency
1	18
2	30
3	11
4	2
5	1
All	62

(Greater Cairo) where buildings are constantly growing taller, legally or otherwise.[20] Much of Giza has been populated since time immemorial, but it is only during the last two decades or less that some areas have been considered urban and are housing unprecedented numbers of people.[21] When I started my research in 1983, there were still some signs of agricultural activity on not so distant borders of the neighborhoods, and one could easily see the desert land beyond. However, by 1994, these neighborhoods had become even more crowded and were no longer considered the frontiers of Greater Cairo.

These areas cannot be considered squatter settlements in the same sense as those found in Latin America. Most owners have legal title to the land but lack permission to build since the land is classified as agricultural; in some cases the landowner has authorization to build only one or two floors. However, except for the occasional *fallahi* (village) style of housing, most buildings have four to six floors. Since these are generally built without professional calculations of height and weight, many collapse and sometimes kill their occupants.[22]

20. Administratively, two of the neighborhoods were in the district of Bulaq Al-Dakrur on the west side of the Nile, which is reputedly among the most densely populated areas of Cairo City. The third neighborhood was in Umraniyah Gharbiyah, to the west of Bulaq Al-Dakrur, which has rapidly transformed into yet another densely populated district since the research started.

21. In fact middle classes as well as more educated people in the area sarcastically referred to the district as the China of Egypt, indicating its population density.

22. These collapses are so frequent that the newspapers often fail to report them. Although I know of no deaths in these neighborhoods due to the earthquake of October 1992, some of the buildings, including the one I lived in during the first year of my research, were seriously damaged and left many people homeless. However, not all the collapsing buildings are those illegally constructed. Many are old and perhaps once grand buildings in the ancient quarters of Cairo that the owners deliberately allow to deteriorate so they can evacuate their tenants and sell the land, which has increased in value as much as a hundred times in the last two decades.

These new areas have developed in traditional Cairene style with sets of crisscrossed narrow and winding alleys running through rows of four- or five-story terraced narrow brick buildings. These two-room flats, without yards or backyards, bear little resemblance to the fascinating mixture of beautiful, if crumbling, architecture of old Cairo. The main streets are the official traffic routes used by buses, minivans, and the occasional taxi. Many well-constructed shops and buildings are built along these main roads and are occupied by higher-income households. Over the years, small entrepreneurs with old, tatty minibuses and minivans have, for a small passenger fee, efficiently if not always safely connected the neighborhoods to the major centers of Cairo or to the city bus lines.

The narrow, unpaved alleys, where chickens abound and the occasional sheep is to be seen, are the site of many different social and economic activities. Men are notably absent, particularly during the day, because most spend both their working and leisure time away from the neighborhoods, leaving women and children as the primary actors. Children usually play in the alleys since they have no other option. Some women perform domestic chores and chat with friends on their doorsteps, while keeping an eye on their children. Those with a balcony overlooking the street prefer to sit there. Passersby see women holding conversations across balconies or haggling over prices with street vendors below. Despite periodic police raids, the daily vegetable markets, where women make up the largest group of petty traders, are constantly expanding, and some informal workshops have recently been established.[23] Many kiosk-type shops sell sweets and household items. There are also numerous itinerant vendors who make daily visits to the neighborhoods, peddling items ranging from cheap plastic toys to drinks and household wares.

During the day, alleys are women's space, and they are laid out in such a manner that unless one makes a point of seeking them out, passersby get little more than a glimpse. The residents, however, have easy contact with the rest of Cairo. They often cross the city to work, to go to government offices, or to visit friends and relatives. Most of the women's contacts are in the nearby main streets, however, where the

---

23. As selling without a license remains illegal, despite being a widespread practice, police periodically raid these markets, particularly if they are on the roads rather than in the alleyways. During these raids vegetables and fruits are deliberately destroyed by the police, and those who object may be arrested and fined. On these sad occasions many women and men lose the small capital that is their only means of survival.

cooperative shops called *gamᶜiyat* (which sell subsidized goods), other bigger shops, hospitals, pharmacies, and schools are located.

These neighborhoods are not ghettos, and the population is not culturally distinct. In fact, they are referred to as *haya shaᶜbiya*, often translated into English as the folk or popular quarter, as opposed to the *afrangi*, or European-style, quarters. *Shaᶜb* means "the people" or "the nation." The people of these neighborhoods were mainly first-generation rural-urban migrants and younger families from the densely populated parts of old Cairo who had difficulty finding accommodation in their own neighborhoods when setting up house. I did not notice that people from the same part of the country clustered together in the same buildings or close to one another as has been reported for other newly developed areas of Greater Cairo (Tekçe, Oldham, and Shorter 1994). Setting up their own independent households at marriage, young people often have to move farther afield, as housing in these neighborhoods becomes more scarce and expensive.

Most of the neighborhoods' inhabitants were Muslim, with a few Copts among them, but there was little in their lifestyles to distinguish them from each other. All, Muslim and Copt, considered themselves Egyptian and spoke the same language, though with various regional accents. The situation has changed somewhat, however, and people are much more conscious of their religious differences as a consequence of the Islamic oppositional movement. Although I heard of no overt tension between Copts and Muslims, I learned that some of the Copt families I had known in one of the neighborhoods had since moved out.

While many educated Cairene Muslim women in other sectors of the city were veiled, in 1983 one rarely saw a veiled woman in the neighborhoods of my study. However, their numbers have increased rapidly since then. During my visit in 1992, I went to pick up a friend's daughter from the local school. I was surprised to see that a large majority of girls, aged nine and older, including my friend's children, wore a white veil to school. There were also a few more Qur'anic schools for young children, with low or no tuition. With no other facilities in the neighborhoods, mothers were particularly pleased about these schools that provided a sort of day care and taught the Qur'an at the same time. The number of small local mosques had also increased. These mosques have reserved space for women where they can attend Qur'anic readings and religious gatherings, a rather recent phenomenon in Egypt where women historically have been excluded from mosques.[24]

PUBLIC UTILITIES

All three neighborhoods had electricity, whose quality and service have greatly improved since the early years of my fieldwork. One neighborhood was connected to the city water supply and another is now being connected, though there were often water stoppages lasting days at a time, or water only in the evenings, and rarely on the top floors due to low pressure. Families in the other neighborhoods had to carry water from the public taps installed on their boundaries. There is no proper sewage system in the neighborhoods, and in most cases refuse is periodically collected and illegally disposed of in a rubbish dump. In Cairo there is a private sector system that works well only if the garbage is valuable enough to make collection worthwhile, so the poor neighborhoods received poor service.[25] Recently, the government has provided some large bins on the borders of the neighborhoods as rubbish dumps, and garbage is occasionally burned there.

The Macro Context:
The Making of Egypt's Modern Economy

To understand why people make certain choices and not others, it is essential to look at the wider society in which they live as well as their individual characteristics and circumstances. People do not create the context of their society but influence it through continuously making choices within the options and possibilities it offers. Here I briefly outline the historical developments that have shaped Egypt's labor market and people's expectations of the state's role in delivering social services and ensuring that basic amenities are available even to the economically disadvantaged segments of the population.

The year 1952, when the old regime—and with it, British colonial

24. I was astonished to find that many mosques have no space for women. Mosques in Tehran and all the other major cities of Iran have always had a reserved space for women.
25. The garbage collectors did not come regularly and often dumped rubbish on the side of the main streets that border the neighborhoods. Therefore, the new government initiative to improve garbage collection with the provision of large bins was greatly appreciated by the residents.

influence—was overthrown in a coup d'etat by a group of young nationalist officers under the leadership of Gamal Abdel Nasser, was a major turning point in the emergence of modern Egypt (Gordon 1992). During the 1950s and 1960s, Nasser's government introduced a form of limited socialism in which the state gained considerable control over the economy, including foreign trade. The expressed aim of the regime was to dissolve class distinctions and to bring about a more equitable society in which individuals' capabilities and talents would decide their gains and their position.[26]

The regime promoted expectations of upward social mobility and made the state responsible for delivering the social conditions that would transform these hopes into reality. To this end, the regime introduced free, universal education, an impressive public health care system, subsidies for basic needs, an elaborate rent control system, and a liberal labor law that gave equal opportunity to women (Abdel-Fadil 1980; Amin 1995). The regime also implemented a radical land reform policy, addressing the entrenched landlessness of Egyptian peasants (Abdel-Fadil 1975; Richards and Waterbury 1990: 152–184; Beattie 1994).

The Nasser regime used the state's expansion to create and expand its own constituency, particularly in urban areas. One strategy was to employ qualified candidates from the poorer and less powerful social strata, who made up the strongest bloc of government supporters (Waterbury 1983; Richards and Waterbury 1990; Amin 1995). Education became a vehicle for social mobility. This gave new impetus to educational achievements during the second half of the 1950s and 1960s, reflected in increases in the standard of living at the national level (Abdel-Fadil 1982; Williamson 1987).[27] For the first time in Egypt's history, sons of peasants and urban lower-income groups had access to higher education and could move to positions of power.[28] Through these policies, the regime created a new form of social stratification with a new ruling class

26. Nasser underlined these hopes in his speeches to the nation: "I want a society in which class distinctions are dissolved through equal opportunities for all citizens. I want a society in which the free individual can determine his own position by himself, on the basis of his efficiency, capacity and character." (Speech delivered on October 3, 1961, quoted in Abdel-Fadil 1982: 352; see also Beattie 1994).

27. The key to secure well-paid jobs in the state and public sectors was formal education: the government guaranteed jobs for all high school and university graduates. The eagerness to obtain educational certificates derives from the Nasser era, and after three decades, social mobility and educational attainment are still closely linked in popular ideology.

28. These were government white-collar employees who form the new middle classes.

and middle classes whose interests were intertwined with the regime's stability.[29]

The embargo initiated by Britain after Egypt's nationalization of the Suez Canal and the subsequent flight of both national and international capital pushed Nasser's government to nationalize major industries, leaving only smaller firms and traditional workshops in private hands. The state became, and still is, Egypt's largest national employer. More than half of the industrial labor force and more than 90 percent of industrial technicians, foremen, and administrators became employees of the public sector (Cooper 1982; Richards and Waterbury 1990; Amin 1995). Both the government and the public sector employed a considerable number of unskilled workers. In fact, many of the older blue-collar workers in the neighborhoods in which I conducted my research were among those who gained government employment in the 1960s, and they greatly appreciated the relatively high wages and the security these jobs had afforded them (see chapter 3). The liberal labor laws brought in under Nasser were imposed primarily in the public sector, and government workers benefited from what the regime called the "basic rights" of citizens. These were the right to free education, health services, employment, social security, an old-age pension, and insurance against sickness and disability, over and above their relatively high income. Their common interest in maintaining this secure situation made the public sector work force a relatively unified constituency, whose continuing support of government policies brought further political stability to the regime.[30]

To extend state benefits to other social groups, the regime introduced subsidies, which became a powerful mechanism for reaching those at the bottom of the social scale and securing their political support (Khouri-Dagher 1986, 1996). In addition to affecting income distribution, this provided an opportunity for the state to manipulate access to consumer goods through selective subsidies (Alderman and Von Braun 1984; El-Issawy 1985; Khouri-Dagher 1986; Richards and Waterbury 1990; Pfeifer 1993). The subsidies covered wheat, rationed kerosene, sugar, lentils, rice, soup, cooking oil, and some cotton tex-

29. As I discuss below, their interests and political positions became much more diverse after Nasser's era. Sadat's "liberalization" of the economy further stimulated the process of fragmentation.

30. In the 1980s and 1990s, it is precisely this segment of society that is the most dissatisfied and critical of the government, as high inflation in the 1970s was not matched by salary increases (MacLeod 1991; Singerman 1995).

tiles. Because of their relatively low initial cost, the regime was able to maintain such wide-ranging income support programs. As a result of urban biases, inherent in the industrialization policies of many developing nations, it was mostly urban populations that benefited from subsidies.

Disproportionate industrial investment and the rapid rate of population growth due to rural-urban migration and improved health status contributed to the rate of urbanization and the concentration of a large group of low-income earners in major cities.[31] This process has gained even greater momentum since the 1970s, when Egypt gradually returned to economic liberalization under Nasser's successor, Anwar Sadat. The increasing demand for subsidized goods by the urban population boosted the cost of subsidy programs, exacerbating pressure on the budget, which was already burdened by the huge cost of war with Israel. When the United States, a major wheat supplier to Egypt, refused to accept payment in Egyptian currency, the Egyptian government faced a major crisis. However, subsidies were too politically sensitive to be suddenly interrupted or dramatically decreased within a short time.

Subsidies that politically benefited Nasser's regime have become a major source of political instability for his successors.[32] World inflationary trends and price increases since 1973 increased the cost of the subsidies so that they have become a major drain on government budgets.[33] This problem was intensified by the fact that under Nasser prices had been generally constant. The government quickly recognized the po-

---

31. Urban development was financed by nonagrarian sources of revenue such as oil, the Suez Canal, tourism, and remittances. In Egypt the agrarian sector has not been subject to any considerable transfer of capital to the nonagrarian sector, especially when the cost of the Aswan High Dam and the extensive subsidization of fertilizer and other state agricultural programs are considered. During Nasser's era, the agrarian sector played a much more prominent role in the country's development plans, but since then, due to its declining rate of growth and new economic approaches, the agrarian sector has lost its status.

32. The association of certain socioeconomic events with certain persons (for instance, Sadat or Nasser) should not be read as a personification of the politics. Rather, it should be understood that collective responsibilities for the development and process of the government in a particular era are often subsumed under one person's name for convenience.

33. The cost of subsidies rose from 9 million pounds in 1960 to 130.8 million in 1973; by 1979 the cost had reached 1,288.4 million pounds, indicating that Egypt would be forced to cut back on its subsidy program, given the very limited government income (Ministry of Supply, quoted in el-Korayem 1982b: 46).

litical cost of passing on price increases to consumers when it announced a sharp reduction in subsidies on some food items, including flour, sugar, rice, oil, and bottled gas, on January 18, 1977. Although the government gave assurances that other basic subsistence items would not be affected and that other compensatory measures such as wage increases for civil servants would be implemented, the public responded the next day with spontaneous protests across the country, from Aswan to Cairo and Alexandria. The government had anticipated some resistance but was not prepared for full-scale riots. The police and the army acted to end the rioting, causing more than one hundred fifty deaths (Cooper 1982; Hinnebusch 1993; el-Sharkawi 1993). The government was forced to cancel the proposed cuts. In 1982, a similar riot took place when the government tried to increase the price of bread.

This reaction was motivated by the important contribution of food subsidies to the daily budget of urban low-income earners, to the extent that any cut in subsidized items takes a heavy toll on their standard of living, which is often very low.[34] Moreover, as Nadia Khouri-Dagher (1996) has argued, to ordinary Egyptians, who have come to see the price of bread and other subsidized goods as a yardstick against which to measure the affordability of other items, a rise in the price of bread indicates a rise in the cost of living in general.

To avoid political upheaval and minimize resistance, the Egyptian state has adopted a policy of gradual removal of subsidies and has largely succeeded.[35] Nonetheless, the gradual reduction of subsidies has meant a huge national deficit and continued borrowing from external sources, plunging Egypt further into debt. Recognizing the political significance of the subsidies, the International Monetary Fund (IMF), the World Bank, and American Aid for International Development, despite their consistent emphasis on abolishing subsidies and promoting conditions in which market forces can function without government intervention, have been tolerant of Egyptian fiscal policies.

Whether due to economic failure or external pressure, Egyptian economic policies have shifted from a welfare to a market orientation through implementing gradual structural adjustment policies known as

34. For more discussion, see el-Korayem 1982a, 1982b; el-Sokkari 1984; Pfeifer 1993.
35. Although the increased cost of living has resulted in a considerable increase in political dissatisfaction, since opting for their gradual removal, the state has experienced no major riots directly related to subsidies.

infitah (often called the Open Door policy). This was officially recognized in 1974, in a government document that focused on the urgent need for foreign currency and the opening of the Egyptian economy to direct private investment from both Arab and foreign capital (Kerr and Yassin 1982; Amin 1995).[36] However, the Open Door policy has not delivered the desired result. Egypt did not attract multinational companies, except in the fields of finance and services. Nor did Arab capitalists show great interest in Egypt. Consequently, the level of production remained low, forcing Egypt to borrow more each year (Butter 1989). Egypt's debt continued to mount, causing high inflation (Lofgren 1993a, 1993b; World Bank 1993: 234–235).

The shift in economic policy did not result in dismantling the old economic system as the economic planners had suggested.[37] In principle, at least until the end of the 1980s, the government was committed to the enounced public gains of the revolution. In reality, however, the quality of public services such as free health care and education have suffered greatly. This has stimulated the private sector to provide services, but they are expensive and beyond the reach of most. These inadequacies have also stimulated the amalgamation of mixed private and public services. For instance, free schooling is combined with widespread private tutorial programs, sometimes held in public school buildings. Similar initiatives have taken place in health care: Christian and Muslim religious organizations offer low-cost health facilities to low-income earners (Sullivan 1994; Singerman 1995). The gap between the citizen's expectation of what a legitimate state should deliver—framed by the Nasserite concept of basic civil rights—and what the state actually delivers, combined with increased income inequality, has created fertile ground for political dissatisfaction, despite popular support for the opportunities that the liberal economy provides.

36. It must be noted that the Egyptian economy was never a closed economy. During the period of socialist development it increased its dependence on the outside world, but this dependence was controlled and selective (Abdel-Khalek 1983).

37. The pressure to keep and continue Nasserist enterprises within the state was too strong (Waterbury 1983; Amin 1995). Indeed, throughout the 1980s, the public sector continued to have a dominant role both in the production of nonagrarian goods and in providing industrial employment opportunities. What has taken place is the development of two parallel "formal" economies: the public sector, which takes little notice of market forces, and the private sector, which is profit motivated. The two sectors have contradictory operating rationales, yet at the same time there is continuous interaction (Waterbury 1983; Amin 1995).

International Migration

Parallel with the economic policy shift, migration to Arab oil-producing countries by both skilled and unskilled workers became widespread. The remittances, which remained primarily in the hands of citizens, have relieved some of the negative effects of Egypt's structural adjustment programs.[38] The sheer numbers of migrants and the relative wealth of remittances from their earnings make it essential, from an academic or political point of view, to scrutinize the impact of migration on income distribution, inflation, the labor market, saving, investment, consumption, and the stability of the present political system. Therefore, it is not surprising that migration has been singled out as the most important agent of social change in the last decade and has been the subject of much debate.[39] Prior to the oil boom of 1973 and the economic shift in Egypt, labor migration was closely controlled by the state and was confined mainly to highly educated and skilled workers such as doctors and teachers.[40] Restrictions were gradually dropped, and by the mid-1970s the government encouraged migration as a source of foreign currency (Waterbury 1983; Amin 1995). Remittances from Egyptians working in the oil-rich Arab states rose from $189 million in 1974 to $1,425 million in 1977, an increase of 400 percent in four years. In 1979, remittances exceeded $2 billion (Amin and Awny 1985), more than the total income from cotton exports, the Suez Canal, tourism, and the domestic oil industry. Since 1980, the upward trend in remittances has been more modest due to the recession caused by the decrease in oil prices. Nevertheless, Galal Amin (1995: 44) estimates that in 1990, workers' remittances amounted to $3,743.5 million (29.9% of total earned foreign exchange). These earnings continue to be an important source of revenue, particularly since the Gulf war, when many of the Yemeni, Jordanian, and Palestinian workers were replaced by Egyptian migrants.

38. This term refers to the general withdrawal of the state from the economy, leaving market forces to operate.

39. For a survey of the literature, see Amin and Awny 1985 and el-Sayed Said 1990; and for a national study, see Fergany 1987. For in-depth case studies, see Khafagy 1984; Brink 1991; Nada 1991; and Hoodfar 1996a.

40. It also had a political undertone and was considered a brotherly gesture between the Arab nations. See Dessouki 1978 for a detailed exposition of Egypt's migration policies since 1950.

There are no reliable statistics on the exact number of Egyptian migrants; estimates vary by as much as 50 percent.[41] Conservative estimates judge the number of migrants at two million. However, turnover is high, and the majority of migrants spend only three or four years in the host country (Fergany 1987: 11). Thus a significant part of the population has been directly involved in this process, as either migrants or beneficiaries of remittances. Migration has enabled manual workers, particularly previously underprivileged unskilled and semiskilled workers, to improve their economic position in two ways. First, the removal of large numbers of workers from the local economy to the Gulf countries has pushed up wages in Egypt, particularly in rural areas. Second, remittances have encouraged demand for basic goods, housing, and durable goods. The remittances of low-income migrants, in particular, are a major force in increasing demands for more affordable nationally produced goods (chap. 7; see also Amin 1995: 45; Hoodfar 1996a).[42]

Summary

Anthropology and anthropologists have come to accept, though not always willingly, that regardless of their training their perceptions and understanding of social issues cannot be divorced from who they are and how they are perceived in the community of their research. I was conscious that my status as an unmarried, Iranian, Muslim woman had an impact on how I was viewed by the people of the neighborhoods, which in turn affected the research and the data I collected.

Survival strategies are affected by the socioeconomic characteristics of individuals and their households, their cultural settings, and the opportunities that are open to them in the wider context of the society. Hence the chapter provided a brief review of both the micro and the macro situations, particularly the role of the state in shaping the labor market opportunities and providing basic amenities such as health care,

41. For different estimates up to the early 1980s, see Amin and Awny 1985: 25. The difficulty in establishing reliable figures arises from the fact that many migrants leave on visiting visas while many others continue to be illegal migrants.

42. Wealthier segments of Egyptian society, which include highly skilled and highly paid migrants, have shifted to consumption of mostly foreign-produced goods, a market that has been vastly expanded since the introduction of the Open Door policy.

education, and employment. Egypt's budget deficit forced the government to revise its welfare state-oriented social and economic policies and implement structural adjustment policies, the result of which has been a high inflation rate on basic needs. The massive migration of unskilled and semiskilled workers to the prosperous oil-producing countries has provided a buffer against the ensuing economic hardship among those who traditionally formed the low-income social strata. While formal and informal private sector workers have benefited from the new policies and have improved their economic situations, those in the public sector have been hit hard as their salaries have not kept up with the steep inflationary trend. As a result, lower-middle-class Egyptians and many urban public sector workers, who were traditionally supporters of the state, are now vocal critics.

CHAPTER 2

Marriage, Family, and Household

Why Marriage?

In Egypt people rarely live alone by choice (Rugh 1984; Shorter and Zurayk 1988). Individuals move out of their natal households when they form their own households through marriage. A household may include extended and nuclear family members, and other kin on occasion, though membership is rarely extended to nonkin. In the lower-income neighborhoods of urban Egypt, most households are formed around the nuclear family (Shorter and Zurayk 1988; Shorter 1989), and marriage plays a significant role in shaping the structure of a household and the position of individuals within it. Moreover, marriage practices in Egypt (and generally) play an important role in reproducing gender ideology.

In practice, at the outset of marriage, a bride and groom together with their families generally negotiate agreements that enhance their positions and their bargaining power within the marriage and the household. In addition to emotional and social factors, economic considerations are of prime importance in the choice of a marriage partner and in the stipulation of the conditions of a marriage contract, since the material well-being of individuals—particularly women and children—is closely tied to the economic situation of their households. After briefly outlining the rights and responsibilities of husbands and wives in Muslim marriage as it is practiced in

Egypt,[1] this chapter reviews the major premarital strategies and the factors that influenced people's choice of marriage partners.

Marriage in Its Cultural Context

Marriage is probably the most important social event in the lives of Middle Eastern men and women. It is through marriage and having children that adulthood and self-realization are achieved. Particularly in the urban setting, the beginning of married life often coincides with the couple setting up their own household. Almost from their children's infancy, parents are preoccupied with improving the prospects for successful marriages. While marriage is often delayed because of financial hardship, the pursuit of education, or family circumstances, the idea of remaining single by choice is beyond the imagination of almost everyone in the neighborhoods—young or old, male or female. "How could anyone choose not to follow the custom of the Prophet?" an elderly woman responded to my innocent query about the possibility of remaining unmarried by choice.[2] In the neighborhoods and in Egypt generally, like most other parts of the Muslim world, marriage is the only acceptable context for sexual activity and parenthood and provides the primary framework for the expression of masculinity and femininity and the fulfillment of gender roles.

Marriage in Egypt is regulated by custom, religion, and the legal system, which dictate different roles and responsibilities for men and women. Muslim marriage gives certain rights to a husband in return for his expected contribution to the family. Men are responsible for providing for their families, which includes their current wives and underage children and may include aged parents, unmarried sisters, younger brothers, and the orphaned children of their brothers. In return for

1. A few households in the wider sample were Coptic, but I will be discussing Muslim marriages in this chapter as many of the issues and concerns are similar, with the exception that Coptic women rarely divorce officially.

2. She was referring to the hadiths: "Marriage is my Sunnah. He who does not act according to my Sunnah does not belong to me"; "A person who marries achieves half his religion, so let him fear God in the other half"; "Most of the people of the Fire are bachelors"; "No building is built in Islam more beloved to God than marriage"; "A Muslim man can acquire no benefit after Islam greater than a Muslim wife who makes him happy when he looks upon her, obeys him when he commands her, and protects him when he is away from her in herself and her property" (Murata 1992: 171–172).

these responsibilities, a husband is assumed to have the unilateral right to end his marriage without the consent of his wife.[3] He also has the right to have as many as four wives on the condition that he can provide adequately and equally for all of them and treat them equally.[4] Furthermore, at least according to the cultural interpretation of Islamic marriage mores and the legal codes in Egypt, a husband has the right to restrict his wife's physical mobility.[5] This has come to be understood as the husband's right to prevent his wife from being employed. Should a marriage end in divorce, husbands have the guardianship and custody of their children beyond a certain age, usually five to seven years for boys and puberty for girls.[6] In recent decades in Egypt, as in other Muslim countries, there has been some attempt to legally limit some of men's rights by favoring a more liberal interpretation of Islamic *sharī'a*.[7] Nonetheless, women, particularly those with children, are aware that they stand to lose more than men should the marriage fail.

In a Muslim marriage, in addition to providing for the family (regardless of his wife's financial status), a husband is expected to satisfy his wife sexually. Failure in any of these responsibilities gives a woman grounds for divorce with or without her husband's agreement. She is also entitled to her *mahr*, which is a sum of money or tangible property agreed on before marriage. Muslim women have always had the right to control and dispose of their own property, including inheritances or any wages they may earn, without having to contribute to the household. While women may inherit from their blood kin, they inherit only a negligible part of their husband's property (although in Egypt, the wife or wives of a government employee will also receive his salary or pension after his death until such a time as she or they remarry). In the case of divorce, however, a wife is entitled to only three months alimony, her mahr, those possessions she brought with her at the start of the marriage, and what she may have acquired with her own income

3. Although in recent decades in Egypt some legal reforms have been introduced to curb some of these male privileges, in practice there is little a woman can do if her husband decides to exercise his traditional privileges.

4. This often means that each wife must be provided with her own residence.

5. This right stems from the principle of *ta'a*. See Fluehr-Lobban and Bardsley-Sirois 1990 for more discussion.

6. In recent years, laws have been enacted to raise the age at which children may be taken by their fathers. However, in practice among low-income communities, men rarely demand custody of their children, particularly daughters.

7. For a general discussion on these issues, see Leites 1991; Esposito 1982; Botiveau 1993.

during the marriage. For these reasons, the security of marriage is an important factor for women and their natal families—who are responsible for supporting a woman whose marriage fails—and thus they strive to arrange secure marriages for their daughters.

The reality of the institution of marriage is much more complex than its accepted ideology indicates. For example, among low-income groups, in which men often depend on their wives' labor, men rarely use their prerogative to restrict women's movements, and women are generally free to perform their errands and social activities. As well, the relatively low incidence of divorce, particularly after children are born, suggests that marriage is a relatively stable institution in Egypt.[8] In general, most women enjoy more rights than are traditionally ascribed to them, and hence they are unlikely to resist or question the status quo on gender relations, despite being very aware of their restricted legal rights in marriage. While the more powerful, wealthier classes have advocated legal reform as a means of social change, the less privileged groups try to protect their interests through manipulation of the resources and avenues they can control. During the last few decades of rapid social change, women and their families have developed initiatives and strategies to circumvent the legal and ideological limitations imposed on them. For instance, kin and in-group marriages have historically been the most common strategies for protecting women from abuse by their husbands. More recently, women have been demanding a larger mahr, and among low-income communities detailed and rigorous premarriage negotiations that cover most aspects of married life are becoming the accepted norm.

Social and economic change has given rise to much higher material expectations, which place greater pressures on men, the ideologically designated breadwinners. For young men, the legal and religious privileges that marriage historically afforded come at a greater cost than for previous generations. Hence many young men try to find ways to minimize these responsibilities. For example, they may marry women who have some cash income, or they may marry women from much lower social rankings whose expectations may not be so high. As we will see in chapter 5, difficulties arise when men attempt to reduce their responsibilities without forgoing their traditional privileges.

8. In Egypt, the rate of divorce has declined from 2.09 percent in 1971 (UN 1971: 752) to 1.42 percent in 1992 (UN 1992: 318, 321). However, the rate of divorce, in relation to the number of children, indicates a decline of 6 times less after the birth of the first child, 13.2 times less after the birth of two children, and 49.3 times less after the birth of the fourth child.

Choosing a Suitor

Both Islam and tradition provide channels for devising strategies for secure and successful marriages. Since marriage is viewed not as a partnership between individuals but rather as an alliance between two families, the equation to determine the best marriage partner is very complex and not easy to disaggregate.[9] All but four women in my sample said that it was best for women to marry kin because their economic status and background are known, leaving little room for deception. Furthermore, they pointed out that should there be a problem between the groom and the bride, the families would try to help patch up the differences, as the consequences of divorce or domestic violence would be grave for both sides of the family.

Women and most younger members of the communities almost always viewed members of their mothers' kin as the most suitable for marriage partners, as opposed to the norm of patrilineal and especially cross-cousin marriage. This choice may stem from the fact that most families in the neighborhood more commonly interacted with their mother's kin (see chapter 8). Fathers, however, often said that the ideal marriage was between parallel cousins from the father's side, but they frequently qualified that statement by saying that in their own case their relatives were not suitable.

While men also expressed preference for kin marriages, their underlying logic was very different. Both young men and their fathers said that kin marriages are best because they are less expensive. Neither the bride nor the groom can demand many gifts or a high mahr, making these marriages less of a burden for the fathers of both bride and groom. Ironically, many women, particularly younger ones, counted this aspect of kin marriages as a disadvantage. Fatin explained:

In Egypt men do not work at home. In fact they do not spend much time at home. Once a man is married and has a wife who cooks and cleans for him, he no longer has a vested interest in providing household goods and so does not work as hard. But if he has to provide these as a condition of marriage, then he probably is more eager to do that. . . . But when one marries a relative the bride's family places fewer demands on the groom. Con-

9. Fortunately, marriage and employment were a favorite subject of discussion for men and women of all ages in the neighborhoods. Apart from many informal discussions, I also conducted semistructured interviews with parents and unmarried young men and women in my sample.

sequently kin marriages give women less economic leverage and a wife has to endure more hardship to improve her standard of living.

Many daughters observed that the eagerness of their fathers to marry them to relatives stemmed from a desire to lessen their own financial responsibilities while ensuring safe marriages.

Despite these preferences, there were few kin marriages within the neighborhoods, and only three couples among my sample had married within their kin group. This low rate of kin marriage may be attributable to the fact that the population of these neighborhoods was primarily first- and second-generation rural-urban migrants who had few relatives nearby.[10] Many marriages in the neighborhoods were between neighbors, which according to parents were second only to kin marriages because of the opportunity to observe potential spouses and their families. Many neighbors who had established close ties with one another planned marriages between their children or family members to strengthen their friendship ties through kinship (see also Singerman 1994, 1995).

Great emphasis was put on the credentials a spouse ought to have. In addition to a pleasant appearance for suitors of both sexes, a potential wife should be a clever homemaker and a good mother, while a potential husband should be able to provide for the family, be a responsible and loving father, and respect his wife. Azza's mother, who had four daughters, explained the difficulties most parents face.

In the old days most people married their relatives or neighbors who were of the same social class. But now there is much more contact between different people and one's daughters may have a chance of marrying into a much higher income group. But this also means that the daughter may not be treated with respect by her husband and in-laws. . . . For my daughters, I wish to find good self-made suitors, educated men who have good jobs but come from similar family and social backgrounds.

Whereas most young and educated unmarried girls in the neighborhood expressed a desire for rich, modern, educated, and handsome men, more traditional and less educated women were skeptical of marrying up. At the age of sixteen, against the wishes of the uncle who was her guardian, Mona married Nasser, a handsome man from a family considered relatively well-to-do. She had no education; he had a high school diploma. Ten years into her unhappy marriage, Mona told me,

10. Other studies indicate a much higher incidence of kin marriages in Cairo (see Rugh 1984; Shorter and Zurayk 1988; Watson 1992).

If only I had the sense to marry someone like myself, I would not be treated the way Nasser treats me. You have seen how he treats me. I don't feel like his wife, he makes me feel I am his and his children's servant. And there is nothing I can do now because if I ask for a divorce, I would have to become a maid to support myself. Worse yet, he may take my children away from me and then I will have nothing in life. So I have to put up with being a servant in my home, as the alternative is being a servant to other people.

Young women from families who proudly associated themselves with *baladi* (urban traditional) or *fallahi* (peasant) culture were inclined to accept the conventional wisdom and marry among their own class.[11] However, they were often considered "backward" by the more educated young women.

Sahar was a friend whose company I enjoyed, though other young women and sometimes their mothers made fun of her and called her "mindless." I was continuously told that I would not learn anything from her. Later I realized that it was her marriage story that had resulted in her "becoming the laughingstock of the educated girls of the neighborhood," as she herself put it. Sahar was the eldest of seven siblings. After her primary schooling she was kept at home to help her mother with the domestic chores, the fate of many elder daughters in the neighborhoods.[12] When she was eighteen, she found a suitor, a high school teacher with a university degree. His family was much better off than hers and he was considered good-looking. However, after three months she broke off her engagement, although he was insistent on the marriage. She told me,

I'm not educated and I may be silly, but I thought, Why would a man of his stature, who can marry many other women from better families and with more education, want to marry me? Is it not because he can rule me, . . . because I am not as educated and knowledgeable as he is? His family would look down on me, and I would have to play the role of subservient wife. . . . I couldn't take it. I know all the girls in the neighborhood think I'm stupid and maybe I am, but my dignity is more important to me than social standing.

Sahar's mother understood. She said, "Sahar's father came, like me, from landless peasants. We have been poor, but he always treated me like his queen."

11. For a discussion of traditional identity and baladi self-images, see el-Messiri 1978a, 1978b.

12. Many families did this: eldest daughters were virtually illiterate because the mothers needed help; youngest daughters may have finished high school and sometimes several years of college.

Months later, Sahar found a new suitor who was the first in his family to have graduated from high school (and not so good-looking in her opinion). He was a primary school teacher. A few months after her engagement, she was disappointed to observe that he did not respect her and at every opportunity reminded her that she was not educated. She said,

I was really hurt by his behavior toward me. . . . I had given up a richer and more educated man because I didn't want to be treated like a servant by my husband and I was not going to put up with him treating me this way, so I canceled the marriage.

Before long she married a young man from her parents' village, who had nine years of education and thought very highly of her. Now, years later, she frequently visits her mother in the neighborhood with her three children, and many middle-aged baladi women praise her for her realism and intelligence. Others still remember that she gave up a real chance to escape poverty, but in 1992 when I visited her, she confidently repeated that she made the right decision and pointed out the marital problems of some of her educated peers in the neighborhood as proof.

There were other factors that women pointed out as important elements of a successful marriage. All women in my sample said that men have to be more educated than their wives. Younger and urban-born women also insisted that a husband should be older by at least five or six or even ten years. When I asked why that was, they explained that a wife should obey and listen to her husband, and, since men do not mature as fast as women do, a woman cannot heed a man of her own age whose judgment is not as sound as hers. This would create problems for a marriage and might even result in divorce. Women consistently used this justification for their preference for older men. Mona, a seventeen-year-old high school student, told me,

I would never marry someone of my own age, education, income, or social stature. . . . The problem is that in our society men like to think they are wiser than women, though if they are equal in age and education it is always the woman who is more clever, as you can see all around you. On the other hand, according to our religion a wife has to obey her husband. But no one can obey someone who is not as wise as she is, and consequently there would be lots of arguments and the marriage will fall apart and what would happen to the children? Therefore, it is better for a woman to marry someone who is older, more educated, who has much more experience in life than she has, and so it would not be illogical for her to obey him.

What this kind of universal justification indicates is that women not only do not consider themselves inferior to men but also see themselves, under equal conditions, as wiser and more capable. Therefore, to cope with the religiously legitimized male expectation that a wife has to obey her husband, women deliberately marry older and more experienced men.

Urbanization, social change, and the trend toward nuclear households have strengthened women's conviction that it is best to marry an older man. A middle-aged woman who was older than her husband explained to me,

In the village age wasn't important; if the families decided the couple was right for each other and if they had the means to live, they could marry. My parents agreed with my mother's brother that I should marry his son, who was about two years younger, so we married. But in the village, men used to do their own work on the farm and women did their own tasks. Men and women did not spend time with each other. One spent more time with one's mother-in-law and should have a good rapport with her more than with one's husband. But things have changed, even in the village.

Men's description of the ideal wife and circumstances of marriage mirrored women's views. Men felt strongly that to be accepted and respected as heads of the household, they had to be older and more educated than their wives. None of my male informants expressed any inclination to marry women of higher social standing since such a marriage was viewed as a continuous test of their dignity. Some men acknowledged that the option of hypergamy (marrying up) was not usually open to men because of financial constraints.[13] But the more successful men in the neighborhoods expressed outright hostility to the idea, saying that even when the couple truly loved each other, marrying up meant a man would be a "henpecked husband."

One of my middle-aged informants told me that while he was at university he fell in love with a classmate.[14] The love was mutual, but she came from a rich and vastly different background, so he decided to marry a young woman from the neighborhood instead. He explained,

At the time I wasn't sure of what I was doing, but as I get older I am more convinced. My wife does not have much education, but when I go home she runs to bring my tea and keeps the children quiet. When my mother

13. Although there were a few examples of men who married into a higher social class, it was usually at the cost of total separation from their own family and social class.

14. He was the first man from the neighborhood to atttend university.

visits, she treats her like a queen. She looks up to me and is grateful to have an educated husband, and that her standard of living is higher than she had at her father's.[15]

Generally, men were aware that society awarded them privileged status within the family, and they were conscious of placing themselves in socioeconomic positions within marriage so as to avoid situations that might cause women to question the status quo. Some of the more traditional older men from upper Egypt said as soon as women earn money, the marriage institution is spoiled and men are no longer men. Other, younger men said they would never marry a woman who earned more money than they do because in that case "the husband becomes a wife" and gave examples of such couples from the neighborhood. Men saw a direct link between their masculinity and their role in marriage as the major breadwinner; any deviations would leave their masculinity and adequacy open to question.

However, both men's and women's responses to questions regarding gender roles within marriage and factors that influence their respective positions often shifted substantially if the discussion took place in the presence of their spouses. In these situations men would rely primarily on culture, custom, and biology, rather than on a material approach, to justify their views. For instance, Ahmed, who had on various occasions explained to me that men should not marry women with more education and income, said in the presence of his wife,

Among Egyptians a man always receives respect and obedience from his wife even when she is highly educated and he is illiterate. For instance, I know of such a couple and I have seen that when her husband arrives home the wife drops everything and brings him tea and massages his feet, as a wife is supposed to.

Of course, Ahmed's friend was a fictitious one, and during all the years of my fieldwork I have yet to see or hear of any wife massaging her husband's feet. That talk was more directed to his wife and the other women who were present, as he remarked later when I probed him about the comment he had made. "Women need to be reminded that in nature there is a place for men and one for women and nothing should change that." A similar tactic is also adopted by women, who point out in front of their husbands that the housework they do is

15. A husband is expected to be able to provide at least the standard of living that a woman enjoyed at her parents' home. His failure gives the wife grounds for divorce.

worth more than all the income their husbands bring home and for that reason God has made men responsible for family expenses. In support of their claim, they sometimes calculate the monetary value of their services. Women downplayed having to obey their husbands or having their movements restricted by asking why a woman would want to go out or go shopping, and so on, if her husband offered to have everything delivered at home.

In other words, gender ideology and the marriage institution provide a framework within which both genders try to manipulate the norms and promote their own interests, within marriage and outside it.

Arranged Marriages versus Love Marriages

Ideally, parents chose their children's partners with the tacit agreement of the prospective couple. The groom's father directly or indirectly contacted the bride's family, and if the response was positive, he then visited them and proceeded with marriage negotiations. By this stage the potential bride and groom have usually seen each other and agreed to the match. Although one hears about women who were married against their will, apart from a young Coptic woman who was married at the age of fourteen, I never came to know of any and none of my informants knew of any such marriages, though a few women had not been sure and their mothers and relatives had persuaded them by reminding them of the groom's attributes. One thirty-two-year-old woman who was always amused by my interest in their lives and views jokingly told me,

Write for your professor at American University that we were poor and we all had to marry among the poor. For our parents, one good responsible poor man was the same as another poor man. They had no reason to force us to marry against our will. . . . Maybe if we were rich it would be very different.

When asked how they chose their partners, women invariably answered that their families or fathers decided who they would marry. However, after I got to know them better, a different picture emerged. Several older women said that their fathers or brothers had found them rich suitors, thinking that it was in their best interest. But through their mothers and aunts the girls expressed opposition to the matches and they were canceled.[16] Many educated women who married in the 1970s chose their husbands from among their colleagues. At least five in my sample had married for love and had decided on their marriage before their parents met the groom, and two of them had married against the wishes of their parents. Others had asked friends to find them suitors among their families or brothers. Many of the older couples (both within my core sample and among others I came to know relatively well) had married relatives or neighbors or someone from their village. Younger and more educated people had found their marriage partners through their network at home or through contacts outside the neighborhoods. However, in all cases, formal steps were taken and the bride's family negotiated the marriage conditions, even in the two cases in which the family had opposed the marriage.

Although an ideology of marriage based on love is gaining popularity, it is compatibility and harmony that are viewed by both men and women as the key to a successful marriage. Love is said to be blind and irrational, as one educated woman who herself had an unhappy marriage based on love told me.

Love may make the best subject for a pleasant song or the basis of a film. Maybe it is good for dreams when you are fifteen, but it surely should not be the only or even the major basis for marriage. How can physical attraction, which is all love really is, be the basis of a marriage?

Marriage in Egyptian culture "is supposed to be primarily for survival, for cooperation between two parties, not for the unification of two souls" (Zaky Nagib Mahmud, quoted in Rugh 1984: 133). This view was conveyed to me by many men and women in the neighborhoods. Umm Shadia, an elderly woman, mother of four sons and four daughters, and a respected community leader who was often consulted by others about marriage and marital disputes, decided to teach me the principles and importance of marriage among Egyptians. She explained,

Here one does not marry a person, but a family. Therefore marriage is much too important to be left in the hands of two kids who have lost their heart to a pair of beautiful eyes or nice hair, who think life is like love films they see on television. What do they know about the difficulties of life? A marriage should be based on compatibility of the couple and their families. Husbands and wives should be respectful of each other and perform their

16. Anthropologists have documented different strategies women adopt to resist undesired marriages when faced with authoritarian parents (Morsy 1978; Abu-Lughod 1986; Singerman 1995).

respective duties within the marriage. . . . A marriage based on respect and harmony brings love, but a love marriage that lacks harmony ends in fights and disaster.[17]

Indeed, children's characteristics are observed very keenly to suggest appropriate marriage partners. For instance, it is believed that daughters who are quiet and obedient are best married within their own kin group to ensure against mistreatment by their husbands. Marriage opportunities are used to bring children, especially aggressive or rebellious female children, in line. To discipline them, children of seven or eight are often told they will grow old and lonely because their behavior and temperament make them undesirable marriage partners.

Although a few men said they would marry a woman they fancied as long as she was from a good family and was decent and modest, even if their parents disagreed, all women, including the younger women who thought love is essential for marriage, said they would not marry without their parents' complete approval. Samia, a very bright eighteen-year-old known for her rebellious nature, told me,

I think loving my husband is essential for me. In marriage, life is tougher for a woman than for a man. At least if one loves one's husband it makes it easier to obey him. . . . But I will not marry a man if my parents do not agree. I may tell my parents it is either him or nobody, but if a daughter does not have the blessing of her parents, her husband is not going to treat her with respect. He will think a woman who does not respect her parents' wishes after all they have done for her will not respect him, a stranger, either.

This attitude is reinforced by observing the lives of those who deviated from traditional marriage practices.[18] Those who had married without their parents' approval were the first ones to point out the problems. Sadia's marriage provides an excellent illustration of this point. Sadia, a white-collar worker, told me,

When I was a teenage schoolgirl in the 1960s we were told about dreams of modern Egypt, not the Egypt of the rich, but our Egypt. Women were going to be educated and free themselves from the traditional binds. Like

17. My own grandmother of eighty who worried about the consequences of the romantic views of her eight granddaughters—including me—on issues of love and marriage used to repeat this last sentence to me every time I went to visit her in Tehran.

18. These observations were possible because there were very few aspects of family life that are considered beyond the scope of discussion among family and friends. Discussing marriage issues with my friends in the neighborhoods, they frequently raised examples from the lives of other women or households to justify their views. I often felt that I was doing fieldwork in a community of anthropologists.

all my classmates at the time, I took that to heart. I believed in love and wanted to marry the man I chose. I fell in love with the brother of one of my friends who was tutoring us. I agreed to marry him and I announced this to my parents, who had already found me another suitor and were waiting for me to complete high school and then marry us off. They were shocked but finally agreed, but they told me that I had to take 100 percent responsibility for the marriage, that if tomorrow I had problems with him, I could not complain to them. So I married him, before receiving my high school diploma, and since he had very little money, we had to move to his mother's at first. There I quickly realized that I was dreaming that marriage was just about love but in fact it was about harmony and mutual respect— that society and parents, too, have to approve of the marriage. I could not go to my parents, as they had warned me, and worse, I became pregnant almost immediately. However, my first child, a son, died. I decided to finish my studies, and had my second child the same year. I got a job at the Ministry of Education, and immediately after that my husband refused to pay any money to me for house expenses because he wanted to spend all his money on himself. Since I married without my parents' support, he believed I could not turn to my parents and indeed it was hard for me to do so, but I did and they forgave me. I also felt stronger because I had what was then considered a good job. I almost got a divorce over this matter. However, I went back to him. Life is different when you have children. . . . My parents helped us to get a small flat and now he pays a little money. But our relationship is not healthy. The love died long ago and the harmony and respect was never there, but I only came to discover this after I had married him. Now, when I take a look at my sisters' marriages arranged by my parents, they are happier and have their husbands' respect. I married for love, but I want my three daughters, who are the apples of my eye, to marry in the traditional arranged way so that I can negotiate on their behalf and make sure they have a good start. I want them to be happy and not suffer the way I did.

Young women are reminded that if their parents are concerned and control their movements, it is because they do not want them to fall in love and ruin their lives. Unmarried women who were employed outside the neighborhood explained that if a colleague approached them and they liked him enough to consider marriage a possibility, they would immediately ask him to contact the family. Only if the negotiations were successful would they start seeing him. Naima, a white-collar employee with a high school diploma, asked me,

Why should I start talking to a man and put my reputation and heart on the line before I know if he is serious? If he meets with my parents and meets their conditions, even if things do not work out and we break an official engagement, at least I and everyone else would know that he was serious and did not just want to play with me.

Some thought that women should show respect for their husbands, but never love, even if they are in love with them. One afternoon, after a few of us watched an old Egyptian movie on television, we had a lively debate on the role of love in marriage. Haleh, a happily married twenty-eight-year-old woman, concluded our long discussion by saying, "One should never demonstrate her love for a man because he will take her for granted. The right way is that men should love their wives much more." Others agreed with her. This view stems in part from many women's belief that expressing such love for their husbands undercuts women's bargaining power. As one middle-aged woman commented, "Men want what they don't have; why would they do anything for you if you are already at their feet?"

Ideologically and religiously, the most important responsibility for any parent was to assure that their children, both male and female, were happily married. However, despite strong views on these matters by all, few parents from low-income households actually were involved in their sons' marriage arrangements, or rather their involvement was more formal than real. Only the richest and, sometimes, the poorest parents in the neighborhoods had a say in the marriages of their sons.[19] This gap between ideology and practice was due in part to parents' inability to pay or substantially contribute to the soaring cost of marriage, which traditionally in Muslim cultures is largely borne by the groom and his family. Also, a large number of parents were from rural backgrounds and felt they no longer possessed the experience and expertise needed to advise their sons or find them suitable wives. Sons, therefore, enjoy much more freedom in choosing partners. Some men considered this a mixed blessing as they believed only a woman could get to know another woman, and without the support of their mothers and sisters they would find out little about the true nature of the woman they intended to marry. Many men under forty had found their wives through their own networks.

19. Richer parents often paid for the wedding expenses and had an important role. However, a few poor men who were obliged to live with their mothers and did not have the resources to rent an additional room had left it to their mothers to find them a wife. "Since they [the mother and the wife] have to live together it is better that she [the mother] chooses the bride. Then hopefully there will be no fights," one son said. Moreover, the poorest men had to rely on their mothers' networks to find a bride who would demand nothing.

While parents can withdraw from involvement in a son's marriage without great social consequences, particularly if there is a legitimate reason, no parent can choose not to participate in a daughter's marriage arrangements. A family's honor and self-respect are very closely tied to the daughter's. Allocating resources to the marriage of a daughter is probably the only time she receives priority over her brothers. However, the cost of a daughter's marriage is much less than a son's. While the parents are expected to provide her with a suitable trousseau, consisting of clothing and personal items, the contribution of other items is much more flexible and is considered a gift, not an obligation.[20] What is important is that the bride's parents play an effective role in negotiating the groom's contribution to the cost of the wedding and establishment of the new household.

Marriage Negotiations:
Strategies to Reduce Marital Conflicts

Marriage negotiations are considered the most important element in setting a marriage on the right path. As one woman who was helping her husband to build their very first small flat put it,

Marriage negotiation is just like a plan for a building. You have to realistically assess your resources and think of every little detail that is important for your comfort and the safety of the flat. If parents conduct a good and smart marriage negotiation for their children, it is most unlikely that the marriage would end in disaster.

Among low-income Egyptian families, in addition to financial matters, every detail of married life considered important by the parties involved is up for negotiation. Some mothers will even go so far as to negotiate whether the bride should use contraception the first year or have a child and then use contraception (see chapter 9).

After an initial meeting, when the groom or his family visits the bride's home and both sides indicate their consent, additional meetings take place to negotiate the details. Ideally, negotiations should take place between the elders from both sides: fathers and uncles, mothers

---

20. This is rapidly changing, though, and the bride's parents are now increasingly expected to contribute more to the cost of setting up the couple in their new household, often at a standard much higher than that of the parents.

and aunts, and grandmothers. However, in the neighborhood, negotiations often began between the bride's parents and the groom, who might take a friend along. I know of only one case in which the groom's father participated and another in which the groom's mother, who paid for the wedding herself, negotiated all the aspects of the marriage with the bride's father. The groom's mother and sisters may be present at the final stage of negotiation to formally give their blessing. The exceptions were instances in which the two families were very close and the women of both sides played the key roles in negotiations.

The primary player in the negotiations is the mother of the bride, who, depending on her position in the household, may participate actively and openly or may sit more quietly and note the details being discussed and afterward convey her opinions to her husband. During formal discussions the bride's father, while making his wishes known, chooses his words very carefully, remaining noncommittal until later in the negotiations.

Negotiations start with the groom revealing information about his family and himself, such as the details of his education, job, income, worldly possessions, and future plans. The bride's father or his representative indicates his demands. Neither side expects that this first serious meeting will end in any concrete agreement, beyond the sharing of several pots of tea. Ideally, if the groom is not well known to the bride's family, after this meeting the bride's mother and friends set out to learn about the man and his family from his neighbors, colleagues, and employers. However, the degree to which families take this character investigation seriously varies substantially. In fact, since nowadays there is typically an engagement period of several years during which the bride's family has the opportunity to know the groom better, the importance of character investigation has diminished.

Marriage negotiations have two components: first, the material contribution of each side to the marriage and the new household; and second, other relational arrangements between the bride and the groom after the marriage. For the most part, the first includes the size of the bride's mahr. This is usually a considerable sum that varies with the social status of the bride's family. Theoretically a bride can demand all or part of the mahr at the time of the marriage or reserve it until some time during the marriage or in the event of divorce. In Egypt, the mahr is customarily divided into two sums. The first payment, called the *muqaddama,* is given by the groom to the bride before the marriage and is used to buy furniture for the couple. Sometimes the groom buys the furniture, which he then puts in the bride's name when the marriage contract is signed. The second payment, called the *muakhkhara*, religiously and legally may be demanded at any time after the signing of the contract but usually is used as a deterrent for divorce, since if a man wishes to divorce his wife he would first have to pay her this remaining sum. Therefore, the larger the sum, the more effective the wife's leverage.

Anyone over the age of forty can tell you that marriage expenses have increased since the 1970s. Elderly women told me that at the time of their marriage, a bed and canopy, a wardrobe, and a few other major items were provided by the groom, while the bride's family provided bedding, cooking facilities, and a small trousseau of personal items.[21] Often they just rented a room near their parents and expanded their quarters as the family grew, but times have changed. Parents, and young people themselves, expect that each generation will have a higher standard of living.[22] A couple preparing to marry now needs a gas stove, a television, a matching bedroom set, settees and a table, an electric washing machine, a food mixer, and a refrigerator. The bride's trousseau includes many nightgowns and enough clothing and personal items to assure she will not need to ask her husband for personal items for at least five years. The greatest expense incurred in setting up a household is the key money needed to rent a small flat, which runs from 1,500 to 3,000 pounds even in the most distant neighborhoods. This means that the groom has to work hard for a few years before he can get married. By contrast, as soon as a daughter is born many families start accumulating items for her trousseau.

The negotiation includes details of all items that both sides have agreed should be provided before marriage, what share the bride's family will provide, and what the groom's responsibilities will be. Once the items are accumulated and the marriage takes place, everything is carefully detailed in the marriage contract as the property of the bride. If the marriage dissolves for whatever reason, the groom must see that all nonperishable items are returned to the bride. All women agreed that this was important, to remind men to treat their wives well. This custom led to deferred marriage and encouraged potential grooms, who normally live with their parents and have few housekeeping expenses,

21. Other accounts of marriage arrangements among the same social group confirm this (Nadim el-Messiri 1975).

22. For further discussion on how families strive to give their children a higher standard of living, see Singerman 1995.

to work hard and save money so that they can begin married life with a higher standard of living.

Many young women expressed bitterness about waiting as long as four years to get married. They were torn between wanting to have most of the basic household goods before marriage and not wanting to wait so long, particularly since many engagements were broken after a couple of years. Women are very conscious that during a long engagement they miss other marriage opportunities. As one mother pointed out, men can always find someone to marry whereas a woman's options diminish with age, particularly since men prefer to marry younger women.

This new trend in marriage practices has caused the average age of marriage to rise considerably for women and men. While the state, family planners, and some feminists may consider this a positive indicator for population control or women's increase in status, most women in my sample viewed it negatively. Women who were neither students nor employed resented having to postpone building their family. Many women agreed to marry older grooms who had worked and saved up enough to be able to marry. One young bride said, "I would rather marry a man just five or six years older than I am, but they don't have the means to marry. So my groom is fifteen years older. But my parents and I felt this was a better choice." This trend, which is increasing in the neighborhoods, has great implications for marital relationships and the status of women in the family. The age and experience of the husbands and the gap between men's and women's monetary contributions to the household place women in an even more subservient position in the marriage partnership. It also means that they will spend long years as widows who will most likely be financially dependent on their children. This in turn has ramifications for population policy as women try to have more sons to secure their chances for later economic as well as emotional support.[23] Many young men find a fiancée and, after an agreement is reached, migrate to the Gulf to work for a couple of years and save money to be able to marry. I asked women why they do not make smaller demands on their fiancés so they could marry sooner. They insisted that such strategies would mean poverty forever. One young woman, engaged to be married, said,

Today I can demand to have a gas stove before marriage. But once I am married, he will not buy it. He wants his lunch, but whether I cook this on a kerosene burner or a gas stove is not his problem.

---

23. Traditionally, sons are responsible for looking after their aged parents.

Another twenty-year-old woman, who was expected to marry within a couple of months, explained that the difficult negotiation of the material aspects of marriage had nothing to do with greed, as she thought I was implying by asking these questions.

When a man has to work so hard to marry, he has a vested interest in trying hard to make the marriage work. Especially since if he divorces his wife, he will lose all that he worked for, because it all belongs to the woman. In this way, too, men who are of modest means are effectively banned from marrying a second wife because to provide all these items again takes them forever.

Given that divorce, even within the revised version of family law, is so much easier for men than for women, women tend to protect themselves through these strategies while simultaneously paving the way for a higher standard of living.

Additional negotiations take place closer to the marriage date. Most women, particularly those recently married, considered these negotiations vital to a harmonious marriage. All details of financial and other responsibilities, the specific contributions of husband and wife, and often the location of the marital flat are discussed. For brides, the location of the flat is very important, particularly if they are employed outside their neighborhood or intend to enter the labor market in the future. Most brides prefer to be close to their mothers so they can help with child care responsibilities. This preference often means putting up with smaller flats and higher rent, but this is a sacrifice many women feel is worthwhile.

Financial arrangements include the amount the groom should pay as housekeeping money, what expenses this covers, and what he can expect from his wife. Some negotiations are so detailed as to specifiy whether he should expect one meal a week with meat, or two. Fatin had divorced her husband at the age of nineteen. Now in her thirties she had not expected to marry again. But she found a suitor, the mahr was successfully negotiated, and everybody was excited and preparing for the engagement ceremony. But the engagement came to a halt because the potential groom had agreed to pay 90 pounds per month but would not consent to buy food or clothing for her. After family members consulted, they decided that if he agreed to bring home a kilogram of meat every week they would agree to the arrangement, but he refused. Fatin had worked as a semiprofessional seamstress in the neighborhood for many years, had bought all her household goods, and had a rented flat of her own. This liberated the groom from providing or paying for all those items. She thought that he was taking advantage of her, that he wanted a wife, a comfortable home, and good food but did not want to contribute very much. She said,

If he only wants to pay 90 pounds a month, then I still have to work many hours to keep our standard of living from falling. He's thinking that if I want to improve our life, I can work and earn money, while he can spend all the income from his second job on himself. I am old enough to know that a man who wants to start in this way will probably be even meaner once we are married.

Women are keenly aware of the importance of these negotiations for relationships with their husbands. Some of the younger women who were experiencing problems with their husbands over financial affairs blamed their mothers for not having negotiated well. Many men try to get out of their obligations, but a good negotiation before marriage helps assure a woman's security. "It hurts a woman's dignity if she has to talk money with a husband she has just married," said one unhappy bride.

Talking about money matters and trying to negotiate and get a better deal for yourself will be interpreted as being too materialistic, when you are supposed to enter into a relationship based on good faith and understanding. It is the parents' duty to arrange these matters in advance and try to prevent future problems for the couple.

Men generally felt an agreement before marriage was fair, because if the conditions are not acceptable, a groom is free to end the negotiations and look for another bride. A newly married man added,

Since parents and others are usually involved in this negotiation, if problems arise the couple can always ask them to intervene and find a workable solution that is acceptable to all sides, rather than leave it to two inexperienced people to solve their problem.

Another groom said,

Beginning married life and putting two people from two different households together to live is difficult enough without them having to solve money matters and other details. Best is to discuss these matters in advance, and if years later they are unhappy, things can be changed.

Premarital negotiations may also include how often the bride should be able to stay with her family. I never heard of this matter being written in the legal marriage contract, but such a discussion was intended to help ensure a smoother marriage with little room for conflict.

According to my older informants, detailed negotiations regarding the daily life of a married couple have emerged only in the last few decades. In the past, people married within their communities, where customs and norms were shared, but now people may marry across regions and social classes with vastly different customs and expectations. Moreover, life is changing very rapidly, and most young couples do not live the way their parents did. Some young women whose mothers were not very influential in the family or had little experience in such matters would ask a relative or a neighbor to participate in the negotiations. On the whole, as a result of social changes, the bride's mother is taking a more prominent role.

Although most negotiations focused on the demands of the bride and her family, increasingly men bring their own conditions to the negotiating table. For instance, more men, especially educated men who choose to marry educated women, are now objecting to their wives working outside the home, particularly if the job is located outside their area of residence. This even includes men who have chosen their brides from among their colleagues. This demand often creates a dilemma for some women who, to increase their chances of finding a secure job, finished high school at great sacrifice to their parents and sometimes their siblings. Men's objection to their future wives' employment is often framed in terms of the costs involved and the threat to a husband's honor (see chapter 4). Though not always successful, women try to make compromises by agreeing to stay home after having children or if they feel they cannot cope with both domestic responsibilities and their jobs. Occasionally they also suggest taking up the veil to protect the family's good name and honor. This situation has encouraged many younger women in the neighborhood to return to more traditional female activities such as tailoring or hairdressing, since these skills allow them to operate from home and circumvent their husbands' objections.

A second, now common, condition men attached to their marriage proposal is that the bride take up the veil.[24] Although until 1986 only a few educated women in the neighborhoods wore the veil, the practice is now quite widespread. It is now rare for women who get married to remain unveiled, particularly if they are educated or aspire to be con-

---

24. For more discussion of reveiling among working women, see Hoodfar 1991 and MacLeod 1991. For a more general discussion of modern veiling, see Zuhur 1992.

sidered modern (though not afrangi, which implies Westernized) as opposed to baladi (traditional). Husbands' demands to this effect are now
far less controversial from women's point of view than they were a decade ago. During the first few years of my fieldwork, women felt very
strongly that veiling should be done of a woman's free will and that a
husband had no right to impose it on his wife. Nahed, for example, was
excited because her friend had found her a handsome, educated suitor
who had the financial means to marry within a few months. However,
her excitement soon withered away after a couple of meetings with her
suitor because he demanded that she take the veil at once. Nahed, dis-
illusioned and disappointed, explained to me,

If he had put forward any other condition I would have accepted to marry
him because he is from a very decent family and I liked him. However, his
demand for me to veil because he wishes and not because I might decide it
is best for me indicates that he will not respect his wife as an equal partner
and also that he has not understood what Islam is all about. I have thought
from time to time that I might like to veil and I admire women who do it,
but I feel I have not reached that point yet. I will veil when God wants me
to and when he gives me the strength, but not when a man demands it of
me as a condition of marriage.

Nahed's mother, an illiterate woman from upper Egypt respected in her
neighborhood for her long struggle to educate her four daughters as
well as her four sons, regretfully agreed with her. Nahed was not the
only young woman in the neighborhood who had resisted a suitor's
demand to veil. Some women had successfully confronted their suitors
and had convinced them that veiling was a matter for the woman, not
her husband, to decide. Many of these women, including Nahed and
her sisters, subsequently veiled of their own accord a few years after
their marriage. By the time of my visit in 1992, the situation had completely changed. It is now rare for an educated woman not to be veiled.
In fact, many young women veil while still in high school and some
even before that. Others veil as soon as they find a job. Most women,
with the exception of those who were least educated and young women
in the neighborhoods who saw themselves as part of the rapidly changing baladi culture of Cairo and still dressed in the traditional manner,
planned to veil at the time of marriage if they had not already done so.

   Though taking up the veil no longer seemed to be a major issue during marriage negotiations, the question of employment remains quite
significant for educated women. In the face of rapid social change,
women and their families feel they should try to safeguard their future

and old age by having a secure formal sector job.[25] However, the salary for low-level clerical jobs in the formal sector has not kept up with the rate of inflation, and many men felt that their wives' employment would not contribute much to the household income but would cause great inconveniences (see chapter 4). Some men added that women's wages may also make them "big-headed" and lead them to question men's authority as head of the household. Other men framed their objections in terms of not wanting their honor tested for nothing.

Once the marriage agreement is reached, the groom brings a piece or two of gold jewelry (among low-income families this can be a very modest pair of earrings and a watch or piece of cloth). The groom and the father of the bride read the *fatiha*—the first chapter of the Qur'an— and shake hands, acknowledging that they honor their agreement, and the groom comes to the bride's home to visit her. However, unless it becomes very evident that the marriage will take place, the bride and the groom do not appear in public together without a chaperone. If after some time it becomes clear that the groom is not serious, the bride's family may cancel the engagement. Contrary to attitudes among the middle classes, breaking an engagement did not harm the bride's chances of finding another suitor or the honor of her family. When asked, women who broke an engagement often said simply that it was not meant to be. Some young women in the neighborhoods had been engaged two or three times.

Polygynous Marriages

According to conventional Muslim ideology, if a man can fairly, equitably, and adequately provide for each wife, he can marry up to four wives. The assessment of the ability to provide equitably has, however, been left to men's conscience rather than to legislation. Historically, though polygyny has been practiced mainly by economically privileged men, at times it also occurs among the less affluent. The marriage of a man with few resources to another wife has far-reaching effects on the family. Many men stop or drastically reduce contributions to the first family. Polygyny was thus an issue both women and men

25. Formal sector jobs were preferred for their stability and fringe benefits, especially the old-age pension.

discussed frequently, often with reference to the polygynous households in the neighborhoods. While women tended to condemn polygyny outright, particularly for poor men, men were reluctant to condemn the practice even when they themselves believed they would never enter a polygynous marriage. "I am happy with my wife and I will never marry another woman, nor could I afford that. But there must be a good reason for its existence if the Qur'an has recognized that right," one middle-aged man told me.

Some men in the neighborhoods had married a second wife because the first wife could not have any children, and in one case that I knew of, it was the first wife who chose the second wife for her husband. The first wife, a middle-aged woman, defended polygyny, saying if it was not for such arrangements, women like her (who did not produce children) would have to sleep in the street. However, there were other cases in which the husband and wife were reputed not to get along well and therefore the husband finally left and married a second wife. I also came to know of one man who married a second wife, a widow in the neighborhood, because he fancied her, although he insisted he had a happy family life with his first wife. The news of his second marriage left his first wife devastated, but at her age with four children, she had no recourse but to pretend she was content with his decision. In all cases, each wife had a separate household, usually not in the same building.

Men invariably said a man in a happy marriage would not marry another woman, thereby indirectly blaming the women. Some women accused men of being greedy and shortsighted, thinking only of their own pleasure. Otherwise, they argued, why would a poor man marry a second wife when he cannot even afford to keep his first wife? Women insisted that for this reason they must be clever and manipulate men to prevent them from exercising their right to marry a second wife. Some younger women said if a man wished to take additional wives, his first wife must be as much to blame as he, since the cost of marriage is so prohibitive that no man would want to go through marriage twice. "Except very rich men, who do not come to our neighborhood anyhow," one woman added. However, when I asked women what they would do if their husbands took other wives, all with the exception of two unmarried ones said that if they had children and the husband continued to honor his duties and support the children and the household, they would remain in the polygynous marriage rather than get a divorce. Most unmarried women, whether educated or not, including women in white-collar jobs, said the same thing. They would contemplate divorce only if the husband refused to provide.

Women's reluctance to consider divorce stems from two major factors. First, children legally belong to their fathers and women do not want to risk losing them. Second, women often lack the financial means to survive; even when they have a paid job, their income is often too meager to support the family. Women are also very aware that divorced women with children have little chance of remarrying, because men rarely accept other men's children in their home. Therefore, the practical choice for a first wife is to stay married to her husband and try to secure support from him. Moreover, women also benefit from the legitimacy of marriage, which affords them more freedom in the community.

One informant who said she would definitely divorce a husband who took a second wife had just turned thirteen, and her father had married a second wife. She was determined to get an education so that she could earn enough to support herself should her future marriage not work and to not have to compromise her dignity and stay in a polygynous marriage, as her mother had, just for money.[26]

Some women became second wives unwittingly and found out about their husbands' domestic arrangements only after the marriage. However, a woman who knowingly becomes a second wife, particularly in a close-knit neighborhood, is often treated badly by other women, unless they see that she had no choice in the matter. Umm Sabah, who sells vegetables in the local suq, is a second wife and is liked by her neighbors. She explained her marriage story to me.

I came from a very poor family and my father was sick most of the time. He had a stand where he sold vegetables and I used to help him with his business. Every time a suitor came along, my father refused. For one thing they didn't have money to buy me a trousseau, and second, the family could not survive without my labor. In the end, my parents died and my brother went to do his military service and I managed to marry off my younger sister and later my brother also married and left me. I ended up living by myself in a dark and damp room even worse than the one I live in now, and I survived by selling vegetables and greens in the local market. I barely earned enough to pay rent and eat. I was very sad, not because I was poor, but because I, like all other women, so much wanted to have children, but

---

26. At the age of twenty-one, she is now one of the very few women from her neighborhood who has attended university. Despite having many suitors, she says she will commit herself to a marriage only when she has a good job.

no one would marry me because I was poor, old, and not pretty. One day a neighbor said the butcher wants to marry a second wife and get away from his first wife. He asked me if I would marry him, and I said yes. Before I knew it, I was married to him and I had two children. That is all I wanted from God. He is not the best husband, but he pays 10 pounds a week and I earn around 5 or 6. He visits twice a week and brings the children some meat. I think, given my situation, this is the best arrangement. I do not want more children, but I am glad that my children have another five brothers and sisters, and sometimes they go there to play with them. I have also lived by myself and have become stubborn and do not really want a husband all the time who I have to obey and cook for and clean after. Now I only have to cook for him twice a week, and almost never do any cleaning or wash his clothes. And he is a good father, and very kind to my children. It suits me fine, and my co-wife, though initially upset, has become more friendly and accepts my children.

Umm Sabah was very content, and glad that her children had more siblings. "Eventually, they [the half-siblings] will support them more than a stranger. They are of the same blood, and blood pulls," she said.

Another woman told me the story of how she became a second wife.

We were very poor. When the groom came, my parents were ambivalent in the beginning, because he had a wife and four children. But then he is rich and has a shop and a building and they thought he can support two households. It is not so bad. I just wish my co-wife would not feel so hostile to me.

Since the marital relationship is primarily an agreement to live together and raise a family with respect and harmony, spouses fulfill their emotional needs through other relationships, particularly in the early years of marriage. For instance, women often have very close relationships with their sisters, mothers, or more commonly with one or two neighbors. Daughters, as they grow up, become a mother's best friends. Men also seek moral support from friends. Often as the husband and wife grow older and bring up children together, they gradually also develop a strong friendship.

Summary

In Egypt households are formed on the basis of marriage and kinship. While blood ties remain important, marriage is a domain within which individuals can influence whom they want to marry or be related to. Hence among the poor (as well as the rich) marriage choices and conditions are important life and survival strategies. The ideology of marriage and gender roles, legitimated by law and by conventional understandings of Islam, prescribes different rights and responsibilities for men and women. This assymetry encourages women and their families to develop marriage strategies to circumvent legal and social limitations.

Unable to challenge the social and ideological constraints that treat women as inferior to men, women, who generally see themselves under equal conditions as equal if not always superior to men, have opted to marry men who are older and have higher social and economic credentials. While this made it more logical for men to act as the head of the household, as they were more educated and more experienced, and for women to obey them, it also meant that through marrying up women translated their social and ideological inferiority to men into socioeconomic advantages. Men felt that they should marry women with lower credentials so as their privileged position as the head of household would not be questioned by their wives. Hence gender inequality and the ideology of inferiority of women are continuously reproduced with little pressure for social and legal change.

Because of the parents' inability to contribute to the cost of the marriage traditionally borne by the groom and his family, men in low-income neighborhoods increasingly choose their partners without their parents' influence. However, women's awareness of their unequal social and legal status in marriage diminishes the appeal of love marriages. Women of modest means prefer to have their parents and in particular their mothers involved in their marriage negotiations. Marriage contracts, demand for a substantial mahr (in cash and household goods), which they keep in the event of divorce, and other strategies are used to circumvent the legal limitations women face.

Similarly, men motivated by their desire to retain their privileged position in marriage devise strategies and bring conditions to the negotiations. In the 1980s they frequently asked their potential brides to wear the veil, which at least symbolically communicated that they accepted the conventional gender ideology. Since veiling has become much more widespread and most women, especially those with careers, wear some kind of veil, it is no longer a sensitive issue in marriage negotiations. However, more and more suitors demand that women give up their employment. This demand conflicts with women's, particularly educated women's, concerns regarding financial security in the event of divorce or widowhood, and yet many women feel obliged to acquiesce as most eligible suitors give this demand high priority in the marriage negotiations.

In short, the marriage institution and gender ideology provide a framework within which both sexes operate, manipulating the norms and conventions to promote their own interests, both in marriage and society. In the process, asymmetric gender relations and gender ideology, which often disadvantage women, are reproduced.

CHAPTER 3

In Search of Cash

Men in the Labor Market

The Rising Need for Cash

In the highly commercialized metropolis, cash is an important part of any household's total income. In Egypt, the rapid commercialization of goods and services traditionally provided at home, together with a growing demand for more modern products, has increased the significance of the household's cash resources. The past decade's high rate of inflation and reduction of food subsidies have also contributed to the household's need for cash.[1] Households and individuals are preoccupied with earning more money. To survive and improve living standards, low-income earners seek to increase their cash income by diversifying their activities and weighing the cost and possible gain of various alternatives.

Labor market conditions provide the context within which individuals assess viable options in relation to their abilities (such as skills, education, network, capital resources) and their position and responsibilities within the structure of the household. Therefore, a man and a woman with equal opportunities, facing similar situations in the labor market, may make different choices, though each decision is equally rational in economic terms. This is due in part to the sexual division of labor within the household, which places different demands on males

---

1. The food and beverage index rose from 100 in 1966–1967 to 1839 in 1990 (CAPMAS and UNICEF 1993: 88).

and females. In Egypt, both traditional and modern views of the sexual division of labor designate men as the breadwinners: hence their primary role and responsibilities are outside the home, in the labor market. A man who does not have a job and stays home is pitied and considered a failure. A woman's primary contribution is considered to be domestic work and child care. Though this does not exclude her from labor market activity, her choices are governed by different criteria. This chapter examines the characteristics of the labor market and then looks at the moneymaking strategies employed by men, who tend to be the major cash contributors to many households. Women's options and choices are explored in chapter 4.

Urban Employment Opportunities

Like many other developing countries, Egypt is finding it difficult to provide jobs in the formal sector for its growing population. The formal sector includes state administration, the public sector, large-scale modern industries, and tertiary services with substantial capital; in short, it covers all economic activities where employees are protected by labor law. High unemployment in the formal sector has coincided with the decline of agricultural employment over the last three decades and limited opportunities in industrial employment.[2] The process of labor reallocation continues to be heavily dependent on the expansion of the tertiary sector.[3]

Egypt's labor market has three distinctive features. First, the state, even after two decades of structural adjustment policies, remains the major employer in the formal sector. Second, despite the lack of reliable statistics, scholars and policy makers agree that a dynamic informal sector accounts for a large percentage of employment (Abdel-Fadil 1983; Kamel Rizk 1991). Finally, international migration is probably the most influential factor in the recent restructuring of the labor market, particularly among unskilled and semiskilled groups.

Theoretically, employment in the formal sector includes those in the government and public sectors and larger private firms. However, in the

2. Abdel-Fadil 1980: 13; ILO 1984, 1991, 1994.
3. The tertiary sector includes activities such as trade, banking, services related to production, state administration, and social services.

absence of large-scale private production or services, the private sector's share of employment has remained small. Furthermore, the jobs available in this sector, primarily in commerce and banking, are among the best paid, and are often reserved for better-educated upper-class workers. The formal jobs accessible to people of the lower social groups, who are the concern of this study, are almost exclusively in the government and public sectors.

The state and public sectors together provide the bulk of formal employment. This is a trend established by Gamal Abdel Nasser's nationalization policies and the expansion of the state machinery in the 1960s. To expand the regime's support base, Nasser's employment policies incorporated not only the educated sons and daughters of the rural and urban lower classes but also many unskilled and semiskilled workers; many of the older male informants in this study were among these public sector workers. Economic and political changes of the 1970s brought a change of policy (Hansen and Radwan 1982). The rate of state and public sector expansion slowed, and these employment policies were practically abandoned by the early 1980s.

Male Employment in the Neighborhoods

Until the mid-1970s, state and public sector jobs were preferred (Abdel-Fadil 1980; Cooper 1982; Singerman 1995). They were well paying, with shorter hours, more security—they were all protected under the relatively liberal Labor Law 91 of 1959—and generous fringe benefits.

In 1985, most of my male informants who had been in the labor market for more than ten years preferred government and public sector employment, and many of them worked in that sector (see table 6). Their greatest problem was the highly competitive nature of the public sector labor market, where education and social connections determined hiring (see chapter 8). However, both male and female informants agreed that, given the socioeconomic conditions in Egypt, technical professions, preferably in the private sector, or self-employment were most appropriate for men. This change of opinion was caused by rapid wage increases in the private sector (both formal and informal) and the rising cost of living while government wages increased only modestly. The fringe benefits, retirement plans, and job security that government em-

Table 6 *Formal Sector Occupations of Male Heads of Household*

Type of Occupation	Frequency
Office clerk (middle level)	2
Junior clerk	9
Technician	2
Blue collar (low level)	14
Total	27

ployees enjoyed did not compensate for the low pay. Middle- and lower-level government employees were among the lowest paid in the labor market, and their salaries hardly met the basic needs of a small household.[4] According to Mahmoud Abdel-Fadil's (1983: 75–78) calculation, in the early 1980s there were about 1.7 million people in the formal sector who earned wages below those estimated by the World Bank as the poverty line for Egypt. He suggested including them in the designation "working poor," a term usually reserved for those working in the informal economy.

By the early 1980s, government employment was no longer a favored option. This had a considerable impact on the education of boys in the neighborhoods. Among low-income earners, education was an investment rather than a luxury and was meant to lead to a well-paying job. Households with few material resources to spare were alert to changes in the labor market, and young men were encouraged to start work as apprentices in workshops or enter technical school rather than prepare for clerical or administrative work. The view of Abu Wa²el, himself a white-collar worker, expressed this change of attitude.

I will send Wa²el [his son] after his elementary education to a technical school to learn a skill. A man needs to earn money to provide for his family. All those who have spent years in educational institutions at great cost to their parents now cannot earn enough money to rent a flat or to marry. Times have changed and one has to be alert. Under Nasser, education was the most important means, but under Sadat and Mubarak it is skills that earn money.

4. Married female informants said the best option for an unskilled male worker without the capital necessary to set up his own business would be a public sector job, as this provides his family with a minimum secure income that can be supplemented with a second job. At the same time, they recognized that job opportunities for unskilled workers in the public sector were declining.

In discussing future plans both with and without their parents present, only one thirteen-year-old from among fifty-four informants' sons aged eight to twenty-two expressed a strong desire to complete his studies in law. Parents of four boys (under ten years of age) said that if their boys did very well at school they would like them to pursue medicine or engineering; otherwise they would like them to go to technical schools. Parents of the remaining forty-nine boys thought that technical schooling or apprenticing in the labor force would be the best bet for their sons.[5] In many families, the elder brothers had graduated from high school or even university, but younger brothers left school to train as plumbers, electricians, or other skilled worlers. Since the households were investing less to educate their sons, they could afford to keep their daughters at school longer, improving the girls' chances for government jobs. Egyptian educational statistics indicate a sharp increase in the number of females who have continued their secondary and high school education.[6]

Skilled manual work was gaining social acceptability, and there was a greater tendency to engage in production work. Ironically, there was little attempt by Egypt's economic planners to encourage such trends, though in the 1970s and 1980s the shortage of trained technical workers was identified as a hindrance to Egypt's economic development (Abdel-Fadil 1982; ILO 1982). The percentage of educated people had increased sharply since the 1960s, but Egypt still suffered from a lack of trained technical workers because few people pursued technical studies, due to their low status. By the mid-1980s and certainly in the 1990s, low-income earners viewed technical professions as the most rational economic option, though these jobs still did not carry prestige or status in Egypt.

White-collar government workers, considered middle class despite their low pay, were forced to engage in manual labor to supplement their income. Although they initially tried to conceal their menial second

---

5. Some social critics blamed migration and the absence of fathers for the high academic dropout rates. What they have not appreciated is that education beyond the primary school had been viewed as a means of access to better jobs, but the new situation had changed labor market conditions so that skilled and technical jobs were higher paying. Therefore, young men chose to join the labor force at an early age to train as skilled workers.

6. During the first four years of my fieldwork (1983–1986), I did not come across any case where daughters who were in secondary or high school gave up their studies. The only exception was a seventeen-year-old who married a man from Abu Dhabi and left Egypt.

jobs, most workers eventually acknowledged engaging in manual labor since it was nearly impossible to find jobs without mobilizing one's network. Ahmed, a white-collar worker with two years of college education, worked as an electrician in the afternoons, although he found it hard to admit this or talk about it. He told me,

My parents tried hard and gave me and my brother the education so that we would become respectable civil servants. But today, in order for me to pay my rent and provide for my three children, even though my wife is also a government employee, I have to work as an electrician. I earn more in my afternoon job than my wife and I together receive from our government jobs. But here in Egypt people are not sophisticated and they look down on manual work. I worry that my labor may reflect poorly on my children.[7]

While there is no national pension or social welfare system, such benefits exist for government and public sector employees. This security, at least for those who had entered this sector in the past, has maintained the appeal of these jobs, despite their low pay. Many people were conscious of the minimal work demanded as well as the shorter working hours. In fact, they saw these as concessions or perks offered by the government to compensate for low wages, allowing employees to engage in a second or even third job. Thus, despite frequent complaints about their low wages, only one government employee had resigned from his job.[8]

Financial insecurity, and its implications for old age, prevented many people from venturing into risky businesses or from capitalizing on opportunities offered to them, particularly when they had family responsibilities. For instance, Abu Azza was approached by acquaintances who offered him a job in a workshop at a wage almost three times his salary, but after a few days of grappling with the proposal he said he would only work for them in the afternoons. He told me,

I know that it is a very good wage and we need the money very much, but I have four children and have to think of their future. Suppose I have an accident tomorrow or get permanently sick. If I am a government employee,

7. They were among the few families who were considered modern and middle class in the neighborhood. Both husband and wife were educated and had white-collar jobs.

8. He was a high school teacher who had taken a leave of absence from his job to work in Saudi Arabia. He returned to Cairo with sufficient capital to invest in a business, and he gradually built two flats and rented one out. The rental income, he explained to me, provided him with more than his government pension would have been. This financial security made his decision to resign much easier.

at least they will be paid a minimum to eat. But if I work in the private sector, at best they will have the employer's sympathy.

His wife agreed with him.

He has had more than ten years with the government and it would be foolish to lose all that. Yes, the government income is very low, but they [government employees] do not have to work hard and they can find another job to supplement the family income. They can get leave and migrate to the Gulf for a few years and improve the family's condition.

Many people pointed out the insecurity of nongovernment work, mentioning those who had once earned enough money in the private sector as young skilled workers and later, in their fifties, had to sell vegetables in the local market to survive.

Government employees adopted three basic strategies to overcome their shortage of cash. First, they routinely worked overtime, particularly the lower-grade clerical, blue-collar, and technical workers. The second tactic was to work a second and sometimes third job. Moonlighting was common (Khouri-Dagher 1985; MacLeod 1991; Singerman 1995, 1996b) despite the law that prohibited government employees from working at a second job. Indeed, people felt that since the government did not enforce this law, it was encouraging and even legitimizing additional employment. While many state employees complained about their low pay, they acknowledged that unlike private sector workers, they still had energy at the end of their workday to augment their income with other employment. A third tactic, though increasingly difficult, was to take a leave of absence without pay and work in the Gulf countries for several years.

Working at a second job was a long-term strategy to counteract low wages and indefinite shortages of cash. The plan was to work as long as physically possible, whenever work was available. Abu Tahar worked as a messenger in a government office and had turned a small room in his ground-floor flat into a carpentry shop. He discussed his plans for the future.

Soon I can retire and I hope then I can spend more time in this shop to earn more cash. For years we have planned to repair and paint our flat, which as you see has deteriorated badly, but we never had the money. Perhaps, in a couple of years after my retirement, we will have enough to do so.

Sadly, his grand plans, like many others' in the neighborhoods, never materialized. He died very soon after his retirement in 1987. His wife continued to work in his carpentry shop, performing small repairs, but within a year or so she closed the shop, which was not generating enough income to support her.

Most people used a combination of different strategies simultaneously. Abu Muhammad was a blue-collar worker in the public sector. He had also worked afternoons as a domestic servant for twenty years. He told me,

My wages from the government job pay only for food. I have eight children and I want them to be educated. I work in the afternoons to pay for their clothes and school expenses. If and when the opportunity arises, I also do all the overtime I can get. Without the extra cash I earn we could not possibly live.

There was a wide range of jobs held by moonlighting workers, according to the individual's opportunities and options. These included running a small local shop or working for a private firm, selling vegetables in the local market or running a taxi, working as a doorman or domestic servant, and other activities conventionally characterized as part of the "informal" economy.

Scholars and government censuses have often disregarded the nature and income of second jobs. In fact, workers often earned more from extra economic activities than from the primary occupation they stated for the census. These practices rendered census classifications meaningless. Thus, in addition to Abdel-Fadil's (1983: 75–78) observation that in Egypt the concept "working poor" spills over into the formal sector, we have a flow of goods and services that connects the two sectors (Portes, Castells, and Benton 1989) and a flow of people simultaneously engaged in both formal and informal economic activity (see Yalman 1991).[9]

Men, particularly married men who were expected to support a household, experienced great social pressure to take on a second job. Those who did not follow this pattern and had no acceptable excuse were seen as lazy and useless, and their wives and children were pitied. Since the prevailing sexual division of labor prevented men from contributing to the household in the form of domestic labor and cash was really their only means of providing, the income from a second job, however little, was still a gain for the household.

Men often preferred to be out of the home, mainly because their

9. The primary difference between formal and informal sectors is in terms of government control and regulation over production and income taxes.

presence in the small and often overcrowded dwellings interrupted the daily activities of the other members. They often mentioned that it was difficult for them to cope with the children and the comings and goings of neighbors. Some men explained that although they loved their children, they did not have the patience God has given to women, and they would get agitated and punish the children or get involved in arguments with their wives (usually over money or children). The men concluded, therefore, that it was best for them to be working or to spend their time in the teahouses.[10] Women found the presence of their husbands disruptive and preferred them to stay out, but they liked to know of their whereabouts when the men were not working.[11]

Employment Opportunities in the Informal Economy

In the absence of any effective social security benefits for the unemployed in developing countries, many of those denied work in the formal sector create their own employment. Activities that take place outside the formal industrial, investment, or government sectors are referred to as informal. Literature on the informal economy in developing countries has grown rapidly since 1970 (Moser and Young 1981; Castells 1989; Portes, Castells, and Benton 1989; Smith 1989; Greenhalgh 1991; Murray 1991; Lobban 1996). These writings have encouraged debate on the interrelation of informal economic activities and the formal sector in capitalist development (Redclift and Mingione 1985; Portes, Castells, and Benton 1989; Smith 1989; Tadros, Feteeha, and Hibbard 1990; Yalman 1991; Lobban 1996) and have fostered a better understanding of the dynamics of development whereby the informal sector is no longer treated as a separate or transitional stage in a capitalist economy.

The informal economy, which Egypt's government defines as estab-

10. It is essential for most men to spend time in at least one of the local teahouses, because the teahouse is the major channel through which men could find jobs (chapter 8).

11. The sexual division of labor and the ideology of segregated domains for men and women have created a situation during the day where the homes and the neighborhoods (except the teahouses) were spheres legitimately dominated by women and children. The presence of husbands was disruptive and was not welcomed or tolerated for an extended period.

lishments employing fewer than ten workers, was a major source of employment and cash-generating activity. Little is known about the actual size and structural characteristics of the informal labor market since the fluid nature of its activity makes it difficult to measure in large-scale surveys. Data are particularly scarce for the lower end of the scale, which includes the petty traders and vendors who were the great majority of my informants, both male and female. Nevertheless, 1986 statistics indicated the informal sector was the most dynamic of the economy and self-employment was responsible for the largest increase in employment opportunities (Handoussa 1991: 17).

The informal service sector covers most very low paid economic activities, although a census comparison of 1960 and 1976 suggests that the employment share of the informal service sector had declined by 45 percent, with domestic services accounting for about 80 percent of the total decline (Abdel-Fadil 1983). With the rapid rate of urbanization during the last decade and the slow growth of new job opportunities, an upsurge in this sector was not surprising (Tinker 1987; Tadros, Feteeha, and Hibbard 1990; Roy 1992; Assaad 1993; Singerman 1995).

Egypt's shifting economic policies dramatically altered the structure of its informal economy. Under the Nasser regime, wages in the informal sector were stagnant. The introduction of structural adjustment policies, labor migration to the Gulf, and an increase in investment, particularly in small-scale construction and commodity production, revitalized the informal sector both in terms of wage increases and job creation. The wages of artisans, craftsmen, and other semiskilled laborers in informal construction and some workers who performed personal services rose substantially (Kamel Rizk 1991; Roy 1992; Assaad 1993).[12] Many earn considerably more than university graduates employed in government offices.

Many of my male informants were wage earners or self-employed in the informal sector (see table 7). The line between the two groups, however, was fairly arbitrary, since many informants were simultaneously

12. General definitions of the informal sector state that its workers are unprotected by labor law and do not enjoy the same wage levels, working conditions, or long-term security that exist generally in the formal sector. This implies that those in the informal sector would enter the formal economy given the opportunity. In Egypt, low formal sector wages encouraged many to join the informal sector, though they regretted not having the security of an old-age pension. Research in other countries indicates that this trend may be a universal response to structural adjustment policies (Portes, Castells, and Benton 1989; Tripp 1991).

Table 7 *Informal Sector Occupations of Male Informants*

Occupation	Frequency
Wage earners	
Driver	7
Cook	2
Imam	1
Plumber	3
Semiskilled construction worker	4
Unskilled construction worker	2
Unskilled casual worker	4
Handyman	1
Self-employed	
Carpenter	1
Butcher	1
Vendor (mobile)	2
Petty trader	5
All	33*

*One husband had never contributed cash and does not appear in this table.

wage earners and self-employed. I grouped them according to the activity in which they spent most of their time. A further problem arose over determining the informants' occupations. Some engaged in four or five different kinds of jobs over periods sometimes as short as three months. This is only one indication of the urgent need to develop an alternative methodology and conceptual framework that reflect more accurately the complexities of the labor market.

Generally, workers with modern technical skills (such as mechanics and electricians) earned higher wages. However, few of the first- and second-generation rural-urban migrants had such skills. The most skilled workers of these generations tended to be engaged in more traditional activities (builders, carpenters, house painters, plumbers, drivers), and often they had learned their trades through long years of apprenticeship. Their skills were rarely acquired through formal training, although this is now a growing trend.

Skilled workers earned between 5 and 15 pounds daily, depending on the area of skill, level of ability, and workplace. Some respondents had experienced an eight- to elevenfold wage increase between 1975 and

1985; however, there has been little increase since then. The wages of these workers were considered relatively good; their incomes covered daily needs and served as a small cushion against probable periods of unemployment. However, they were preoccupied with finding a secure income for their old age because even the most skilled workers are pushed aside by younger newcomers. In these occupations, age and youthful appearance are the decisive factors in the chances for employment; for this reason male informants tended to underreport their ages.[13]

All wage earners viewed self-employment as their eventual destiny since, as Abu Samir said, "Why would anyone employ an old man when there are at least five young men begging for the job?" The more skilled technical workers aspired to set up small workshops of their own, but the initial cost of establishing these businesses was often prohibitive. Many semiskilled men had migrated to the oil-rich countries in hope of saving enough to start small workshops of their own, but few succeeded. By the time they reached middle age, they often lost such hope and left their trades to invest their savings in petty trading or a local shop, to secure a small income for old age.

Abu Nasser was an electrician and among the more successful men of the neighborhoods. In 1983, he talked enthusiastically about his plan to amass some capital and open a shop. He reckoned that he would earn at least 30 pounds per day after expenses, if he had even a very small shop. In 1984, he migrated to Iraq for sixteen months and on his return in 1986, to my surprise, set up a retail shop with his wife. When I asked him why he did not establish an electrical shop as he had planned, he said,

I tried, but my money was not enough to buy the minimal equipment necessary and pay key money for a shop. Worse yet was the cost and headache of getting a license. You know, we do not know anybody in those government offices. I was worried that I might get hassled by the police and tax office: we know of people who have lost their capital in this way. So, with disappointment, my wife and I decided it was safer to open this shop. I work as an electrician whenever I find a job.

Since they saw no future for themselves in their professions, skilled workers did not try to update their skills. In a system without financial

13. During the first year of my fieldwork, I noticed that, contrary to my expectation, it was men who lied about their age—often claiming to be thirty to thirty-five regardless of their physical appearance. A simple calculation would determine that they were at least ten years older. Only later did I realize that as people get older their chances of finding waged work diminish and they therefore tended to present themselves as younger than they really were.

security, everyone had to look after his or her own future. Many of my informants agreed with Ammu Tahar, who explained,

A man has to think about his old age, starting from when he is in his twenties. . . . Two sources are the most secure ones: first, one should have many sons so that at least one or two of them will have the means and desire to help you in your old days; second, you have to make sure to have some income because nowadays no one will help you.

Both male and female informants were aware that a bleak future awaited waged workers who did not secure some other means of earning a living by the time they reached middle age; examples were not rare in the neighborhoods. For this reason, the very low pay of the public sector still held some attraction for the low-income strata.

Casual workers had the least resources. While young and strong they moved from one construction job to the next; this common pattern was encouraged by their relatively high wages. Later in life they worked as shop assistants, doormen, handymen, or vendors. Abu Batta recounted his employment history.

I was brought to Cairo to work as a handyman at the age of ten, because I had lost my parents and had nobody to look after me. When I was fifteen, I started to work at the construction site until six years ago, when I had an accident at work and hurt my back. Since then I have worked as a shop assistant, first in a *kushari* [a dish of cooked rice with lentils] shop, and now selling ful and tam'iya outside the school for my employer. Perhaps, with the help of God, one day before I am too old I can set up a small shop or kiosk of my own.

Abu Karim had a similar story.

As a boy of only five or six I worked at a bakery. When I was older, I worked as a construction worker most of the time, though I did other things too when there was no construction work until I grew sick and weak. Then I worked as a cook, then a vegetable seller, then I drove a cart with a donkey [distributing vegetables in the local market]. Then I migrated to Saudi Arabia in vain and now, as you know, I am a mobile vendor selling plastic toys and housewares.

Many casual workers were out of work for a considerable portion of the year, though few of them remained unemployed for extended periods. If they could not find jobs in their principal occupations, they took any other job that came their way. As a last resort, they sold vegetables in the market. The income from these activities was often negligible. Thus, although casual workers had received wage increases, they were still among the poorest householders in the neighborhoods. In fact, they often sold vegetables or secondhand clothing with their wives (and sometimes children) to supplement their sporadic employment. Many, like their skilled counterparts, migrated temporarily to the Gulf countries, though there was a high rate of failure among casual laborers.

Self-employed men from the neighborhoods were often small-scale traders, shop owners, or producers. Petty producers were mainly involved in some aspect of the food business, though a few small furniture workshops had opened.[14] Most of these businesses were located close by and consisted of a very modest shop, kiosk, or simply a few baskets and trays arranged on a table. Many of these male traders were middle-aged and had retired from wage earning to self-employment. Abu Ahmad, who sold homemade pickles, had a typical work history.

I was a construction worker until I grew older, when few people were prepared to employ me. Then my wife and I sold our television and a few other items and opened this small shop [which measured 1 meter by 1 meter by 2 meters high] and started to make and sell pickles. Now we earn little, but at least we do not starve. I supplement our earnings with occasional wage work I am offered in the neighborhood.

In fact, wage earners commonly combined petty trading with waged work. If they could not rely on members of their households to run the business, they simply closed the shop, kiosk, or stand until their next period of unemployment.

Migration as a Cash-raising Strategy

International migration has emerged as one of the most prominent features of the Egyptian labor market and the economy.[15] Until the mid-1970s, migration was an option open mainly to highly skilled laborers and specialists such as teachers, doctors, and engineers. The oil boom of 1973 and subsequent development projects in the oil-rich countries increased demand for unskilled as well as skilled manual

14. In older neighborhoods, artisans produced traditional and some modern items. Most of these businesses had benefited greatly from the economic changes (see Meyer 1987; Stauth 1991; Roy 1992; Singerman 1995).

15. For a review of literature on migration, see Amin and Awny 1985 and el-Sayed Said 1990.

workers. This situation, coupled with changes in Egyptian migration policy,[16] altered the occupational composition of migrants in such a manner that unskilled and construction workers formed the majority (Amin and Awny 1985; Fergany 1987; el-Sayed Said 1990). This feature of international migration is significant to this study in three ways. First, it presented low-income workers with a new economic option. Second, the removal of large numbers of workers from the Egyptian labor market constrained the supply curve and thus pushed wages up to the advantage of laborers who had remained in the country. Third, the flow of remittances into consumption and investments also contributed to an increase in demand for labor.

Migration profoundly affected the lives of agricultural wage workers, construction workers, and craftspeople. An estimated half-million workers left the rural areas for the oil states or for Egypt's urban centers to replace those who went abroad. This had a positive effect on the historically very low wages of the agricultural sector, where the majority of rural workers lived below the poverty line. Between 1973 and 1983, their wages more than doubled in real terms (Amin and Awny 1985: 132–136). Although their wages remained lower than those of urban workers, rural workers' standard of living increased considerably, which many of my informants remarked was a sign of real development in Egypt. Even the efforts of Nasser's socialist programs had failed to have any appreciable positive effect on the lives of those at the very bottom of the social scale in rural Egypt.

Construction workers have probably been the largest group to benefit from migration (ILO 1982: 154). The investment of remittances in formal and informal sector construction increased demand for construction workers (Assaad 1993). Wages in construction work increased three- to sixfold during the 1970s. The increase in wages attracted rural migrants and other casual workers to this sector (Amin and Awny 1985; el-Sayed Said 1990).

Apart from construction workers and craftsmen, many other people migrated to perform personal or other unskilled services: cooks, drivers, servants, gardeners, and doormen flocked to the Gulf countries where salaries were much higher than in Egypt and opportunities for employment were greater. Migration played a substantial role in reducing unemployment (particularly among less-skilled workers), although this

16. See Dessouki 1978 for a detailed exposition of Egypt's migration policies since 1950.

was neglected by statisticians until the economic recession of the Gulf countries caused a sharp fall in the rate of increase in labor migration.

Fifty percent of Egypt's population is below twenty years of age. To avoid an increase in the level of unemployment, 350,000 to 400,000 new opportunities must be created each year. Using the most conservative estimate of 1.5 million migrants for the past decade, migration accounted for a sizable reduction in Egypt's unemployment.[17] As temporary migration continues despite some reduction in wage differentials, similar arguments hold true in the 1990s (el-Sayed Said 1990).

The migration of craftsmen (and occasionally craftswomen), construction workers, unskilled workers, and agricultural workers affected the income of those who did not migrate as well. Remittances stimulated the demand for goods and services, which in turn stimulated the need for labor. As migration removed considerable numbers of workers from the labor market, workers were aware that they had more bargaining power than ever before in the history of modern Egypt. One informant, a plumber, said,

Why should I migrate? *Hamdullah* [Thanks to God] my friends have migrated for me. I used to work for 2 pounds a day, just a few years back. Now I am paid 15 pounds a day and my family is much better off.

Another middle-aged construction worker said,

Prior to migration, at my age one could never get a job, but thanks to migration I get fifteen or twenty days of work most months. Without migration, who knows how we would be living now?

National data show a considerable increase in labor income during the late 1970s and early 1980s (ILO 1982: 237–238). There is less information on how migration affected income distribution among wage earners of different groups, but there is general agreement that wage earners were positively affected, to varying degrees (el-Sayed Said 1990; Amin 1995). These wage increases have been criticized as inflationary, since it is often assumed that inflation is negative regardless of its social implications. However, the inflationary impact of migration and consequent wage increases should be evaluated against its impact on in-

17. There are no reliable statistics on the exact number of Egyptian migrants. Estimates vary from 2.98 million by the Ministry of State to 9.9 million by the National Specialized Council (see Amin and Awny 1985: 25 for other estimates). There is tacit agreement that 2 million is an acceptable, if low, estimate. For examples of calculation of reduction of unemployment as a result of migration, see ILO 1984 and Amin and Awny 1985: 95–96.

come distribution. In fact, in Egypt wage increases served as a corrective measure in favor of the least privileged groups. Migration allowed a sizable number of workers to upgrade their standard of living by redefining their position in the labor market. Moreover, considering that the Egyptian labor market had been diagnosed as having strong institutional barriers to labor mobility, such advances should be viewed as conducive to a healthier labor market structure. Migration's effect on wages also helped members of less privileged sectors to absorb the shock of structural adjustment policies, which often hit the poor harder than the middle classes (Vickers 1990; Beneria and Feldman 1992; Meskoub 1992; Thomas-Emeagwali 1995).

In many households, one or occasionally several members had worked in the Gulf and many, particularly younger men, eagerly planned to migrate in the future. Many regretted the reduction in migration opportunities for wage workers.[18] Migration was generally viewed as a short-term strategy to raise cash, although some of the men in the sample had been away for as long as fifteen years. Most people considered migration in terms of a three- to four-year period. However, it was as much market and political conditions that affected the length of stay as it was personal circumstance and the fact that the family was left behind (see table 8).[19] Several informants returned to Cairo but, not finding employment, migrated again to the Gulf.

Migrants' occupations were diverse (see table 9), showing that this cash-earning strategy was not limited to those working outside the "formal" sector. In the past, the government organized the migration of civil servants and public sector employees. By the late 1970s, government employees (white and blue collar) were applying for up to four years of leave without pay to migrate and supplement their meager, but secure, income. The government welcomed this trend as a means of reducing underemployment in government departments.

18. Migration was viewed as a predominantly male option, although many women also migrated and continue to do so to the oil-rich Arab countries as doctors, nurses, teachers, and maids. Among my core sample and their friends were women who had left children as young as six months old in the care of husbands in Cairo to work as nurses, hairdressers, maids, and nannies in well-paying job opportunities in the Gulf countries. The literature has overlooked the extent to which women migrate.

19. People were especially aware that national politics play an important role in the stability of migration patterns. Some of my informants had to leave Libya as a result of national dispute, yet recently after the Gulf war some migrated to Saudi Arabia conscious of the fact that they are replacing Yemenis and Jordanian/Palestinian workers who were practically deported due to their national governments' lack of support for the allied forces during the war.

Table 8 *Duration of Migration among Returned Migrants*

Duration	Frequency
Under 1 year	6
1–under 3 years	12
3–under 5 years	8
5 or more years	5
All	31

Table 9 *Occupation of Migrants in Cairo and in Host Countries*

Cairo	Host Country	Frequency
Skilled		
White collar	White collar	2
Engineer	Engineer	1
Technician	Tech./Instructor	1
Junior clerk	Accountant	1
Junior clerk	Junior clerk	1
Semiskilled, manual		
Construction worker	Construction worker	6
Plumber	Plumber	2
Electrician	Electrician	1
Carpenter	Carpenter	1
Driver	Driver	5
Driver	Cook	1
Driver	Semiskilled construction worker	1
Cook	Small shop owner	1
Unskilled		
Government worker	Construction worker	2
Government worker	Casual worker	1
Vendor/petty trader	Casual worker	1
Unemployed	Factory worker	1
Unemployed	Cook	2
Casual worker	Casual worker	4
All		35

All but two of my male informants viewed migration as the best strategy for raising cash. However, many recognized the multiple factors beyond political and market conditions that made migration difficult, if not impossible. The decision to migrate often involved long-term planning, including gathering information about employment opportunities in different countries, matching them against their own credentials (skills, education, and physical strength), and then comparing overseas opportunities with those in Cairo.[20] But perhaps the most influential factor was having a social network in the host country to ease integration into the labor market and provide the information essential for day-to-day living in the new environment. Few people were prepared to migrate without having some kind of social support in the host country. Those who did take such a risk were often men with sought-after modern skills, such as mechanics, who had no financial worries at home. For instance, they were either single or married to wives who had incomes of their own, which made it easier to cope until they found jobs. A second group who took the risk of migration with little information were those with no chance of employment at home (often middle-aged casual workers).

Skilled, formally educated men tended to work in jobs similar to those they had held at home. Sometimes they even improved their skills because they worked under trained supervisors. Occasionally, because they were members of ethnically diverse work teams (many Europeans, Americans, Indians, and Filipinos also worked in oil-rich countries), they had to learn a minimal amount of English, which later improved their marketability in Cairo. Semiskilled and less educated men, however, rarely had the same opportunities to upgrade their skills. Although they sometimes found technical jobs in their own field, often they engaged in any job (often as a casual worker or unskilled construction worker) that would bring them money. As one migrant worker said, "There one does not have to worry what one's neighbors or colleagues would say. I, like everyone else, was there to earn as much money as I possibly could in any *halal* [religiously permitted] job."

Besides job opportunities, other factors played a decisive role in whether a man could migrate. These factors derived from a man's po-

---

20. This decision-making process mirrors many aspects of classic migration theory as described by Lee 1966. It is important to recognize, however, that the locus of decision making is the household and not the individual. See Hoodfar 1996a; Grasmuck and Pessar 1991.

sition within his household and other characteristics of the family: the age of his wife; the number of children; the wife's character and personality; the number of other adults in the household; the financial situation; and the strength of the network of relatives and neighbors who could help in difficult situations during the husband's absence (Khattab and el-Daeif 1982; Hoodfar 1996a).

The family cycle was extremely important in the decision to migrate, as it is not considered acceptable for young women to live on their own. Nor do women want to live alone. Women felt that the absence of an adult male in the household curtailed their freedom, since they were then scrutinized more closely. Consequently, the young wife of a migrant would have to move in with relatives. However, among the poor, few people could afford to take in another family member since accommodations were often very small and overcrowded. The few exceptions were cases in which the wives had no children or only one child and moved to the home of their parents or, less commonly, of their husbands' parents. Young wives resented this situation since it undermined the newly acquired independence offered by marriage. Moreover, women felt that the first few years of marriage were the time to build their families and secure their marriages, an attitude that both their husbands and their community saw as legitimate. Thus only under exceptional circumstances would young wives allow their husbands to migrate. Most women preferred their husbands to migrate after their engagement and before marriage, or after the birth of two or three children. For this reason, many men postponed their plans to migrate, and those with more children felt a more urgent need to migrate to improve their lives. (Table 10 shows the size of migrants' families at the time of migration.) Larger and more nationally representative research in Egypt confirms that a higher number of children, as opposed to the absence of children, increases the chances of migration (Fergany 1987).

Another factor that determined the possibility and timing of migration for many low-income households was finding cash to cover the initial cost: obtaining a passport and other documents and minimum living expenses for a few months for the migrant and the members of the household left behind.[21] This money was usually obtained through loans or the sale of the wife's gold or household goods, because it was rare for low-income earners to have substantial cash savings. In poorer

21. For a discussion of the involvement of wives and other family members in decision making regarding migration, see Khattab and el-Daeif 1982; Brink 1991; and Hoodfar 1996a.

Table 10 *Size of Family at First Migration*

Family Size	Frequency
Premarriage	2
Married, no children	2
Married, 1 child	6
Married, 2 children	6
Married, 3 children	9
Married, 4 children	4
Married, 5 children	1
Married, 6 children	3
Married, 7 children	2
Married, 8 children	1
All	36*

Table is based on 1988 data.

*One man had migrated once before his marriage and once after the birth of the first child.

households, the husband could afford to migrate if the wife (or perhaps another family member) worked outside the home, as her meager earnings could pay for the household's basic needs until the migrant managed to send money. The rate of failure among migrants of these households appeared to be lower; without the worry of immediately sending money back for the family, the migrants could afford to stay longer without reasonable employment, hoping for a better job.

Cash Contributions from Other Male Members of the Household

As we have seen, low-income urban households, particularly in the newly urbanized areas, seldom include people outside the nuclear family of husband, wife, and children. While a man is responsible to assure the support of his mother and sisters if necessary, and so they may become part of the household, this responsibility is rarely extended to include male family members. Traditionally, children were expected to contribute to the household as early as they could, and once formed a significant percentage of the labor market in Egypt. During the past decades, this situation changed considerably, particularly in urban areas, because of the introduction of public schooling and a legis-lated minimum working age. As many informants remarked, the most important factor in reducing child labor was that households earned higher incomes and were therefore not as desperate to send children out to work. Even so, it was not rare to see male children as young as eight years old working in the artisan shops in old Cairo, often as unpaid family members or unpaid apprentices (Abdalla 1988; Singerman 1995). Since there were few workshops and craft activities in the newly urban-ized neighborhoods, it was rare for children there to do paid work until they entered the labor market in their early teens.

As workshops are being established in and around the neighbor-hoods, parents try to engage their young sons as apprentices during the summers. Umm Reza was very happy because the small mechanic shop just outside her alley had accepted her eight-year-old son to work over the summer. They would pay for his lunch, and if he worked well during the first month, they would also pay him 50 piasters each day as pocket money. I asked if he was too young to go to work. Umm Reza told me,

You don't know here in Egypt men have to earn money or like my husband they will always be poor. Nowadays, technical skills pay well. If he learns how to repair cars, by the time he is eighteen years old he can earn 20 pounds a day. Then who wouldn't want to marry him? Anyway, if he isn't busy working, which is just doing small tasks, he wants to run around in the streets and get into fights and be a nuisance for me and the neighbors.

Adult sons who lived at home but were not the main cash earners of the household were expected to contribute some cash, but rarely on a regular basis. Sometimes they took on fixed financial responsibili-ties, such as paying for the private lessons or the clothing of younger brothers and sisters. Once the sons were earning money, they began saving for their marriage, since few parents could afford to participate in fulfilling the groom's material responsibilities. Few parents received fixed financial help from their sons once they left the household, how-ever, although some gave frequent gifts, including occasional small cash presents.

Summary

Within the neighborhoods, which are highly integrated in the urban and commercial economy, earning cash was the primary material preoccupation of the households. As the designated breadwinners, men felt pressure to improve the household's cash resources. To ensure a constant and adequate level of cash income, men who worked in both formal and informal jobs adopted a combination of strategies at any given time. Since government and public sector salaries have not kept pace with inflation, low-ranking government employees were forced to find second and even third jobs to make ends meet. Consequently, there is considerable overlap and movement between different kinds of cash-earning activities and between the formal and informal sectors, rendering such a categorization confusing and analytically unhelpful.

Another strategy men employed to raise cash was migration to the oil-rich Arab countries. Migration decision making was influenced by a comparison of opportunities in Cairo and the potential host country. Another important factor was the family cycle. Most men and women felt that migration was most suitable either before marriage or after the birth of several children, which indicated the stability of the marriage and also meant an increased need for cash. The work history of the informants, their alertness to the changing market conditions, and their courage, dynamism, and willingness to try every possible option to improve their situations were striking, and all of this contradicted the assumption of apathy among low-income groups.

CHAPTER 4

Women and Employment

Official data for Egypt and the Middle East suggest a lower overall rate of female labor participation compared to Latin America and many African nations (Scott 1986; Hijab 1988, 1994; UN 1992). While this is due in part to inadequate (and incompatible) statistical methods and the massive underreporting of women's participation in the Middle East work force (Beneria 1981, 1992), this alone does not entirely account for the low rate. It is probable that women in distinct cultural, social, and economic locations respond differently to industrial development and the evolving global economy.

Women's participation in the labor market continues to be considered one of the most important measures of "emancipation." Ideological and cultural practices that impede labor market participation are branded patriarchal and are assumed to harm women (Scott 1986; Hijab 1988; Ecevit 1991). This chapter looks at women's cash-generating activities and examines the appropriateness of using labor market participation to measure women's emancipation. Women's apparent conservatism and their adherence to Islamic traditions have a material basis, as they defend their privileges in the face of rapidly changing socioeconomic conditions and commercialization of the economy, which increase their dependence on their husbands. When terms are agreeable, women take full advantage of the labor market.

Urban Women in the Labor Market:
The Historical View

Urban women of Egypt have traditionally been involved in trade and cottage industries. Middle- and lower-class women worked in family enterprises with their husbands or independently as members of the numerous women's guilds that were active up to the beginning of the twentieth century (Ibrahim 1980: 51). Judith Tucker (1976, 1985, 1993b) documents women who bought raw materials and traded the final products in the market, often independently; this was particularly true of women from the Delta. Records from 1889 list many women as green grocers, midwives, servants, pastry cooks, cotton workers, singers, and dancers (Ibrahim 1980; Tucker 1985; Danielson 1991).

In Egypt's initial short-lived phase of industrialization, Mohammed Ali (reigned 1805–1848) established a state-controlled "putting-out" system. The state took over entire guilds, provided workers with raw materials, and paid them for the finished product (Sullivan 1981; Tucker 1985). According to the registers, many of these pieceworkers were women. When factories were established during the same period, many women participated, especially in the textile industry. However, during the period of colonial influence, the British, who were opposed to the industrialization process in Egypt, pushed the economy into the production of raw materials, mainly cotton for British factories. This left the guild system, which had become dependent on the government after more than two generations of state intervention, in considerable disarray. Cottage industries, in particular, women's guilds, never regained their economic significance (Gran 1977; Tucker 1993b).

Despite the destruction of the cottage industry, women remained integrated in the urban economy and participated in petty production independently or as part of household enterprises, with little professional gender segregation. This pattern still prevails in the old quarters of Cairo. For example, Sawsan el-Messiri and others have reported on women who were butchers and important traders (el-Messiri 1978a; Rugh 1979; Tucker 1985; Singerman 1996a). Although my own research was based in newly urbanized, informal residential neighborhoods, I also found many "traditional" women who engaged in a variety of occupations they had established or inherited, including bicycle repair, trading, and baking. Nevertheless, women were marginal to waged labor during the first half of the century, when new factories were being established. Tucker (1985: 71–99) specifies two reasons for this. First, the availability of male labor for wage work, particularly in rural areas, distanced women from opportunities in commercial agriculture and wage work in general. Second, following the decline of the cottage industry and the displacement of women workers, the transition to factory work took almost a century. By the time large-scale industries emerged in the second phase of Egyptian industrialization, women's role in the production process in home industry was a distant memory.

The impact of capitalism on Egyptian women of different classes is diverse. While upper-class women moved into public life and politics (el-Sayyid Marsot 1978; Nelson 1991; Badran 1995), the women of the newly emerged petit bourgeoisie became more isolated due to the separation of domestic and production units. With much of the economic activity moving out of residential areas, women were no longer able to move between the family enterprise and home, or to share their husbands' professions. The sexual division of labor became more rigid: men became producers of goods and services for the formal labor market while women remained in the informal market so they could also attend to their domestic responsibilities.

The Legal Position of Women in the Labor Market

The revolution of 1952 improved women's legal position in the labor market. Women's organizations had participated actively in the anticolonial movement and had developed influence in nationalist parties, such as the Wafd, and successfully brought to the fore the position of women as one of the most pressing political issues needing redress (Abdel-Kader 1988). Across the spectrum, nationalists, modernists, and socialists saw the education of women and the development of Egypt as closely linked (Jayawardena 1992). Nasser's new state, anxious to win the support of the more liberal factions of society, gave equal importance to female and male education. At the same time, by the standards of the 1950s, very liberal labor laws were passed and women's participation in the labor market was actively encouraged. In fact, Nasser called it a duty for women to participate in building the national economy (Ibrahim 1980; Abdel-Kader 1988; Badran 1995).

Female employment is governed by Law 91 of 1954, which makes it illegal to discriminate against women (art. 130). Women are entitled to fifty days of maternity leave while receiving 75 percent of their wages (the laws covering white-collar workers are much more generous). Female workers are also protected against dismissal during their absence, and employers with more than one hundred workers must establish a nursery. These new attitudes toward women's work outside the home and neighborhood by the new government contrasted with the conservatism of Egyptian religious elites and influential ʿulama (religious scholars) of Al-Azhar University, who used Islamic arguments to oppose any suggested change in the status of women.[1] The sweeping revolutionary fervor and optimism for modernization of the country introduced acceptance of new ideas and ways of life and tolerance in the society.

The willingness to introduce these changes was partially based on the belief that modernization and building a strong Egypt required the participation of women. As Nasser's regime moved toward a more limited socialist ideology, primarily as a result of the hostility and economic pressure of the Western world (Waterbury 1983; Gordon 1992), its views on the integration of women as an integral element of its approach to development were reinforced. Although the government explicitly recognized that there were problems and obstacles to women's full participation, it appears to have concerned itself mainly with ideological obstacles, not practical ones. The National Charter of 1962 reads, "Woman must be regarded as equal to man and *she must therefore shed the remaining shackles that impede her free movement,* so that she may play a constructive and profoundly important part in shaping the country" (cited in Tucker 1976: 9; emphasis added).

Nasser's state has always been credited for its liberal attitudes toward women; indeed, no other single factor has exerted comparable influence on the legal and actual position of women in the recent history of Egypt. However, his eagerness to encourage women's entry into the labor market brought about the early stage of official devaluation of women's domestic labor in Egyptian social history. Women's participation in reproductive activities, both on day-to-day and generational

---

1. The state made these concessions because the women's movement at the time was quite strong and integrated in the nationalist movement (Abdel-Kader 1988; Hoodfar 1989). It was also a means by which the new state could communicate its emerging power to the religious leaders and curtail the extent of their influence.

bases, was not considered significant and noteworthy. Women's domestic responsibilities were seen unproblematically as the extension of a
woman's biological function. Neither the facilities nor the new educational system was designed to influence the prevailing domestic sexual
division of labor. Thus the state completely disregarded the reality that
in both rural and urban areas the survival of many households depended on the hours of labor contributed by women, despite the value
that Egyptian culture traditionally attached to women. The fact that
women were simply expected to extend their efforts into the two domains with a minimal change in the domestic sexual division of labor
has been an important influence on the existing structure of female
labor participation, an issue I will return to later in reference to my
informants' views.

Anwar Sadat (president of Egypt, 1971–1981) has often been accused
of being more conservative than Nasser, particularly on questions per-
taining to women and labor market participation (Gran 1977; Sullivan
1981; Badran 1995). However, women continued to secure more rights
under Sadat, especially with the enactment of the Personal Status Law
in 1979, which curtailed the rights of men to obtain a divorce or marry
a second wife without the consent of the wife.[2] Chapter 2 of Law 44
(1979) also gave married women the right to be employed outside the
home if the family's economic circumstances made it necessary (Sullivan
1981: 11–12).[3] Though this is a conditional rather than an absolute right,
it has meant an immediate improvement in the situation of those in
need, although one might argue that a historic opportunity for giving
the unconditional right to participate in the labor market to married
women has been missed.

A major reason for the charge of conservatism leveled against Sadat
is based on the wording of section 2, article 11 of the 1971 constitution,
which declares, "The state shall be responsible for making a balance
between women's duties toward her family and her activity in society,
as well as maintaining her equality with men in the fields of political,

---

2. Many of these rights evoked heated controversies after Nasser's death. Parliament,
under pressure from Muslim "fundamentalists" and the more conservative social forces,
reviewed these laws to make them appear more compatible with Islamic law.

3. Because women need to have permission from their husbands to leave the house,
it has been conventionally interpreted that women also need the permission of their husbands to enter the labor market. Apparently, by inference, the modern law also makes it
possible for husbands to object to their wives working at home, a right men never had
under Islamic law. The new law has made it possible for women of poor households to
enter the labor market without the consent of their husbands.

social, economic and cultural life without detriment to the laws of the Islamic shariᶜa."

Consequently, the state at least, if not other institutions, had to provide special provisions for its female employees, to enable them to combine their jobs and domestic responsibilities. For instance, it became possible for married women in the government sector to have up to two years leave without pay—over and above paid maternity leave—for each of their first three children, in addition to many other considerations.[4] This situation has made working in the government sector the preferred option for most women. By inference, the state also recognizes the considerable contribution that women make to the national economy through their domestic activities.

The issue, then, should not be between "revolutionary" legislation, which breaks away from tradition, and the more conservative position, but between practical consideration for social change and unreflective support for more "progressive" legislation that remains underutilized. Legislation is among the most important factors that influence the position of women in the labor market and must be appropriate for the social and economic conditions of the society concerned.[5] The recent legal histories of Middle Eastern and other developing countries contain many examples of laws that, in theory, were instituted to promote the interests of less powerful groups. However, because they were not carefully designed or because they were not based on economic and social realities, they remained unimplemented or in some cases even worked to the disadvantage of the very group they were meant to help.[6]

Major Issues in Measuring the Female Labor Force in Egypt

The inadequacy of the ILO convention for statistical measurement and the collection of data (to which Egypt was an early

4. Theoretically, such a law should apply to both blue- and white-collar workers. However, as I will discuss, in practice blue-collar and unskilled female workers were prevented from using the leave-without-pay option.

5. For further discussion, see el-Korayem 1981.

6. For instance, Algerian law requires divorce to be adjudicated. The necessary infrastructure such as legal offices did not exist, nor was the majority of the population skilled or educated to deal with the bureaucracy of such a law. The result was that many women were being deserted without a legal divorce, which meant they could not remarry, while the men simply took other wives or migrated to the city (Newland 1979: 26).

adherent) is an issue discussed by many since the 1980s (Beneria 1981, 1992; Anker 1983; Ibrahim 1983). Critics have argued that women's work is varied, complex, and organized differently from much of the work men do. Moreover, the organization of women's work varies by culture and class. Therefore, to accurately document women's work, new culturally sensitive perspectives are required. Other scholars demonstrate that much of the data currently collected on women's labor market participation is underutilized.[7]

Lack of cultural sensitivity and consideration for the differences between male and female unpaid work have resulted in the statistical capture of disproportionately male unpaid family workers in rural areas. Earl Sullivan (1981: 13) points out by way of example that, according to Egyptian national statistics in 1960, only eighty-six women were employed in private agriculture. Anyone with minimal knowledge of the Egyptian countryside would immediately discern the extremely wide gap between reality and statistics. Furthermore, the same census recorded that only 4 percent of the total agricultural force was female, but a detailed rural survey (Dixon 1982; Papanek and Ibrahim 1982) found that 25 percent of nondomestic labor was performed by women.[8] A 1990 sample survey in lower Egypt indicated that between 55 and 70 percent of wives were involved in agricultural production, including plowing the land. In upper Egypt, between 34 and 41 percent of wives worked in agricultural production. However, both sets of figures indicate substantially higher female labor force participation than the 11 percent reported by official statistics collected after the definition of economic activity was revised (Hijab 1994: 3).

Our knowledge of Egypt's urban economy outside the formal sector is even more sketchy than that of rural areas. Furthermore, since the participation of women and children rarely falls into the categories under which data are collected, little is known about the nature and extent of urban female labor participation. The low official figure for the participation of women (10 to 12 percent) stands in sharp contrast with the impression of anyone who observes the intense economic activities of women and children in the residential streets of Cairo and reads the findings of small-scale studies of urban districts. Field studies in the poorest districts of Cairo suggest that as many as 40 percent of all

---

7. See, for instance, Zurayk's 1985 analysis for the Middle East.

8. Research and debates on this subject resulted in the revision of some survey questions and the improvement of data collection. Already this has indicated a much higher level of low-income female labor market participation.

households contain women who are involved in various forms of gainful employment (Papanek and Ibrahim 1982). In extremely poor neighborhoods in Cairo, Andrea Rugh (1979) found many women engaged in piecework for manufacturers, food vending, domestic service, poultry raising, and water carrying. The census fails to capture these activities because the vast majority of women are categorized as housewives and are only included in labor force data if they hold jobs in the formal economic sector.

Abuse of the concept of the *sitt al-bayt* (homemaker) in collecting data has been a major source of underreporting and misunderstanding of women's gainful employment (Ibrahim 1983).[9] The official definition of "housewife" precludes gainful employment (Ibrahim 1983), whereas the popular notion of the term can also accommodate other statuses (i.e., self-employed) simultaneously. Among the sample of my field research, many of the women, engaged for long hours in activities that sometimes brought in more cash than those of the working males, assertively introduced themselves as sitt al-bayt. That is because the concept of work came to mean a paid job for which a woman has to leave her home. Umm Shadia was one of the many women whose home was the base for her income-generating activities. She traded in clothing and bed sheets, and she also raised chickens, rabbits, and pigeons for retail to the neighbors. She earned an income of 80 to 100 pounds per month, while her husband's total salary was 60 pounds. However, she considered herself a "housewife" only and insisted that her daughters must receive formal education to be qualified to become working women. Her case was typical of many women engaged in varieties of home-based, cash-earning activities.

A further implication of the popular notion of "work" was that those unpaid contributors to the family business did not perceive themselves, nor were they regarded by their social groups, as working. All women of families who had a neighborhood business—regardless of size—participated in running the business. At times they were putting more labor into the business than were their husbands, but only one out of ten such wives among the informants considered herself a "working" person.

9. Ibrahim (1983: 49) points out that while the official definition of housewife (which includes any female above the age of six who is not a full-time student or a worker) and the indigenous and popular understanding of housewife diverge, in some crucial respects they also share the implicit assumption that the "natural" condition of the vast majority of women is to hold housewife status.

It is important to recognize indigenous definitions of economic roles and explore the meanings attached to the concepts used to express these roles. The following two cases illustrate this. Su'ad's husband had been a migrant in Saudi Arabia for five years. They invested their savings in a small sweet shop near their home, and for two years she had been running the shop on her own. When I was discussing the question of occupation with her in the shop, while she was serving her customers, she declared that she was a housewife but that she would like her daughters to be educated and to hold good jobs. She added that nowadays women who have no income of their own can never feel secure and that, in any case, a woman who is earning money is more respected. When I suggested that she was a working woman since she spends many long hours in the shop, she disagreed and said that it was her husband's, that she was merely running it in his absence.

On a different occasion, I visited Umm Abir. Her husband owned a tamʿiya and ful shop, which sold cooked beans and a variety of traditional sandwiches. Every day she peeled over twenty kilograms of potatoes and many kilos of onions and cleaned a huge amount of beans, then carried them on her head to the shop, which was a ten-minute walk from their home. One day while I was helping Umm Abir prepare the vegetables, we discussed women and work. She told me every woman should work and earn money because men have no respect for the wife who doesn't earn. She added that if she had had an income when her husband married a second wife, she would have left him. But with four children and no income, her only option was to accept his second wife. While talking, she finished the morning batch of vegetables, and with the help of her oldest daughter, we delivered them to the shop and picked up the second batch for the evening. On our return to her home, she explained that if she did not do this work, her husband would have to pay two workers to do it. Despite her recognition that she did what two paid workers would otherwise do, she considered herself "only a housewife."

By overlooking a category of unpaid workers in an urban economy that encompasses many thousands of small-scale, family-run businesses, statistics portray a misleading view of labor force composition. This is particularly true in the Middle East. Mary Chamie (1985: 99) reports that when Syrian men were asked whether their wives worked, a large proportion answered they did not. However, when the question was rephrased as "If your wives did not assist you in your business, would you be forced to hire a replacement?" the majority answered yes. Since interventionist policies are based on existing national statistics, the needs of these ignored workers—mostly women and children—are not considered. Thus these workers, who are often among the most vulnerable social groups, have less access to national economic and social programs (Dauber and Cain 1981; Dey 1981; Beneria and Feldman 1992; Thomas 1994).

Another reason for the underreporting of women's economic activities is that while men are more inclined to report their activities—since "unemployment" has the lowest status in the popular mind—women hide their low-status jobs by using the "respectable" title of homemaker. Many women who worked as maids or handywomen would not admit it. It was only through more intimate contact that one could know about these activities. In the case of work history, the issue is even more problematic because those who once held low-status jobs but have since changed professions tend not to mention previous low-status jobs.

Gainful Employment among the Informants

Many women in the neighborhood were engaged in gainful employment at the time of my research or previously. The range of their activities was varied (table 11) and often difficult to subsume in one category.[10] Here, those activities that were conducted in an ad hoc manner (for instance, once in a lifetime) or whose income did not make any significant difference to the material life of the members of the household were omitted. Furthermore, although in some households there was more than one adult female, since the nature of their cash contributions to the household is often different from that of the female manager, I have concentrated on the female heads of household. Other contributors are discussed in a separate section.

Women with better educational credentials and social networks tended to work in the formal labor market. In fact, of all the women I

10. To avoid the kind of shortcomings reflected in official data, for this study I developed an economic activity inventory model along the lines suggested by Ibrahim (1983: 51), with modifications to suit this case study. Ibrahim suggests that women's activity be recorded along a continuum, starting with domestic activities, those in the informal sector and those in the formal sector. In this manner the problem of "either/or" is eliminated and those who are engaged in more than one activity can appear in more than one category.

Table 11 *Cash-earning Activities among Married Women*

	Number	Percentage
Formal employment		
White-collar worker	7	11.6
Blue-collar worker	3	5.0
Looking for employment*	0	0
Informal employment		
Home produce for exchange	3	5.0
Family business**	7	11.6
Self-employed**	16	26.6
Maids and handywomen	4	6.6
Not engaged in cash market	20	33.3
Total	60	100

* One woman was looking for a white-collar job while also working in her husband's business and is therefore counted in "Family business."

** Some women in these groups did not view themselves as cash earners, although they thought their labor was important for the family business.

came to meet or to know of in the neighborhoods (whether they were part of my core sample or not), those who had more than ten years of education were either employed or were actively in search of a job in the formal labor market, mostly in the public sector.[11] Very few women in the neighborhoods had skills such as tailoring or hairdressing at a level they could sell in the formal market. Many women, faced with the very small disposable income generated by their husbands, were forced to supplement their households' cash resources through informal activities.

Economic factors, though the most significant, are not the sole determinants in choosing an occupation. Status is another important factor, one that weighed even more in influencing a woman's choice of employment than it did a man's. Low-status jobs are not always low-paid jobs.[12] For instance, in 1989 an experienced maid in Cairo earned

11. In Egypt, in contrast to other Middle Eastern countries, the advent of free education and Nasserist ideology made it possible for many urban lower-class women to gain an education and have access to jobs in the state sector (see chapter 1, on class mobility). See also Abdel-Fadil 1982.

12. Because of the rapid structural changes in recent years, the wages for manual work have been upgraded at a much faster rate than that for government, white-collar work. This process, however, has not yet been matched with corresponding status.

100 to 150 pounds monthly for eight-hour workdays, while a teacher (albeit without accounting for fringe benefits and old-age pension) earned 50 pounds monthly. However, few women chose to work as maids if there were other options available (although employment as a maid, an option once open to many poor urban women, as I will discuss below, is becoming increasingly limited). One of the peculiarities of Egyptian society in this period of transition from a more state-controlled to a free market economy is that wages do not necessarily correspond to job status. Therefore, in choosing a job people have to strike a balance between their financial needs and how they wish to be perceived by others.

Employment in the Formal Sector

WHITE-COLLAR WORKERS

Seven women in my core sample were white-collar workers. Though they identified themselves as working women, all said that their domestic responsibilities had priority over their jobs. This included two informants who had broken their engagements because their prospective husbands did not approve of their employment. On many occasions, all seven women said that they considered themselves lucky to have a job with the government, which has made some allowances for women's special circumstances.

They all claimed that access to a vertical social network was fundamental to obtaining a public sector job. To encourage higher education in the Nasser era, the government guaranteed a job to every high school graduate. However, by the mid-1970s graduates sometimes had to wait as long as three to five years before jobs became available. (This law is still on the books, but aware that there are few opportunities in the public sector, few people take it seriously.) All male and female government employees, particularly the younger ones, had some family or neighborly connection who had influenced their employment. Many of them had a father or an uncle whose boss had intervened on their behalf (see also Ibrahim 1981; Singerman 1995). Although all the women talked of influential connections, these were almost always relatives and friends who were at the bottom of the office hierarchy. White-collar employees thought it had become more difficult to obtain a clerical job in recent years, particularly if the candidate had neither a special skill nor a very important connection.

Another important factor pointed out by many of my informants—particularly younger women still in high school but aspiring to become white-collar workers—was the change in male attitudes toward women's employment. While I found no evidence that men who married during the 1970s resisted having their wives employed in the government/public sector, in the 1990s many young suitors did object. As Umm Halah put it,

Men were not stupid. A white-collar worker in the past brought home as much as a well-paid man. Even if she did not spend her money on basics, she would buy durable goods and so on. Any man married to a government employee, then, considered himself lucky. But now things have changed, our salaries are so low that it hardly covers the inconveniences a woman's absence causes to the family, so men say they don't want their wives to "work."

Steady changes in socioeconomic conditions since the 1970s have effectively eroded the financial advantage of white-collar workers, whose real wages and purchasing power have declined considerably as result of high inflation. Those middle-class individuals whose education and social contacts have made it possible have moved to private sector activities such as banking and insurance where salaries are much higher. Men from low-income groups (as I have already discussed in chapter 3) are forced to take a second or even a third job to make ends meet. In general, women neither can nor want to look for a second afternoon job or other jobs, for two reasons: first, they rarely have the opportunity to find work that pays better or that is more interesting than their regular jobs; second, women themselves attach a high value to their role as mother and wife, which despite being devalued in the processes of modernization, still carries considerable prestige and status in Egyptian society. Arlene MacLeod (1991) points out that women enjoy and value much greater autonomy in the home than in most office jobs.

These circumstances have made households more dependent on the husband's cash income and have reinforced the husband's role as provider, dashing the hopes of a younger generation of women who studied, often at great cost to their parents, to gain financial independence by becoming white-collar workers. Facing this, women have a vested interest in trying to uphold the traditions and legal situation that hold men responsible to provide for the family. Ironically, this has put the husbands of these wives in a stronger position to oppose their wives' employment.

Men present the demand that their wives stay home in terms of both family reputation and the cost to the family and children of wives going to work. All women agree that when one considers the cost of clothing and other miscellaneous items, the remaining income does not compensate for the inconvenience to the family. Many of them pointed out that child care is a major obstacle to employment. Rising prices and housing shortages have forced the younger generation to establish their households farther away from their relatives. This has robbed women of the valuable child care support they could get from their kin or, at best, made it difficult to take advantage of this support.

Sadia's case exemplifies the problem. She worked for the Ministry of Education. She had three daughters aged two, six, and eight when I first met her during the first year of my research. At that time, the elder daughter was in the morning shift of her school.[13] Every school day, Sadia prepared and packed all the necessary toys and books for all three children, then all of them walked to the school, which was some distance away. There, she would drop off the older daughter, take a twenty-minute bus ride to her mother's house, and drop the other two children there. Then she took two more buses to her office. The eldest daughter finished school at noon, so Sadia had to arrange for a neighbor to baby-sit the girl in the afternoon until she returned. She compensated these friends with gifts or by teaching their children in the evenings. At half past three, she would return to her mother's house, pick up the smaller children, and be home by five to cook, clean, shop, and supervise the daughter's homework.

Her family life became much more complicated the following year when her daughter's class switched to the afternoon shift. This situation caused a great deal of friction between Sadia and her husband. She told me,

This is not a life, this is misery. If only I could trust my husband, I would stop working at least for a few years because I have to spend all I earn on child care and buses. But I do not trust him. One cannot trust men these days, life is getting harder and they want to get out of their family responsibility. I feel I have to work so I will have enough to survive in my old days should my marriage fail.

Whereas women readily articulated the financial contribution to the household as their primary motive for entering the labor market, clearly

13. Due to a shortage of space, most elementary and intermediate government schools in Cairo operated in two or three shifts, starting at 7 A.M. lasting approximately three hours each.

other motivations such as financial security—particularly in the case of divorce, widowhood, or old age—were at least as important and were constantly on their minds. Although many married women accepted that their employment no longer made economic sense, it was these other factors that made them insist they wanted to continue to work. To do so with minimum conflict with their husband, they adopted different strategies.

The most common was to return to the veil. Reveiling appeared among university students in the early 1970s (el-Guindi 1981). By the late 1970s, it had become a widespread movement among the lower middle classes, of which the most visible group were low-grade white-collar workers in the public and government sectors. By 1985, the majority of younger women in most government offices were veiled (Hoodfar 1991; MacLeod 1991).

The modern veil is a style of dress very different in appearance from the clothing worn by more traditional baladi and fallahi women. The most popular version of the modern veil is an outfit consisting of a long, Western-style dress or skirt worn with a kind of turban or scarf. The headgear covers the hair and sometimes the shoulders too (Rugh 1986). This outfit serves to separate the modern educated woman from the traditional woman, whose style of dress among "modern" urban Cairenes carries the implication of backwardness and lack of sophistication. This startling picture has evoked a great deal of attention and speculation, but very little systematic research has been conducted to examine the phenomenon from the perspective of the women who have chosen to veil, not merely out of custom, but as a strategy that enables them to continue to have access to some independent cash income. At the same time, they are undermining religious conservatives, for whom veiling means women's exclusion from the labor market. Here, by examining Sommayya's case, I hope to shed light on some of the factors contributing to young women's decisions to take up the veil.

Sommayya was the only daughter of a female-headed household. She was in her last year of teacher training when she became engaged, and she planned to marry a year after graduation. When she was about to begin her teaching career, her fiancé began to raise objections. His mother and eldest sister came to intervene on his behalf while I was present. A summary of this five-hour visit and discussion will help demonstrate how these questions are examined by the people involved.

Sommayya's fiancé's family calculated that she and her future household would lose more money than she would bring in if she went out to teach. She would have to pay for bus fare and on occasion would eat lunch at work and buy cold drinks for her colleagues. She would also have to spend quite a lot on clothes because it is not acceptable for a teacher to go to work poorly dressed. This would account for virtually all the 40 pounds per month that she would bring home. Furthermore, people would talk and her reputation might be questioned, because who would know where she really spent her time? In overcrowded buses men who have lost their traditional respect for women might molest her, and of course this would hurt her pride and dignity as well as that of her husband and brothers. Such were the arguments of her future mother-in-law.

When her fiancé's family left, Sommayya said that she accepted their logic, yet she did not want to give up her career. She explained,

If I wanted to sit at home I could have been married four years ago and by now have a complete home and family. I studied hard and my mother suffered to provide the money for my education so that I could work. I cannot imagine staying at home all day. I have gone to school every day since I was seven years old. I never thought I would live the way my mother does. I can be a good wife and mother and yet have a job where I can have contact with other women like myself. Perhaps one day, if I have everything I need and have children, and my housework demands that I stay at home, I would give up my job. But not now. What if my marriage does not work out? Who knows? My husband might die when I still have young children, like my father did. My mother suffered so much bringing me and my two brothers up after my father died. She did everything she could so that I would not suffer her fate.

I left her then and came back to visit a couple of weeks later. She was happier and had solved the problem in a way that satisfied both her and her fiancé. She had gone to the Ministry of Education and demanded her right as a soon-to-be married woman to work near her future home. Her new workplace was a short bus ride away, a distance she could also walk. After discussing the situation with many of her friends and colleagues, she had decided to take up the veil. She had previously declared on many occasions that she would never veil because she did not see it as essential to being a good Muslim. While showing me her new clothes, she explained,

I wear a long skirt and this scarf. First, it is not that bad; it suits me better than many other women because my face is small. Second, if I have only two sets of clothes I can look smart at all times because nobody expects *muhaggabat* [the veiled ones] to wear new clothes every day. This will save me a lot of money. It will also prevent people from talking about me or questioning my honor or my husband's. In this way, I have solved all the problems, and my husband's family is very happy that he is marrying a muhaggaba.

She continued to explain that none of the women in her fiancé's family were educated or worked in an office. They had felt a little uncomfortable before because they thought that educated, working women generally do not attend to their homes well and do not respect their husbands. Now that they are assured she is a good Muslim and will respect her husband, they are at ease with her. And her fiancé was comfortable with the resolution of the problem. Of her own accord, she had told him that when they had children she would give up her job and stay at home if they did not need her income. Apparently he had taken her willingness to compromise as an indication of her thoughtfulness and sincerity. He did not continue to insist that she should not work.

She arranged to work two shifts until they were married so as to buy the items they would need for their future home. She repeated many times to me, "A bride with no wealth wins no respect." After marriage, she would work only one shift, and so that she could continue to work as long as she wished, her mother promised to help with the child care and with shopping and obtaining subsidized food. To facilitate this, Sommayya had negotiated and obtained a condition in the marriage contract that she would not live far from her mother.

Clearly, veiling saves a lot in clothing expenditures because muhaggabat are no longer compared with women in Western attire, who as a rule are expected to have a colorful wardrobe.[14] But the function of veiling is not only an economic one. The veil is a powerful symbol that communicates loudly and clearly to society at large and to husbands in particular that the wearer is bound by the Islamic idea of her gender role.[15] A veiled woman indicates that, despite her unconventional economic activity, she respects traditional values and behavior. By wearing the veil, women lessen their husbands' insecurity; they convey to their husbands that, as wives, they are not in competition but rather in harmony with them. Further, wearing the veil puts women in a position to expect and demand that their husbands honor them and recognize

14. This economic advantage is being eroded considerably now as more and more elite and upper-class women are taking up the veil and fancy Islamic fashion boutiques are emerging.

15. For more discussion on the issue of reveiling, see Hoodfar 1991 and MacLeod 1991.

their Islamic rights. Husbands should not claim wives' wages, and they should fulfill their duty to provide for the family to the best of their ability.

It is not only young women in the early stages of employment who are forced by conditions in contemporary Cairo to resort to conventional veiling to defend their unconventional activities. Sadia was thirty-seven with three children and had worked for thirteen years when I met her in 1983. A few months after we met she decided to take up the veil. When I asked her why, she replied that she had never imagined that she would. She went on to explain that although she had always disagreed with veiling living conditions had changed. With much nostalgia for the past, she continued,

The last time I had an argument with my husband because he is never around to at least help me with shopping or to stay with the children when I shop, he demanded that I give up my job and stay at home if I could not handle both home and the job. In any case, he thought I spent most of my money on clothes for myself and presents for my parents and sister because they look after the children. I disagreed and fought with him, but the fact is that he is right. My wages have been spent mostly on these things for the past few years, but I'm not well dressed like I used to be, and I have no comfort. All the same, I don't want to give up the security of my job even at the cost of divorce. Who would look after me if tomorrow something happened to him or if he divorced me? My brothers don't even come to see me, much less look after me and my three children. I need the security. These days life is difficult. Women need security. So I decided to follow suit and take up the veil. I'm much more comfortable now. I wear a long dress and a turban. People are more respectful, particularly in the buses and shopping queues.

It has been argued that the veil is inconvenient to wear (MacLeod 1991). It may be, but a look at the cultural context and the reality of women's daily lives explains why many women consider it more convenient. It saves time because veiled women are not expected to be meticulously or formally dressed or to follow fashion trends, particularly regarding hairstyle. Also, in the Middle East and the Islamic world, women's clothing has always been associated with the rules and conventions of sexual behavior. Western styles of clothing often implicitly associate women with the "immoral" behavior and images of Western women—images based on American soap operas and not on the reality of Western life. The veil indicates that the wearer supports conventional sexual behavior and is not attempting to be sexually attractive to men.

The relief that the veil brings to these women has made their physical movements in the crowded streets of Cairo and in overcrowded public transport considerably easier.[16]

BLUE-COLLAR WORKERS

There were only three blue-collar workers in my sample.[17] That is because the cost of this category of employment outweighs its benefits. These jobs may involve up to nine or ten hours away from home for a small income of about 30 pounds (albeit with fringe benefits), which has to cover transportation and other costs of going to work. The remainder does not fully compensate for the inconvenience and the material losses that a household may suffer as the result of the wife's absence.[18] Furthermore, factory work conditions often continue to be very bad (see Hammam 1979).

The losses that can be incurred as the result of a woman's absence from her home include hiring baby-sitters, not having the time to use public services such as hospitals or to line up for subsidized goods, and having to repay the neighbors' or relatives' favors in purchased goods rather than in personal services. When these costs are tallied, few women find these jobs more rewarding than selling vegetables (or other similar jobs) in the local market, where they can also keep an eye on their children, attend to household chores, or take time off to deal with family crises. This attitude is reinforced by the fact that there is little difference in status between the two kinds of jobs. A few informants who had been working in the public sector as blue-collar employees had given up their jobs after marriage or childbirth. Although they always regretted giving up the security of their jobs, they recognized that the work was not economically viable.

Zaynab, who sold soaked beans in the local suq, complained that it was difficult to support her family (herself, her unemployed husband, and their two sons) on the little money she made. When I asked why she did not go back to the factory job she had held before her marriage, she explained,

16. See Hoodfar 1990 for further discussion and cases.

17. The low figure also reflects the general structure of female labor market participation. In Egypt, contrary to Europe and most developing countries, the majority of women in the formal labor market are white-collar workers. For more discussion, see Hoodfar 1994.

18. For a telling example, see Wikan 1980: 120–123.

Working in a factory is hardly an answer to my problem. They pay me around 30 pounds per month. But I have to get a bus there every morning and I have to take my two children to my mother who does not live nearby. I also have to pay some money toward their food, as my parents are too poor to be able to feed my children every day. Even if I take my lunch like most women do, there are still occasional miscellaneous expenses that arise in the factory. Worst of all, I cannot go to work in my old and patched *gallabiya* [loose, shirtlike garment]. I have to buy some clothes. By the time you add up all these expenses, more than half my income is gone. That will leave me with about the same money that I earn in the market. . . . If I am around the neighborhood, occasionally the better-off households call me to give them a hand, for modest pay. I can also look after my children and my home.

She added that if her salary in the factory were at least 50 pounds, then she would go back to her job, though if that were the case she would never have given up the job in the first place.[19] Her response was typical of many of my informants.

Participation in the formal sector had a number of disadvantages besides the low salary level. Using public services and obtaining subsidized goods, though costly in terms of the women's time, accounted for even more substantial savings in low-income households. The inflexible and long hours of factory work critically impeded taking advantage of savings opportunities. For example, a kilogram of subsidized meat sold for 3.75 pounds at the government shops, while in the open market it was 8 pounds.[20] This represents considerable savings for a household, even though a shopper may sometimes have to stand in line for as long as three to four hours.

Moreover, a shortage of subsidized goods meant they were only sporadically available in the cooperatives. Women who were not in the neighborhood at the time could not take advantage of these items. Such potential losses were important in discouraging women from participating in the formal labor market. Umm Sabah, who sold green vegetables in the local market, explained,

I earn little by selling *girgir* [a kind of watercress] and parsley, but because I am here in the vicinity I learn when there is meat, chicken, eggs, or other items in the gamʿiya and I can always leave my basket with either my chil-

19. Since then, blue-collar salaries have gone up, but so has the cost of living. Removal of considerable subsidies for foodstuffs has reduced the necessity to queue at co-ops, but now, with the new high prices, astute shopping has become even more important.

20. For more examples and discussion, see Khouri-Dagher 1986 and Hoodfar 1990.

dren or a friend and run to queue. Sometimes other people queue for me so that I can attend to my business. This way I can buy items that otherwise we could never afford to eat. But if I worked in the factory, since I am unskilled and illiterate, I would perhaps earn ten more pounds and I would have to buy more clothes and spend the rest on transportation. When I come back home in the evening I would have to buy everything from the open market at higher prices and we would lose more than my extra wages.

Despite the reduction in subsidies that has pushed the cost of food much higher, the informal sector remains attractive to women, because it offers them the flexibility they need to cope with a double day. One woman, the mother of five children, told me,

Here I sell green vegetables and when I have a little more capital I also sell some cheese. At times I carry my *babbur* [a small kerosene stove] to the suq and cook there, so that when my children come home from school their food is ready.

While some women may do some of their food preparation at the market, others operate from their home or their doorstep. In times of crisis, a woman might stop her business operation for a while, perhaps for as long as a few months, and then return to it.

To maximize income, women often simultaneously engage in quite diverse activities. For instance, a couple of informants had managed to buy a sewing machine and were making simple clothes for the neighbors. They also raised chickens and rabbits on their roofs. Others worked as *dallalat* (traders, usually in cheap clothes and bedding), midwives, handywomen, and so on. Most women were interested in finding ways to increase their income, though their very small capital (often not more than a few pounds) limited them. If they had to invest more than a few pounds, they were extremely cautious about entering a risky business. Because the local suqs were periodically subject to police raids, which always resulted in the destruction of their total stock by the police, they were reluctant to invest in fruit and the more expensive vegetables that would yield higher profits.

Fatigue and loss of good health were additional costs of working in blue-collar jobs. Mona gave up her factory job because after deducting all costs, her net gain was about 5 pounds a month for spending more than eleven hours away from home and her children each day. By the time she arrived home she was so tired that she could not even tend to her basic domestic responsibilities. For a large majority of women, participation in the labor market is only a means to earn income. If this

income is not enough to improve their material life, then it is a point-
less exercise. I was often reminded that, in contrast to white-collar desk
jobs, low-grade factory jobs were hard work. Those who had worked in
a factory were the first to speak out against it.

It is demanding. Working conditions are often terrible. The foreman treats
you badly. Worst of all, the time schedule is very inflexible: it starts too early
in the morning, often way out of town. By the time one returns home, one
has no energy to do housework. When there is a family crisis women feel
torn between home and the factory.

These ideas were echoed in Mona Hammam's report (1979) on the
working conditions of female factory workers. A female interviewee
told her, "What woman in her right mind wants to be a factory worker?
I am glad it is not encouraged in the text (she was referring to the adult
literacy book taught in the factory). We do it because we have to, not
because we choose to" (Hammam 1979: 7).

The time a woman offered to the labor market was very carefully
assessed against the reward, whereas a man, because he has no designated responsibility at home other than as the provider, can work overtime or accept errands outside his primary job to increase his income.
A man can also use his workplace network much more effectively to find
a second job. It is in this differential context that the situation of men
and women in the labor market should be assessed.

Since few informants had actually given up their jobs in the formal
labor market, I wondered if their preference for the informal market
could be merely a rationalization of their situation, guided by awareness
that access to formal sector jobs was very limited. When asked if it was
difficult for women to find jobs in the formal sector, one out of forty informants (twenty-nine of whom did not have cash-earning activities on
a regular basis) said it had become very difficult for educated women.[21]
Nineteen women said that there were plenty of jobs available; thirteen
said the problem was that they were too poorly paid. Seven women said
one needs good contacts for the better-paid jobs and that it was possible
to find such contacts through neighborhood networks.

Although it is clear that in the 1980s, jobs for unskilled women were
not plentiful, this was not the reason they did not participate in the

21. This informant had been looking for an office job before she married. After her
marriage she worked in her husband's shop to be close to her two babies and hoped to
get an office job when her children were older. Now that they have sold their shop, she
mostly tutors high school children in the neighborhood for a fee.

formal labor market. Many women did not even attempt to look for jobs beyond their residential areas, because their absence would place too great a burden financially and otherwise on their households. Others employed in this sector had resigned after having children.

Women use the same cost-benefit analysis as men, but because of the sexual division of labor, their opportunity costs are much higher than men's, particularly during the family-building cycle. The irony is that it is often at this period that households go through severe income stress. Therefore, women resort to finding other ways of contributing cash income to their households (Moser 1981; Khouri-Dagher 1996; Singerman 1996b).

Examining the situations of the three women in my sample who continued with their blue-collar jobs after marriage and childbirth will throw more light on the complex web of issues involved. Preference for the informal market seems clear. Karima completed primary school and since then had worked as a skilled employee in a pharmaceutical factory. She said she had continued to stay with her job because she was considered well paid (as an educated, skilled blue-collar worker, she was paid a little more than unskilled workers) and workers were provided with transportation.

Eighteen years ago, it never crossed my mind or my husband's that I should give up my job. Just before my first child was born we moved into the same building as my mother so that she could look after my children. All along I had hoped to continue my education and get my high school diploma, which would qualify me for a white-collar job. But once the children were born it became increasingly difficult to study and after some years I gave up. Since I had more education than most other workers in my factory at that time, I was appointed to a better position. So I continued to work. But in the last ten years inflation has made a mockery of my earnings. However, since I have worked there for eighteen years, I feel it is a pity to give up my pension now. If I work a few more years, perhaps I can retire with a small pension.

She and other older informants explained that blue-collar jobs were considered well paid and there was much competition for them. No one would think of giving up such jobs on the grounds of marriage. Mothers and relatives used to help with child care, and since in those days there were less severe housing problems in Cairo, most people could live near their relatives.

Another woman, who worked serving tea in an office, said that she continued to work because her husband was not reliable: he was lazy, incapable, and very often unemployed. Her job provided her with some security, and to supplement her income she also raised some chickens and rabbits on the roof of the apartment building. Moreover, her office was only a half-hour walk from the neighborhood. As she put it, "I am lucky my mother lives in the same alley and looks after my two children so that I can go to work. I do not know what would happen to me and the children if my mother were not here." Her mother, who after the death of her husband had to bring up her three children single-handedly, insisted that this woman continue with her job because it offered her an old-age pension. Her advice was that "a husband you cannot count on in his youth would not be better in his old age."

All three informants who had continued with their blue-collar jobs had their mothers and families living very close to help them with child care and shopping; this reduced the cost of going to work. As Cairo grew in physical size and population, however, it became more difficult for women, especially those from low-income households, to live near their kin. For women, this meant the loss of a support network that traditionally could be counted on. In the absence of substantial wage increases or other improvements in working conditions, we might expect to see increasing female participation at the lower level of the job hierarchy in the informal, rather than the formal, labor market.

As women have lost much of their traditional network of support (particularly in terms of child care) due to the geographic mobility that commercialization and industrialization encourage, neither the state nor the modern sector of the economy has responded to women's special circumstances in any meaningful way, even though the society and economy would be in disarray without their services (Folbre 1986a, 1986b; Waring 1988; Glazer 1990; Smith 1990). This situation effectively marginalized women, especially as new standards of child care place more demands on women's labor. Moreover, domestic responsibilities have caused women to concentrate on similar cash-earning activities (for instance, selling vegetables in the same neighborhood, or competing for domestic service jobs or even white-collar employment such as teaching, which offers more flexibility). This situation further disadvantages women because such concentration and competition result in a lower profit margin or wage.

SELF-EMPLOYMENT

Self-employment remains the most viable option for most women with little education or professional skill. Although there are no reliable statistics on the number of women who are self-employed (including petty trading), a walk around any major urban residential area, particularly in Cairo, makes it clear that the local suqs are dominated by women.

Petty trading continues to be an option. These women generally trade in foodstuffs and clothing and use either their homes or a nearby market as their base. Women who trade in clothing often have more capital and are more likely to work from home. Their customers are neighbors and friends, who often pay in installments. These traders are less likely to be first- or second-generation migrants, mainly because they require knowledge about where to buy wholesale goods and need established personal contacts, sometimes so that they can buy goods on credit or even on commission from wholesalers. These female dallalat are often Cairenes who had to move out of their neighborhood in old Cairo because of the housing shortage.

Most small traders, however, are vegetable sellers with very little capital. They buy vegetables from nearby villages and sell them in the market. Their income varies from one-half pound to one and a half pounds per day, depending on the variety of vegetables they sell. More expensive vegetables yield a higher income but demand more initial capital. Income from dealing in fruit is even higher, but fruit is traditionally men's domain and it is rare for a woman to sell fruit in the market.[22] The number of hours women put into this business varies; a few times a week they must leave their homes as early as dawn to purchase produce.

Women often identified lack of capital as their major problem. Many thought if they could put together enough money to buy a proper kiosk or open a small shop, they could earn much more money without investing more time.

Another type of employment for a woman was involvement in her husband's business. Many of the small shops or kiosks were set up to supplement the household's cash income, and wives and occasionally other household members were expected to participate while the husbands were away at their other jobs. (This was a strategy favored by many households, particularly those whose male heads were low-paid public sector employees.) Many of the informants (both male and female) said this kind of employment was most suitable for women because it did not break either traditional or modern codes of conduct,

22. Customers too were often men because the tradition continued whereby men buy fruit and women buy vegetables.

and when there was a family crisis, a workable schedule could easily be arranged.

It is ironic that out of my ten female informants who worked—some of them over eight or ten hours a day—in the family business, only one saw herself as a "working" wife. This was one of the two Coptic women among my informants. In fact, dissatisfied with her husband's contribution to the household and with the help of her brothers, Umm Sahar had established a small business dealing in small clothing and decorative items. She used to travel to the port cities of Port Said and Alexandria to buy stock at lower prices, but her husband had disagreed with the idea and, fearing financial catastrophe, took over managing the shop. Although she continued to invest more time and energy in the shop than he did, he gave her only housekeeping money, which she thought was not even half the combined income from the shop and his salary. She believed he was unimaginative, timid, and generally not very good with money, but because he is a male/husband, he thought that he should control the finances.

Umm Sahar was frustrated by her husband's action and many times reminded me that Muslim men do not take over their wives' business or their money. She thought that was because Muslim wives could get a divorce, while the Copts have no easy way out of their marriage and the men know it. It was also a question of what belonged to whom: for Muslims this was more clearly defined in religious terms than for Copts, who consider husband and wives one unit, usually under the control and guidance of the husband. Moreover, Muslim men, according to religious principles, are obliged to support the family regardless of their wives' income. Umm Sahar thought Muslim women have a better chance of making their men work hard for the family and of protecting their own wealth without appearing too materialistic.

The situation, however, was not as clear-cut as Umm Sahar presented it. I had noticed that husbands never helped or interfered with their wives' businesses, and women were very careful to avoid any conversation in the presence of their husbands concerning what they earned. When a husband occasionally asked, the wife would jokingly warn him that the man of the house shouldn't have his eye on the woman's few piasters (100 piasters equal one Egyptian pound). Other women would pretend they did not hear, or, more often, they would complain that they did not make much money even before their husbands began to speak. While the husbands regarded asking their wives and children to help with their businesses as a right, and many wives accepted that, the reverse case was never true: a husband almost never helped with his wife's business. When I discussed the issue with my informants, they were all convinced that they should not ask their husbands to help because, as one women said, by nature men have sticky fingers and would develop an appetite for the few piasters their wives earn. Another woman said if something came up and she could not attend to her business, she would ask her children or a friend to take over. If they could not help, she would simply close her business because, as she said, once men take over, that is the end of your business.

None of the women handed over their income to their husbands, but they made a point of telling me that they usually spent their money on what the husbands could or would not spend on the family. Women who participated in their husbands' businesses did not receive an independent wage from this activity, but since it provided them with a good knowledge of the level of income, they felt they were in better bargaining positions vis-à-vis their husbands (Nadim el-Messiri 1977; Hoodfar 1988).

Petty production among women was mostly limited to foodstuffs. Some women cooked the food at home and sold it with or without the help of their husbands in the street. Other women cooked and sold types of traditional "fast foods" outside the doors of their homes. The capital to buy the necessary inventory for this job was usually the cost of a babbur (kerosene burner) and one or two big pots, which most women possessed in any case. As a result of the gradual removal of subsidies, the price of vegetables and bread had increased sharply and the highly competitive market reduced the profit margin, which was already quite low, and many were forced out of the market.

Raising chickens, pigeons, and rabbits was another form of production that women normally engaged in. Although most women raised a few chickens on their balconies for subsistence use, only those with roof space could raise larger numbers for trading.[23] In any case, many women who had been raising poultry in the past had to give it up, for as the buildings in Cairo grew taller, space had become more of a problem. As well, factory production and cheaper imported frozen chicken meant raising poultry was no longer profitable as a small home enterprise. In Egypt, women have traditionally controlled the production and mar-

23. Looking from the roof of the building I lived in, all visible roof space was covered by chickens, rabbit cages, and geese. A few of the better-off households also kept a lamb on their roof or tethered to their door.

keting of poultry and rabbit. However, men usually owned and staffed the modern factory production facilities, even though women were more knowledgable about the product.

A smaller cash-earning group was made up of self-employed artisans such as hairdressers, tailors, and traditional midwives. These women had often learned their trade as part of their upbringing. A few women hairdressers and tailors had served their apprenticeship with other women who were in business locally. Generally, households with longer urban experience were more likely to send their daughters to a formal training center, if they could afford it. Tailoring and hairdressing were considered by most informants as occupations suitable for women, but very few women were qualified enough to be considered skilled: top tailors and hairdressers in the neighborhoods were men. This was partly because men had more capital to invest in their enterprises and partly because women had not had the chance to improve their skills. The majority of these female tradespeople had turned a room of their flat into a workshop or rented a room in the neighborhood for their business. It was rare for these women to want to move out of their locality, where they were able to attend to their domestic responsibilities while they worked. At times, women would forgo the possibility of a bigger profit to work near their homes.

WAGE WORKERS: MAIDS AND HANDYWOMEN

It is almost universally assumed that in an urban setting, women can always find jobs as domestic servants (Jelin 1977; Chaney and Castro 1989). However, the Egyptian case is much more complex. Domestic work is not the monopoly of female workers; it is estimated that in Egypt up to one-fourth of paid domestic workers are male (Youssef 1976; Scott 1985).

During the 1980s, many Egyptian maids (particularly older women) migrated to oil-rich countries where they were paid at least ten times what they earned in Egypt. Higher wage levels, primarily as a consequence of migration, made it possible for many households to keep their children, particularly their daughters, at school or at home rather than send them to work as maids and servants in Cairo. Concurrently, the rapidly rising cost of living and new job opportunities in the private sector encouraged upper-middle-class women to enter the labor market. Hence the need for child care and other domestic services increased while the supply remained limited. The acute shortage of maids inflated their wages from about 20 to 100 pounds or more, a wage higher than the basic salary rate of a university graduate in any government office.

However, although domestic service was relatively well paid and increasingly considered a feminine job, few women among the very poor had access to such a job. To be a maid was no longer an unskilled job, even if the market, because of its tendency to undervalue domestic skills, failed to recognize this. In the past, most maids worked under the supervision of the female head of household and were trained to perform certain tasks. However, those middle-class female heads of households were no longer at home, and they needed a person to manage the housework and child care in their absence. Most low-income women did not qualify for these positions, because they lacked the necessary skills required to work in middle-class households. Leaving aside the ability to use many different types of electronic household gadgets, a wide gap had developed between the low-income strata and the middle classes in the knowledge and practice of hygiene.[24]

There were other serious impediments for poor women who wished to take advantage of a maid's lucrative wages. To find a job as a servant in a middle-class household required very good vertical social contacts who could introduce a woman to potential employers and supply references for her. Without such assurances, few people were prepared to hand over their house keys to strangers. However, very few poor women had such contacts. Among the middle classes it is often assumed that the low status of the job prevents poor women from taking advantage of these job opportunities. My data, however, do not support such assumptions. Not surprisingly, the very poor women were often younger ones with young children and few if any marketable skills and without an influential network as many were married to unemployed or underemployed husbands. These women were under continual financial stress and accepted any earning opportunity that arose. Some of these women worked, as maids or handywomen, in lower-middle-class households, which were generally more accessible to the poorer strata. However, as inflation ate into the income of these households, it became less possible

24. In the past and in more traditional communities in Egypt, there was little difference in taste and hygiene practices or in the values held by the rich and poor (Rugh 1979). The major difference was that the poor could not afford to practice those values whereas the rich could. However, the gap between the cultural values of the rich and the poor has greatly widened in modern society as the rich adopt more global consumption values.

for them to afford a maid, even one who was paid far below the market wage. Other women worked for wages close to nothing for their better-off neighbors who would call on them to work as handywomen on occasions such as weddings, childbirths, and funerals. It appears, therefore, that the shortage of domestic servants was not caused by the unwillingness of poor women to work as maids but by the dearth of skilled and well-connected maids.

Attitudes toward Gainful Employment

In spite of radical socioeconomic changes, the bases of the ideology of the sexual division of labor and responsibilities within the household have remained fundamentally unchallenged either by men, women, legal jurisdiction, or government policies. In the popular cultural setting, men and women are believed to have different natures that make them suited to different but complementary tasks. Women belong to the home because their caring nature makes them suited to looking after children and the husband, while men must provide for the family. Islamic ideology and the Qur'an are heavily used as justification for such beliefs (ait-Sabbah 1984; MacLeod 1991; Early 1993; Fernea 1993).

The history of capitalist development both in the West and in the Third World suggests that where the ideology of the male as the breadwinner did not exist, the state actively participated in creating one (Boserup 1970; Rogers 1980; Pinchbeck 1981). This appears consistent with the Egyptian context, where the state does not challenge the existing basis of such an ideology. Nasser's socialist ideology never questioned women's role as homemaker and mother; rather, it extended a woman's duty to the labor market without providing the basis for any change in the sexual division of labor within the home. Nor was any major consideration given to shaping the labor market to suit the special situation of women: rather, it was left to women to adapt themselves to the labor market. The result was a heavy concentration of women in jobs that are more flexible, suit their domestic skills, and accommodate their time schedule.

Furthermore, under the pretext of effective and rational investment in human resources, men received a much larger share of public funds in the form of training programs and education facilities. This policy, in turn, was supported by individual households that by the same ideology and logic invested more in their sons' education and training than their daughters', perpetuating the actual biases of the situation.

At the individual level, a man had little reason to challenge this ideology since his high status in the family was based on his role as provider. Furthermore, this role legitimized his access to a wider range of opportunities in the job market. Men's resistance to change was further supported by the flexibility of this ideology since failure to fulfill their role simply results in women taking on men's responsibilities.

Women, for their part, had even less reason to question this ideology since their main resource was often their domestic expertise. The rate of illiteracy was much higher among women and they possessed fewer marketable skills, hence their participation in the labor market was often concentrated in low-paid, low-status activities. They were best equipped with their domestic skills, which were becoming increasingly commercialized, while their performance of domestic work was becoming dependent on commercialized goods such as gas cookers. Fulfilling traditional domestic duties was increasingly cash dependent. Since a husband was the most reliable source of financial support for most women, they had no reason to contest the male obligation. If anything, they often tried to reinforce it by referring to Islamic rule and customs, and by ridiculing men who broke the rules of the sexual division of labor. Women of low-income groups—often more disadvantaged in the labor market—found traditional ideology even more appealing.

Those few fortunate women with relatively better paid jobs were treated as honorary men by the community. They drew such prestige from their unique situation that, far from calling into question the gender ideology, they actively promoted it. Even men treated them as exceptional women who have raised themselves above other women and men. Therefore, there was little opportunity for any fundamental change of ideology. Instead, the convention was manipulated to adjust and adapt to the new situation.

When discussing women's responsibilities, all female informants—married or single, with or without formal education, working or not—declared that a woman's chief responsibility and priority was to attend to her home, her children, and her husband. There were only two conditions in which a woman should "go out to earn money": if the survival and functioning of the household at acceptable standards could not be achieved without her wages (that is, where the husband failed to provide) and if the management of her domestic affairs could be

Table 12 *Question: Do you think that women should "work" or stay at home?*

Answer	Frequency	Percentage
Stay at home	16	27.0
Work if they have to	2	3.3
Work if they are educated	9	15.2
Should work	32	54.2
Total	59*	100

*Informants who did not have daughters were not asked.

performed at least as well as if she were staying at home. Some added that the permission of the husband was also essential. Clearly, both working and nonworking women, including the more educated, regarded cash-earning activity as optional for women.

However, acquiescence to traditional gender role ideology did not prevent women from assessing the fundamental economic changes and their impact on the household, particularly marital relations. When the women were asked whether a woman should "work" or stay at home, the majority answered that she should work (see table 12). Some qualified their answers by adding a woman should work only if she is educated or if her husband has no objection to her working.

Fourteen out of the sixteen women who said it is better that women stay at home were those who were or had been working as petty traders in the local vegetable market and were conscious of the low status and low rewards of these jobs, which represented their only earning option. However, when I asked them whether they would like their daughters to work or stay at home, five said they want their daughters to be educated and have good jobs. Another three women said they would educate their daughters and give them the resources to work if they wished to. Four said they would like them to work only until they marry and have children, and only two said they do not want them to work. Of the latter, both of their daughters were adults and did not have any education; for them, working meant engagement in unskilled and low-status jobs. The majority of these informants wanted their daughters to have paid jobs, and all, with the exception of five, stressed that they wanted them to be educated and have white-collar, prestigious jobs (see table 13).

Most women explained in detail that, given an economic situation of continued inflation, it was impossible to live on only one income. The second most frequent reason given was that a woman must have

Table 13 *Question: Would you like your daughter to "work" or stay at home?*

Answer	Frequency	Percentage
Stay at home	3	5.4
Work until she has babies	6	10.1
Up to her	4	7.2
To be educated and work	42	76.3
Total	55	100

security if her marriage should fail. Few parents or brothers can support their divorced daughters or sisters and their children, many of my female informants explained. The other most frequently stated reason why a woman should work was the respect she received from her husband for helping to support the household. The partnership is thought to become more equal. Often nonworking women pointed out the relationship of a working woman and her husband as an example.

I asked whether they would wish their sons to marry a "working" woman or a housewife (see table 14). Twenty-six of the informants said they would prefer a working to a nonworking wife for their sons. Only two emphasized that she should be educated. Sixteen said they did not have any particular interest in the issue. Six said they would rather their son marry a housewife because she could comfort him better and would always obey him.

Generally, women felt much more strongly about the issue of women working as it concerned their daughters. Although they recognized that men faced increasing demands in fulfilling their duties than did their fathers and grandfathers, they did not feel that men had lost their status and position within the marriage partnership. In contrast, they felt women's position had become less secure, a situation they wished to address by enabling their daughters to have access to gainful employment.[25]

This account makes clear that women's adherence to traditional ideology serves their interests, given their possibilities, and justifies financial dependence on their husbands. However, women recognized that the process of commercialization and the introduction of new con-

25. Since it is not socially acceptable to complain about one's lot in life, people often invested their hopes for change in their children. For this reason, questions were included to elicit information about the direction of changes the informants wished to see.

Table 14 *Question: Would you like your son to marry a "working" or a "nonworking" woman?*

Answer	Frequency	Percentage
I hope he marries a "nonworking" wife	6	12.5
It is up to him	16	33.3
It is better if he marries a "working" wife	26	54.1
Total	48*	100

* Because of the informal nature of the interviews, I did not have the opportunity to discuss the question with all the informants. In addition, the question was omitted when it was not relevant to the circumstances of the informant.

sumer demands had increased financial pressure on the male provider. They also recognized that this process had adversely affected their status in the eyes of their husbands, and they wished to prepare their daughters for contributing to household cash resources—a capacity more socially valued than domestic work. Furthermore, they wanted their daughters to have the means, however modest, to survive if a marriage were to fail or become too difficult.

The informants shared similar views of which jobs were suitable for women. Since there was a conflict between going out to work and attending to home affairs, a woman's choice of economic activity was strongly influenced by her domestic responsibilities. All the women favored those jobs that had the most flexible schedule and were least demanding physically (see table 15).

Factory work was among the least favored choices for reasons already discussed. To avoid the problems facing factory workers, the majority of less educated women tended to participate in jobs that were more flexible and usually locally based, so they could attend to their domestic responsibilities and not feel torn between home and work. As one vegetable seller explained, "Even if the pay is less, my mind is at peace: I know that my children are safe. I try to save in other ways to make up for my small income."

However, if factory work was taken up as a temporary job by single women until marriage, it was considered acceptable and suitable. The strong objection centered around its schedule and the physical demands that prevented women from tending to their domestic responsibilities. Moreover, many mentioned that factory work provided young single

Table 15 *Acceptable Jobs for Women in Order of Suitability*

Educated women

   Government employee (teacher, white-collar worker, nurse)

Skilled women

   Tailor (very suitable), hairdresser

Illiterate women

   If they have to work:
   1. Worker in the market and petty trader within the neighborhood;
   2. Unskilled work such as cleaner or tea lady in a factory or any other
      large institution (hospital, hotel, large business);*
   3. Where there is no other choice: maid or handywoman.

I discussed the question with 55 informants whose answers were very similar. The major difference was in the kind of jobs they chose as examples.

* Large companies provide insurance and pensions. In fact, many women assumed that all large companies were owned and operated by the government.

women with a legitimate reason to get out and meet people and gain experience. More important, they might also find a suitor. The money they earned could be put aside to buy items for their trousseau, since daughters were not expected to contribute to the financial support of the household.

Education was seen as a gateway to clerical jobs, where the liberal attitude of the government toward married female employees was much appreciated and was seen as a way to resolve the conflicting commitments of women to home and work. The informants articulated two reasons for their preference for government employment: being able to stay home if their children fell ill, without fear of losing their job, since the government explicitly recognizes that domestic responsibility is a woman's first priority, and the very light workload.

The low rate of labor market participation among Arab women is often viewed critically without much attention to women's double commitment and the resulting contradictions they face (Hijab 1988, 1994; Hoodfar 1996b). Women are not being credited for the enormous effort they invest in adapting and combining these roles. Removing individual women from the coordination of family and household and placing them into the labor market is a delicate balancing act, likely to be misunderstood unless we know a great deal about the allocative rules determining decision making within the family (Hoodfar 1996b). The economic analysis that is intended to explain individual behavior, particularly that of women in a given society, must start with the broader unit of which she or he is a member. It is not possible to understand an individual's labor participation without considering the dynamic inter-action among individual, familial, and social constraints.

Women are caught in the process of the devaluation of their tradi-tional role as mother and wife, yet both old and new gender ideologies prevent them from effectively seeking new roles. The gender ideology and the economic realities of society are evolving in contradictory di-rections, and women are trying to adapt and accommodate themselves to the new situation by acquiring new resources, finding jobs with maximum flexibility to suit their situation, and at times reverting to traditions, such as veiling, that their predecessors once struggled to dis-card (Hoodfar 1991; MacLeod 1991).

The centrality of the family as an institution and its importance as a channel of redistribution of resources (Singerman 1995; Singerman and Hoodfar 1996) perpetuate the ideology of gender roles and prevent women from consciously giving a high priority to their economic role. Although all married women with postsecondary education whom I came to know in the neighborhoods were working and did not foresee giving up their jobs, most unmarried educated daughters said if they have a choice they would not "work" after their marriage. They would rather be sitt al-bayt who look after their children and husbands and command considerable respect in Egyptian society. In contrast to the emphasis married women placed on the relationship between respect and equality in marriage and a woman's cash contribution, most edu-cated single women denied that a successful and mutually respectful marriage had anything to do with women's cash contribution.

The Male View of Women's Paid Work

Male informants had much more diverse ideas about women and "work." Traditional and older men said a woman should go out to work only if her husband fails to feed her and her children but should participate if there is a family business and her husband needs help. Men defined their responsibility to provide as limited to feeding the family. Women tended to elaborate that the role of the male bread-winner was to provide for all the needs of the family. This difference was often a source of family disputes.

Younger men agreed that if a woman was educated and had a good job (by which they meant a job with status, such as that of an office clerk) and she was able to manage her home at the same time, she could "work." However, all the men, married or not, were adamant that it was a husband's prerogative to deny his wife the right to work. None of the informants was asked to express his view on this issue, but all volunteered an opinion.

Few women contested men's claim to the right to stop their wives from "working" or leaving the house. The majority said that by custom, tradition, and religion, husbands were entitled to such rights. Quite a few of the female informants, however, said that if a man married a working woman and he did not raise any objection at the time of marriage, he would have no right to stop her later, unless the wife failed to fulfill her domestic duties. Other women said that if a woman worked for the government, the husband lost his right to object. Such a belief was based on an unfounded but widely held assumption, by women and sometimes men, that the right of the government was above the right of a husband.[26] This assumption finds its roots in the ideology of Nasserism, which made participation of all men and women in building the national economy a duty.

The legal rights of a husband in this regard are unclear. In Egypt, there was no legal requirement that a married woman get permission from her husband to be employed. However, a husband could raise legal objections to his wife working by using an argument based on his interpretation of shariʿa (Muslim laws), though he must prove that he is an adequate provider. The current Personal Status Law makes it a legal right for a married woman to work if her husband fails to fulfill his obligations, and the state employment law makes special concessions to married women, such as coordinating the proximity of their workplace with their residence.

Five of the female informants said that the husband had the right to prevent his wife from being employed only when he could provide her with all the luxuries she desired. Since few men were able to do this, few had such rights. They added, however, that a woman must calculate the gains and the losses incurred by her employment, and if it was deemed detrimental to her marriage and family, she should not go out to work.

26. Ibrahim (1980) has also found similar beliefs.

Summary

Women's choice of labor market participation was strongly influenced by their domestic responsibilities, which they considered a woman's most important contribution to her household. Therefore, those with formal education preferred to be state employees because of the concessions the state makes to married, white-collar female workers. Inflexible work hours, physical demands, and low pay made unskilled jobs in the formal sector unsuitable for women with domestic responsibilities, who preferred to engage in the locally based informal sector.

Women adhered strongly to traditional and Islamic gender roles, primarily because traditional and Muslim gender ideology justified their claim for financial support from their husbands regardless of their own abilities to earn. Therefore, not only did they not want to discard these privileges, they often guarded them rigorously by adopting a variety of tactics, including wearing the veil and promoting traditional conservative gender ideology. However, conservatism and traditionalism did not prevent more-educated women, who faced more favorable terms in the labor market, from taking full advantage of the market. Moreover, women's strong desire for their daughters to have secure and respectable jobs is evidence that their acquiescence to the traditional gender role had not prevented them from observing economic change and its impact on marital relations.

Cultural and religious practices as well as economic choices should be viewed as a whole and from the point of view of those who live within them. Through a contextual approach, I have demonstrated that the benefits "Islamic ideology" offers to low-income women outweigh its disadvantages. Hence women find this ideology attractive, particularly since their nuanced interpretations of it enable them to take advantage of what modernization offers.

CHAPTER 5

Money Management and Patterns of Household Budgeting

Until recent years, studies of money management and other household assets rarely addressed the welfare of the "working poor." The upsurge of interest in this area has been provoked by feminist scholars examining the nature and source of power relations between husband and wife and their implications for the welfare of household members (Beneria and Roldan 1987; Dwyer and Bruce 1988; Pahl 1989; Gonzalez de la Rocha 1994). These studies contested the assumptions of pooling resources, a high degree of stability, power sharing and egalitarianism in decision making, and consumption within the household.[1] Cross-cultural studies have documented that household budgeting takes many different forms, and men and women in different societies may have different responsibilities toward their households and their offspring (Dwyer and Bruce 1988).

Another phenomenon that has attracted the attention of those interested in family welfare and poverty issues is the widespread incidence of differential expenditure patterns by men and women in many societies. It appears that women often place more emphasis on communal expenditure than men do (Roldan 1985; Mencher 1988). However, studies have rarely discussed the underlying reason for this phenomenon.[2] While my findings confirm such a trend among my informants, my anal-

---

1. The gap between ideology and practice was not recognized in many of these earlier studies that helped to create a blueprint for social reform.

2. Statements of differential patterns of expenditure between men and women without analysis of the underlying social and material basis of such patterns implicitly favor the ideology of "maternal altruism," which implies that the differential attitudes are caused by biological (genetic) factors.

ysis indicates that it is related to the fact that women's interests are often more closely tied to those of their children and their households than are their husbands', evidence of a material basis for their so-called maternal altruism.

Money management is an important aspect of any study of household subsistence strategies.[3] In this chapter, I examine the patterns of financial arrangements in the neighborhoods, the factors influencing these patterns, and their consequences for respective household members. I pay particular attention to households where women had independent cash earnings and households affected by international migration, since these represent a deviation from the "ideal" model of family structure.

Financial Arrangements

As discussed in chapters 2 and 4, according to the tenets of Islam and tradition, men are responsible for providing for their families. Islam gives a wife the unconditional right to financial support from her husband, even when she has a substantial income of her own. A husband has no right to his wife's income, and, at least among the low-income households of Cairo, there was great pressure on men to observe this rule and fulfill their obligations to their households. This religiously sanctioned arrangement, which few social scientists have paid much attention to, has given Egyptian women of the "working poor" an advantage over many of their counterparts in other parts of the Third World such as Latin America.[4] However, this is not to suggest that women freely spend their wages on themselves; rather, it has helped give them discretionary power over their wages and expenditures. Indeed, my findings indicate that women spent almost all their income on communal items, most often on durable goods and their children's education.

In fact, the situation was much more complex than suggested by the

3. In this study I have concentrated on cash, since I am dealing with urban households, but the discussion can be extended to any other household resources (see Whitehead 1981; Dwyer and Bruce 1988).

4. For instance, an important demand of women in the Nicaraguan revolution was that fathers and husbands be legally obliged to give financial support to their families and children (Molyneux 1985).

homogeneous ideology expressed by all male and female informants. As the need for cash increased, men who had limited incomes were torn between their own needs and those of their families. They strove to find ways to limit their financial obligations to their families, while their wives searched equally for ways to ensure their husbands' commitments to the households. Conflicts erupted over the interpretation of "providing." There was no universal understanding of this term that has always been very fluid. While Islamic rules specifically refer to food, shelter, and clothing, cultural practices, class background, and redefinitions of the absolute minimum standard of living and basic needs have always had an impact on defining what is considered an acceptable level of providing.

Men tended to present the provision of anything beyond food, shelter, and clothing as a favor for which family members should be grateful. Women chose a much broader and more specific definition, which included good food, housing, clothing, education, and health care, and some also added leisure. This difference in views was the greatest cause of family tensions.[5] These tensions were heightened by a lack of specific legal or religious instruction on how men should provide, which was usually decided according to cultural practice, the specific conditions of a household, personal preferences, and personality (of the husband and, to a lesser degree, of the wife or other household members).

Household financial arrangements varied from situations in which women had total control of cash and family expenditure to the exact opposite. Studies of financial arrangements in other communities have suggested that they are profoundly affected by specific cultural practices, the family cycle, the age of the couple, the nature of the subsistence activities of the spouses, and the level of aggregate income (Beneria and Roldan 1987; Wilson 1987; Pahl 1989). However, each factor may weigh quite differently in each community, particularly in fast-changing urban communities of "developing" nations.

In explaining the different methods of budgeting, women often referred to regional traditions. However, I found a remarkable degree of flexibility and lack of any consistent pattern or "custom" being continued or transformed. For example, people of Upper Egypt, *saʿidis*,

5. To assess the difference between expressed ideology and practice, I also carried out semiformal interviews. As I discussed in chapter 1, I had intended to ask the husbands' views on these issues. However, these interviews resulted in family disputes, so I changed my plan and discussed the issues with the husbands informally when an opportunity was presented.

traditionally favored male control of financial matters, particularly cash transactions relating to the household. It is up to the husband to decide which of his wife's needs, and those of their children and the household in general, are to be fulfilled. Some male saʿidis expressed the view that women should never touch money, even if they wear kilos of gold. Furthermore, a woman is not expected to ask for any information about her husband's income; she is supposed to know only what he is willing to tell her.

Unfortunately, in the social sciences, unspoken rules are often overlooked (Betteridge 1980). Although the verbalization of saʿidi budgeting arrangements may give the impression that women are disadvantaged, some of the happiest and most contented wives of my sample were from this region. Saʿidi men were trained to be sensitive to the clues that women gave about their needs—a quality noticeably lacking in men from the Delta region—and felt proud in fulfilling them. Women were taught to assess their husbands' financial ability and not to embarrass them by directly or indirectly demanding things that were beyond their means to provide. Umm Samir told me how she felt embarrassed because once, in the early years of her marriage, she had talked about the beautiful dress that her sister-in-law was wearing and her husband overheard her. He subsequently borrowed money from his uncle, went to town, and bought her a new dress. She said, "I knew he did not have money, and I did not mean he should buy me the dress. Anyway, I learned my lesson and have done my best not to embarrass him again."

Nevertheless, though some saʿidi households had retained their traditional financial arrangements, most did not. Men regretfully acknowledged that since much of their time was spent away from their neighborhoods at their places of work, they could not practice the old customs. Many of the younger women, however, openly welcomed the change.

In contrast to the Upper Egyptians, women of the Delta traditionally participated in public life and many established their own businesses or collaborated closely with their husbands. Women were expected to play some role in the management of their households' financial matters. This ranged from total control of all financial affairs, including those of their husbands, to receiving a daily allowance from their husbands for vegetables and other family needs (Nadim el-Messiri 1975, 1977; Wikan 1980; Early 1993).

Though age and domestic cycle played a role when renegotiating financial arrangements, they were not as significant in Egypt as is suggested for other communities (Beneria and Roldan 1987). Similarly, the nature of a woman's occupation seemed to have no effect on the financial strategies that the household adopted, except when the husband did not contribute to its support. In some cases, however, the fact that a woman had her own income made it possible for men to migrate (Hoodfar 1996a). In addition, aggregate family income was not associated with any particular pattern of financial arrangement. For example, total pooling was practiced by both the richest and poorest families in the neighborhoods.

The flow of information from husband to wife about his wages and available resources seemed to play a more decisive role in the way women felt about their household budgeting than cash flow itself. In most low-income families cash resources just covered the basic and immediate needs; the concern, therefore, was for budgeting, rather than for access and control of the cash. Thus, once the spouses (especially the wives) were assured of their partners' trust and good intentions, little value was placed on who had access to the households' cash resources, and often small differences in priority of expenditure were tolerated.

Certain patterns of domestic financial organization documented in other urban societies were absent in Cairo. For instance, the model in which husband and wife shop together, with the wife choosing the purchases and the husband paying, did not occur in the poor districts of Cairo, where cultural practices and economic possibilities preclude such a system. Men and women rarely go out together except when traveling. Furthermore, preference for fresh food, lack of storage space and refrigerators, periodic shortages of some goods in the market, and lack of large sums of money made shopping a daily, if not more frequent, task. Where women did not receive a household allowance, they had no say in family expenditures. Women could directly intervene or exercise control over family expenditures only insofar as they had access to, and control over, the income.

I could not trace any consistent pattern of "customs" being continued or modified. The husband's economic activities were the most important determinant of how a household organized its financial matters. There was a strong correlation between the degree to which men remained involved in the family's daily money matters and the type and location of their economic activities. Women's influence on household expenditure was correlated with their access to money.

Patterns of Budgeting in the Neighborhoods

As the incidence of marriage between people of different regions increased, it became common to negotiate the financial arrangement between the spouses in detail prior to the marriage. The bride's mother played a significant role in this negotiation, trying to secure a fair deal for her daughter. The couple was bound to keep the arrangement for the first few years at least. Breach of the agreement without mutual consent could involve kin from both sides, particularly those present in the premarriage negotiations.

Women strongly defended this practice and were critical of parents who failed to participate.[6] Azza, who was engaged to be married, expressed her gratitude to her mother for having secured an acceptable financial arrangement for her. She explained the agreement between the groom and her family.

He will give me all his basic monthly salary, which is 70 pounds, for the day-to-day expenses and rent. He will keep any extra he earns, but he will also pay for the clothing and medical expenses.

Her mother continued,

I made sure that we reached this agreement before we publicly announced the engagement. . . . The young may not understand, but these matters must be sorted out clearly before the wedding. Otherwise, women will face problems because men do not have a good sense about what a woman wants, and women are too shy to ask outright in the early months of marriage.

Such negotiations, in a culture that encourages women to act modestly and show little concern for money, are designed to protect women and make it possible for them to start from a more powerful position in the marriage union. They also prevent many of the financial disputes that might arise in the early years of marriage.

Sabah had found a suitor and all the negotiations were settled except for marital financial affairs. He had agreed to pay 80 pounds a month for all expenses except clothing. However, Sabah and her family insisted that he should pay for meat and medicine separately. He would

6. Although some of the more educated, unmarried women were skeptical of the importance of such arrangements, particularly when the marriage was based on mutual love, the more traditional single women supported the practices and many referred to love marriages among their friends and neighbors that had gone sour because of financial disputes.

not agree, and after two months of negotiations they decided against the marriage. Sabah later explained,

It was not only whether he pays or not now, but I was worried that a man who is a little tight with his money from the beginning may start to be more mean later in the marriage, when I have children. So, despite the fact that I had liked him much more then any other suitor I have had, my mother and I agreed against the marriage.

Men also thought that the negotiations provided an opportunity to reject the conditions before entering into a marriage contract. Like women, they agreed that financial matters were the primary source of marital disputes, and they welcomed means that would reduce friction over these matters, particularly in the early years of marriage.

In contrast with many other cultures, financial arrangements were discussed openly among women, who consequently knew how each other's households arranged money matters.[7] Prices, daily family expenditures, and budgeting for the day, week, or month were popular subjects of conversation. Budgeting and financial arrangements in the neighborhoods can be broadly grouped in seven categories: wife as financial manager, wife as family banker, full housekeeping allowance, partial housekeeping allowance, husband as financial manager, "guest husband," and migrants' household (see table 16).

WIFE AS FINANCIAL MANAGER

In this arrangement, men handed over the whole of their wages to their wives, who had to meet all the family's needs including rent, food, school fees, clothing, and presents. Men asked for their personal expenses, which normally included cigarettes, tea, and food (many men had to eat out due to their working hours or the distance between home and their place of employment). Sometimes, men handed over whatever they earned from their first and second jobs and kept for their personal expenses whatever they earned from overtime work or odd jobs.

Despite the fact that being financial manager meant many more responsibilities and worries over how to make ends meet on a small in-

7. For instance, it took me some time before I learned that in England one must not ask people about their earnings or the cost of items they had bought. In my experience these matters were common topics of conversations among friends and neighbors and those barely acquainted with one another.

Table 16 *Patterns of Household Financial Arrangement*

Arrangement	Waged Women	Nonwaged Women	Total	Percentage
Wife as manager	5	6	11	17.7
Wife as banker	1	2	3	4.8
Full allowance	6	5	11	17.7
Partial allowance	–	8	8	12.9
Husband as manager	–	5	5	8.0
Guest husband	4	–	4	6.4
Migrants' household	10	10	20	32.2
Total	26	36	62	100

Note: This table is arranged according to the degree of women's access to their husband's cash income.

come, all women preferred this arrangement. Many took pride in the fact that their husbands trusted them with money, and they often explained that they had won their husbands' trust by being good wives. Umm Azza's words are typical of most women in this group.

From the beginning, my husband saw that I was saving the money and not spending it on myself or on my relatives, but rather I preferred to buy things for our home and our children. It is for this reason that now he doesn't even bother to ask me what I do with the money.

Invariably they gave examples of other women who were incompetent money managers or who spent all the money on themselves, and therefore their husbands could not trust them with the money. However, I do not know of one case in which a husband later charged his wife with misuse of funds or incompetence and revoked her role as financial manager. The reverse was often true: many men, particularly among the poorer households, said they left financial matters to their wives because women can stretch the money further.

Eleven of the sixty-two households had adopted this pattern, some from the beginning of their marriage. Other research in the old Cairo quarters suggests that this arrangement was more widely practiced among low-income urban households in the past (Nadim el-Messiri 1977; Singerman 1995), but by the 1980s, fewer men were willing to accept these terms. Wives outside this group considered such women lucky, clever, and capable of controlling their men. Younger and more urbanized men in the neighborhoods regarded such husbands as stupid and peasantlike and openly mocked them.

WIFE AS FAMILY BANKER

There were only three households in which the wife acted as family banker. The major difference between this group and the previous one is that while these women had detailed financial information and access to the family earnings, they did not have the unilateral authority to spend it. Usually the husband undertook the major shopping and allocated money for various purposes. The wives participated in decision making to varying degrees, but this often went unrecognized. These wives often took their husbands' trust as a gesture of goodwill. They felt that being trusted with information and money indicated that their husbands placed the interests of the family before their own needs.

FULL HOUSEKEEPING ALLOWANCE

Women in this category received a monthly, weekly, or daily allowance and were responsible for all normal family expenses (usually with the exception of medicine). Husbands occasionally bought some extra food or clothing, but these were seen as presents. These women had little knowledge of their husbands' income, and there were continual problems and arguments over money.

There were eleven households in this group: in five of them, women had an income of their own, and although they were very critical of their husbands, they had stopped arguing with them and concentrated instead on making ends meet with their own earnings. Some of them said that their husbands' contributions were only enough for food (a very simple diet) and rent. Other daily expenses—clothing, medicine, household utensils, and education—had to be paid for out of their own income, if they had any, or the family simply had to go without.

Without exception, informants (male and female) saw disputes over money as their major marital problem. Women believed this was because of men's selfishness, while their husbands attributed these problems to women's greedy and demanding nature. On closer observation, however, the basis for the bitterness seemed to be the unwillingness of husbands to share information about their incomes and actual (and presumed extravagant) personal expenses. Saida, referring to her husband's suit, said,

You see? That is how he spends his money. And he eats chicken and kebab for his lunch and dinner while we do not see meat more than once a week.

He spends his time in the cafés and cinemas while we cannot leave the neighborhood from year to year.

In almost all cases, husbands in this category spent more money on personal expenses than other husbands in the same income group. However, a simple calculation of maximum income and prices makes it clear that they could not possibly be as extravagant as their wives imagined. The problem arose from the fact that men were not at all involved in the routine shopping and they did not have, or try to develop, an awareness of the rising cost of living. Although their incomes had often increased over the last few years, they had not increased the household allowance accordingly.

PARTIAL HOUSEKEEPING ALLOWANCE

In eight households, the wives received a fixed daily, weekly, or monthly allowance for vegetables and some small items, and the husbands were responsible for all other expenditures including meat, schooling, and rent. This method was adopted by the younger couples. Among some older couples in this group, the husbands had handled all the finances until a period of migration or a second job forced them to turn over some financial responsibilities to their wives. These wives may or may not have had knowledge of their husbands' income, but all of them accepted this arrangement since it saved them from standing in long queues at government shops and provided them with a fixed sum and some latitude in spending it.

All women in this group said that as long as they bought what they were supposed to, their husbands did not ask them to account for their allowances. This encouraged them to save. Some had entered into saving clubs with their friends and neighbors, with or without their husbands' knowledge.[8] With their savings they bought small household goods or items that the husbands were unwilling to buy. The older women bought clothing for their daughters, paid their children's educational fees, or bought presents for their friends and relatives. Occasionally they bought some gold, not only for its prestige but also as an investment.

Generally the women in this group were much happier with their financial arrangements than those with full housekeeping allowances.

8. See chapter 8 for a discussion of saving clubs.

Since men remained involved in the shopping, they had a better sense of prices and the cost of living. The degree to which a woman expressed satisfaction with this method of budgeting depended very much on how she evaluated her husband's household contribution relative to his earnings and what she estimated he spent on himself. The husbands in this group generally spent more time at home and usually ate with the family, in contrast with husbands in the full allowance category, all of whom only occasionally ate their main meal at home.

HUSBAND AS FINANCIAL MANAGER

In five households, men were the financial managers and bought everything except vegetables, a task culturally designated as a woman's job. Usually, but not always, the men of this group left a small sum of money with their wives for bread and vegetables, but there was no fixed amount or fixed schedule: it could be every day or every week. The wives were expected to ask for what was needed for the kitchen, children, house, or themselves, and the husbands would try to meet these demands. In cases in which husbands worked in the neighborhood, the wives demanded money and goods whenever the need arose.

Women in this group, mostly middle-aged Upper Egyptians, often expressed a desire for more decision-making power with respect to shopping and often advised their daughters or sisters to encourage their husbands to give them some of the budgeting and shopping responsibilities. They did not, however, want to change their own system at this stage in their lives, because "shopping is *fan* [an art] and one has to practice it for years to become expert." They felt a change in their budgeting system would risk a loss that their households could not afford. These wives could not articulate how much they would need to manage their households, nor did they know how much per month, week, or day their husbands spent.

An exception was the youngest couple in this group (married for ten years). The wife told me that if her husband only gave half his income to her, she could manage so much better, but he would not agree. She remarked,

He likes himself too much, and his needs and comforts come first. I know it is his money, but we are his responsibility. You can see how much he spends on his suit, jeans, and shirts, and goes to the cafeteria and not to the tea-houses. He goes to the cinema regularly, and, worst of all, he goes to bars with his friends and gets drunk. You see, if I was not living with my five children in this tiny room, I would not complain, but life is difficult for me and my children.

"GUEST HUSBAND"[9]

In some households where women had incomes of their own, the husbands refused to contribute at all, or they contributed irregularly. In two households, the husbands paid only the rent and occasionally brought some meat or sweets as a present to their wives. They also sometimes paid for medicine or clothing, or bought a durable item for the house, but this was infrequent.

In one household, the husband paid the rent and had bought a cheap electric washing tumbler (his only large purchase during four years of marriage). Whenever they had an argument about money, he mentioned this purchase. The wife's wages were spent on food and daily expenses, and, as she put it, she had nothing to show as proof of her financial contribution. She was particularly bitter because her husband asked her for detailed information about her earnings and how she spent them, but he never disclosed anything about his income or spending.

Another wife in this group had worked since the age of eight and had bought all the furniture considered necessary to start a good life in the community. When they moved to an apartment that her husband had rented, she left her job as a maid to be a housewife. She had thought that being a housewife was one luxury that marriage could offer her, particularly since she already had all the household goods that she needed, but her husband refused to pay anything except rent and came home demanding food. After months of bitter arguments she demanded a divorce. He refused, unless she paid him 2,000 pounds in cash. Because she could not raise such an amount of money, she was forced to drop the idea and find a job instead. She stopped demanding money for household expenses and continued to cook for him while he paid only the rent. She said, "This way at least I don't get any headaches. Maybe he will change with time." But when I visited them in 1994 the situation was the same. She had several jobs as a maid and a cook while he often did not go to work despite the fact that he is a good barber. During my last visit she told me,

9. I have coined the term "guest husband" because within the Egyptian context the guest expects to be entertained to the best ability of the host household and may or may not bring a gift. In fact at least one wife in this group often jokingly said that her husband was the permanent guest of her household.

He is not stupid like I am. I work hard outside, and I work hard at home to feed him and treat him like a king. Why should he work and tire himself out? Worst of all, he can't even give me a child. I don't have a good marriage. But a woman's life is always hard.

Yet in a different household, the man had two wives, both of whom had to work to support their five children. He contributed toward rent and sometimes brought home meat or fruit. Umm Ashraf, who worked as a janitor in a hospital, told me, "This is my lot. What should I do? At least my children have a father." Every time the husband was criticized for failing to contribute, he threatened to move to the other wife's household. By playing the two wives against each other, he managed to arrest many of the arguments sparked by his failure to provide for his households.

In another household, the husband had migrated to Libya. During his ten-year absence, he only brought presents once a year, and occasionally sent some money. After he returned to Cairo, he continued this pattern: although he bought expensive household goods and took the children out, he did not contribute any housekeeping money. The wife was most unhappy about the situation and told me that she often thought of giving up her job. The only thing preventing her was the loss of her retirement benefits: she had given eighteen years of service.

All the women in this group wished they could give up their jobs and stay at home. In fact, one of the informants, while expecting her second child, had applied for a two-year leave without pay, since there was no one who could look after the new child while she worked. She had hoped that this would make her husband act more responsibly and pay at least a minimal housekeeping allowance. However, a month after her paid maternity leave was up, she had to return to work, leaving her child either with neighbors or a relative who lived a half-hour bus ride away. When asked if she would stay at home at her husband's request, she readily agreed, but added regretfully,

Young men today choose to marry working women because life is expensive and they want to have a home and a wife and also continue the fun they had before marriage, such as going to the cinema, cafés, and bars and buying expensive clothes.

She concluded that husbands who chose a working wife would never ask them to stay at home. "Didn't you see how I had to go back to work because he refused to pay any housekeeping money?" she asked me.

Another working wife offered a detailed account of her husband's refusal to pay for the household expenses as soon as she acquired an income of her own. They argued, and she even demanded a divorce, until he finally agreed to pay a fixed amount toward food, medicine, and part of the rent. She said that in this way she was able to save part of her income to buy household goods.

All the women, all of whom were wage earners, had chosen their own husbands and the conditions of marriage had not been fully negotiated, either because they had lost their mothers before marriage or because they had announced their intention to marry against their parents' wishes. Hence they had relinquished the opportunity to have their families negotiate a marriage contract and secure a suitable financial arrangement. The accepted rule was that if a daughter married without her parents' consent, she lost the right to demand their support in time of dispute. Therefore, with the exception of one woman whose husband had migrated, the women had little moral support from their families of origin in dealing with their marital problems. The husbands, well aware of this lack of support, took advantage of the situation. The support of a woman's kin appears to be among the crucial factors influencing men's attitude in respect to their responsibilities and attitudes toward their wives. There were two other wage-earning women whose husbands had tried to withdraw from their financial responsibilities, but the women, after securing the support of their parents and immediate kin, protested and managed to improve the situation.

Impact of Male Migration on Budgeting

When the first stage of this research concluded in 1986, the primary male contributors in twenty households were migrants to the oil-rich Arab countries. In many other households the husband had been away as a migrant for some time and had since returned. Although declining oil prices and the political situation resulted in slowing down the pace of migration to the oil-producing countries of the Middle East, my subsequent visits indicate that out-migration continues. A significant change, however, is that the financial rewards of migration are generally smaller than in the 1970s and 1980s. Naturally migration affects the budgeting arrangements of these households. Using the original data I collected as a baseline (see table 17), I briefly look at the major changes resulting from migration.

Wives who had always managed the entire financial affairs of the

Table 17 *Budgeting among Migrants' Households*

| | Before Migration | | During Migration | |
Types	*Waged*	*Nonwaged*	*Waged*	*Nonwaged*
Wife as manager	2	1	–	–
Wife as banker	–	1	–	–
Full allowance	1	4	4	7
Partial allowance	1	2	1	–
Husband as manager	2	1	–	–
Mother-in-law as manager	1	1	–	2
Guest husband	3	3	5	1
Total	10	10	10	10

Note: Waged refers to wives with cash earnings of their own; nonwaged are those with no cash income of their own. The table is arranged according to the degree of women's access to men's cash income.

household experienced no significant change in their situation as a result of migration. In these cases, the husband either sent home all his income periodically or entrusted his wife with the money when he visited. The only change was the wife's increased ability to spend on daily household needs and durable goods. In six households, prior to migration, men were either financial managers or gave only partial allowances to their wives. During migration, however, these households had to adopt the full allowance system. One wife moved back with her parents, but her husband sent her an allowance periodically.

Wives living in extended households often lost their partial allowance, at least for the first few months, but they considered it a temporary phase. Many of the households with working women did not receive an allowance; migration increased the number of these households from three to six. Some wives knew that their husbands were not successful; others did not object to this situation because they believed their husbands were keeping the money to buy household goods. In the early years of my fieldwork, I found the women did not worry that this might be the beginning of a continuing pattern. However, the experiences of migrants' wives whose husbands returned changed this optimism.

The budgeting history of the former migrants' households suggests that some of these changes were permanent. Wives who had received full allowances to manage their households during the migration either continued with this same system or became financial managers of their households, despite the fact that in some of these households the husband had been the financial manager prior to migration.

The husbands' migration had affected the cash-earning wives quite differently. None of the husbands sent regular or substantial remittances for the upkeep of the family, although many of them returned with presents. They continued this system of contribution after their return. This represents a reversal of the premigration pattern of budgeting, in which men paid for daily expenses and women invested their wages in durable or other items.

As daily expenses were considered a husband's responsibility, this role reversal was resented by women, who felt the extra efforts they made became a compensation for their husbands' dwindling contributions. They felt that neither their children nor the community credited them for their extra contribution to the household. Karima expressed her view.

What does working do for me? That I buy the beans and the bread, while he buys the color television and takes the children out. I do a double day of work and he draws status from it, in the eyes of both my children and the neighbors.

Many women, however, adopted strategies to combat or prevent this reversal of roles. After her husband's return and failure to contribute to the daily expenses, one white-collar worker took a two-year leave without pay. A few months later, under the pretense that they needed more time to attend to their children, two other women adopted the same strategy when their migrant husbands continued to refuse to send money. The husbands were then forced to pay a housekeeping allowance. Some unskilled wage workers stopped their cash-earning activities after the return of their husbands, leaving it up to their husbands to support their families.[10]

As a result of these observations, many white-collar women now demand to migrate with their husbands or to join them shortly after they are settled, particularly if they are migrating for more than one year. Contrary to their husbands' warning about the lack of jobs for women, many succeeded in finding jobs once there. Often kin and parents supported their daughters' decision to insist on joining their migrant husbands. Umm Sahar, who was not well and missed her daughter who had joined her husband in Abu Dhabi, told me,

10. For more detailed discussion, see Hoodfar 1996a.

I knew that her absence would be very hard for me, but I encouraged her to go and join her husband who hopes to stay there for four years and save money to buy some land and build a house. You know men who live on their own for a long time then become accustomed to being single-minded and to not listening to their wives. Most of them, too, do not send much money for their wives because they know she has a salary and can spend on herself, and even after they returned they don't want to pay for housekeeping, like Abu Rammi and Abu Wa'el [two of the neighbors]. Men are like that, though Islam has made it their duty to pay for their families. So I told her to go and keep the company of her husband and hopefully she will find a job there because she is a good typist.

The Contribution of Women's Wages

Women who held men responsible for providing for the family saw their own cash contributions as a means to improve their standard of living, particularly those aspects of it that men could not or would not contribute to. Women remained in control of their wages; I never heard of or observed any working woman handing over her wages to her husband or father, a practice that has been reported for other Muslim communities.[11] Men did not make any claim to their wives' wages, although sometimes they borrowed from them. The Muslim principle that women are entitled to their own wealth and income was never broken except indirectly, by men who did not provide adequately for the household.

Women preferred to invest their money in household goods or items not viewed as a husband's responsibility. They drew prestige and power from providing expensive household items or giving their children what their fathers could not or would not provide. Family members and neighbors were aware of these contributions. The importance of tangible proof of women's contribution was mentioned either directly or indirectly by all earning women who were insistent that their contributions over and above their domestic services be recognized. They raised strong objections to spending their income on daily expenses, which they saw as the unquestionable responsibility of their husbands. Exceptions occurred when the husband was very poor or unemployed and so could not meet basic needs.

11. Taking over the wages of young wives was a widespread practice among the households in the shantytown where I conducted research in Tehran.

Cash-earning women were alert to the fact that their efforts in providing more cash for the household might result in the reduction of their husbands' contributions. To prevent this, they adopted strategies such as buying items on installment, not revealing the amount of their income, or, as a last resort, leaving the labor market.

In fact, the model that Pauline Hunt (1978) first documented for budgeting in working-class British families is relevant to understanding low-income, urban Cairene households. She points out that men's wages were allocated for essential and recurrent expenditures such as rent and food; therefore, their wages were seen as the primary family income. Women's wages were spent on bulky consumer items such as electric washing machines and accordingly were viewed as not essential to the survival of the household. Hunt points out that such a distinction reflects the economic realities of female employment. Women were more likely to leave the labor force due to their higher opportunity cost, particularly during the family-building cycle, and the nature of their employment was often insecure and precarious. Therefore, the family budget had to be organized to withstand a sudden loss of female earning power. The Egyptian case does not contradict Hunt's analysis but does add a new dimension to it. Women were conscious that the social dynamic increasingly removes men from involvement in the day-to-day life of the households. Yet the households' need for cash is expanding. Women entered the labor market to cover the gap between what their husband could or would contribute and the actual needs of the household, and adopted any strategy—including appealing to traditional ideology—that secured their husbands' commitment to the household.

Several facets of Egyptian society supported these tactics. The first was that women could legitimately pressure their husbands to provide for basic needs such as food, shelter, and clothing, while other needs were debatable. Second, in case of divorce or death, the wife only received those items that she had purchased using her own money. Third, women could leave the labor market without inflicting too much hardship on the household, since the husband was providing the essentials.

However, these strategies were not always successful, and some women were forced to put up with guest husbands who had consciously chosen working wives. These women resented their situations and viewed their jobs as mixed blessings, since it appeared that the husband benefited most from the wife's labor. However, they feared the possible repercussions of not having their own income. Their neighbors—male and fe-

male—profoundly sympathized with them and pitied them. Nevertheless, these working women often ended their complaints by saying "*Allah karim*" (God is generous) or "*Kul shay nasib*" (Everything is according to one's fate). They were thankful that they had their own
money to spend on their children and pitied those women who were in
similar positions and did not have their own source of cash: "*Miskin
sittat gawzuhum mishkways wa humm ma andhumsh flus min nafsahum*"
(Poor are those women whose husbands are not "good" and do not
have any money of their own).

Despite their grievances against their husbands, these women recognized that, given their small income and the social constraints imposed
on women in their society, they were still better off within their marriages. When I asked why they remained married if they were so dissatisfied with their husbands, they explained that a woman's primary
desire is to be independent of her parents and to have children and a
home of her own. But most women did not earn enough to have a place
of their own. Even if they did, it was unacceptable for a single woman
to set up her own home; an unmarried woman must always be part of
her parents' or other kin's household, where they remain "children"
whatever their age may be. The exception is when the woman has
no blood kin or family of her own.[12] Furthermore, there was a social
stigma attached to an unmarried or divorced woman. Even if they sur-
mounted these obstacles, they needed to have children, which was impossible outside marriage.[13] Women often referred to their children as
their world, and the reason for their efforts.

Men's Pocket Money

While all women acknowledged that men held back a
portion of their wages for personal expenses, their complaints were di-

---

12. I became aware of two exceptions. One young woman had been sent to be a maid
at the age of six. Later, she trained as a seamstress and rented a room in the neighborhood.
Another woman moved to her own flat after she divorced her husband. At the age of
twenty-eight, she appealed to some of her more "modern" relatives to convince her
brother who was living in a village to allow her to live on her own. However, soon after
their independence, both took the veil so as not to be judged loose women.

13. Egypt is a very child-centered society, and few are childless by choice. People, especially women, without children are deeply pitied. Despite this, having children outside
wedlock is not an acceptable option, a situation that stands in sharp contrast to many
African and Latin American societies.

rected at the husband's extravagance relative to the family's standard of living. None of the working women envisaged such a personal budget for themselves. Their own personal material desires were so molded by their households' needs that it was difficult for them to distinguish between the two. One white-collar worker, in reply to whether she had any personal budget, said that she had to pay her bus fare to work. Another woman said that every month she would buy some small items, such as china teacups or glasses, for her home (in fact, she was accumulating them for her daughter's trousseau).

This difference of attitude was a consequence of the structure of everyday life in the neighborhoods. Men were physically removed from the home for long hours and their consumption often took an individual form, whereas women spent much of their time in close connection with their children and in their households. The opportunity, therefore, to develop habits and tastes for individual entertainment was limited.

The literature on money management suggests that in many communities, men set aside a considerable portion of their wages for personal expenses (Beneria and Roldan 1987; Pahl 1989). While my findings indicate similar patterns among the married men, much of their personal expenditure was very closely tied to their networking efforts. Men's networks were usually their job-hunting lifelines (see chapter 8). Many men spent much of their free time in teahouses, a male social institution where they could find out about new jobs and employment opportunities, get information on migration, and join saving clubs organized by regular teahouse customers.

Though the cost of a glass of tea was as little as 5 or 10 piasters, many men could not afford to go to teahouses and felt disadvantaged. Zaynab, whose husband had been unemployed for over two months, complained that he would never find a job. When I questioned her pessimism, she said,

We can't afford for him to go to teahouses where one can hear about jobs. He has lost all his friends there because he has not been there for so many weeks. But with my earning as little as 20 pounds a month, we cannot afford 40 or 50 piasters a day for him to buy tea in the teahouses.

Another major expense was food. With many men working outside their neighborhoods from early morning to late at night, they rarely ate at home. Despite the claims of many wives, they often ate bean sandwiches, not chicken or meat, which their income made impossible.

However, while few men spent disproportionate amounts of their salary on clothing, many bought more stylish clothing because their jobs—as barbers or hotel bellboys, for example—required it, something their wives failed to appreciate.

Men's major personal expense was cigarettes, and for young men, the occasional movie. Some younger husbands were also members of the local soccer club, where membership fees had recently increased. Though some wives accused their husbands of drinking because they would not disclose their whereabouts, I never knew of any man being drunk in the neighborhood. Some younger men said that, on occasion, they might drink a bottle of beer.[14]

My findings indicate that except for the guest husbands, most men spent a small portion of their wages on what the wives categorized as personal expenditures. Yet some wives complained bitterly about these expenses, while others seemed content. What emerged was that a husband's unwillingness to share information with his wife about his income and expenditure was taken as an indication of illegitimate motives, notably putting himself before the family. Many men, however, felt they had no obligation to give their wives information on these matters and believed their wives should trust them. For the men, it was a deliberate power game: they reasserted their status as heads of their households by keeping their wives guessing and making them feel helpless. This had a negative consequence on marital relations. Sometimes even the relationship between parents and children was adversely affected.

Summary

The aggregate wages of husband, wife, and other members of a household only rarely represented the sum of what was invested in communal consumption in the neighborhoods, a point that has been identified in other communities (Dwyer and Bruce 1988; Pahl 1989). The contribution of different members of the household to the

14. In Egypt, drinking alcohol was more common among the more Westernized middle classes. Clearly the women in these neighborhoods were not exposed to the physical violence that can result from drunken husbands, an unfortunate problem facing many of their counterparts in other countries (Johnson 1985; Beneria and Roldan 1987; Gonzalez de la Rocha 1994). Nor can drunkenness be used as a legal defense for violence toward women, as it has in Canada by a Supreme Court ruling (*Montreal Gazette*, 7 November 1994).

common pool was affected by cultural practices, ideology, and actual social relations. In Egypt, ideally men/husbands pay all household expenses. This meant few men demanded to control their wives' cash income, which the women spent primarily on durable household items and their children's education. Nonetheless, there was considerable variety in the way households managed their cash income, which ranged from total control by the wives to control by husbands or mother-in-laws. The different budgeting methods had considerable impact on the power and status of the wives as access to cash is tied to power over the pattern of expenditures.

Changes in the economy and labor market increased the access of some women to their husbands' wages, while others (notably many from the Delta) lost control of their husbands' wages, which they viewed as belonging to the household. The rising cost of living, on one hand, and increased opportunities for personal expenditure and entertainment, on the other, encouraged many men to adopt strategies that limit their financial responsibilities. These strategies ranged from marrying women in gainful employment so as to withdraw from making a financial contribution to marrying women from a much poorer background whose expectations were minimal or defining their responsibility as the bare minimum of food, shelter, and clothing. This limited definition of the male responsibility toward the family has brought them into conflict with their wives and sometimes their children.

Male migration, which is a common strategy for raising cash and promoting the household's standard of living, had a varied impact on salaried and nonsalaried wives. My field observations indicated that the husbands of nonsalaried wives sent remittances home and these wives often gained more access to their husbands' income on their departure and after their return. However, the husbands of salaried wives were less likely to send remittances, knowing that their families had some other means of support. To the dislike of their wives, many did not volunteer to revert to their premigration budgeting arrangement, thus forcing their wives to pay for the daily expenses. This represented the loss of women's access to their husband's income. Women have used several strategies to counter this problem, including leaving their jobs temporarily or insisting on accompanying their husbands during the migration. In short, men and women try to resist what they see as the negative impact of socioeconomic change while promoting and protecting their interests within the parameters of their own culture and society.

CHAPTER 6

Nonmonetary Contributions
to the Household Pool

Nonmonetary contributions are a substantial part of household resources. Accounting for these contributions is particularly important among the low-income strata of any society, where such activities do not merely improve the level of household welfare but often represent the margin that makes survival possible. Moreover, they influence and shape much of the economic decision making. In particular, these activities affect the economic choices that women make since it is women's labor that accounts for most nonmonetary contributions. The composition and relative importance of these contributions vary, according to the extent that a household is drawn into the market economy, cultural practices, and ecological factors. For low-income Cairene households, I have distinguished three broad categories of nonmonetary economic activity: domestic work, cash-saving activities, and dealing with public institutions. Here I will provide an overview of the factors influencing the extent of these contributions and the way in which they are assessed by my informants.

Domestic Work

Domestic work is the most underacknowledged subsistence activity in modern societies; until recently, it rarely featured in any social science discussion. In the West, an important outcome of the women's movement and the development of feminist consciousness was to highlight this hidden aspect of the economy and its consequences for women, especially vis-à-vis their social position. Much of the early "domestic labor debate," however, took place on an abstract level and was primarily concerned with demonstrating that the low social position of women was caused by their domestic and reproductive role (Delphy 1976; Werlhof 1980). Feminists, in their attempts to reintroduce women into class theories and to establish the revolutionary potential of women, became engaged in debates on the "productive" and "unproductive" nature of women's domestic labor (Molyneux 1979; Werlhof 1980, 1984; Hartman 1981). Whatever the success or failure of this debate, it has deepened our understanding of the complexity and dynamic of the interplay of socioeconomic factors that influence women's social position.

Despite substantial theoretical discussion, the literature on the economics and sociology of domestic work is sparse.[1] Few scholars, feminist or otherwise, have carried out research on the components of domestic work, or its transformation; references are often made as if domestic work were transhistorical and unchanging. Also neglected is the variation of what may be considered a domestic task from society to society. The definition of domestic work is affected by the social organization of economic activities within a society, the level of "technological development," ecology, and class.

Domestic work, much the same as other work, evolves and changes within any given society. In a unique study, Caroline Davidson (1982) documents the great transformation of housework and its components in the British Isles from the seventeenth to the twentieth century (see also Berk 1980). Such studies encourage closer attention to the differential meaning of domestic chores for a woman who has to fetch water and fuel miles away from her home and a woman who lives in a Western city. Not recognizing these major differences has created further obstacles to developing methods of evaluating and incorporating domestic work in gross national product (GNP) calculations (Goldschmidt-Clermont 1982, 1987; Folbre 1986b, 1991, 1993; Waring 1988; Kessler-Harris 1990).[2] Such inclusion would have a positive impact

---

1. Ann Oakley (1974a, 1974b) made exceptional and early contributions to this field. Her work did not generate interest, however, and there were few follow-up studies until much later in the 1980s.

2. The inclusion of domestic work in gross national product will indicate official recognition of women's contribution to the economy. Housewives would no longer be automatically categorized as dependents, which may bring about a greater awareness of the female population's needs by legal and social policy makers.

on the social and economic evaluation of domestic work and women's contributions to their household and to the national economy.

This difference in the nature of domestic activities, however, should not be seen as an indicator of less or more hours of work. In fact, the popular belief that Western women are now spending less hours on their domestic chores than their forbears, due to labor-saving devices and other amenities, has proved to be a fallacy.[3] Although the physical burden of domestic chores may have declined, levels of expectation and standards of hygiene and domestic comfort have risen. The evidence suggests that domestic work has remained an important contributor to the standard of living at all levels of development and therefore should be incorporated in any study of living standards (Goldschmidt-Clermont 1982).

The status and value that society attributes to a given job influences how the performers feel about it. Part of the assumption that housewives are dissatisfied derives from the very low status that most industrialized societies ascribe to domestic work, often presented as mundane, repetitive, and unrewarding—work no one would willingly engage in. Until recently many feminist scholars have not questioned these assumptions (De Beauvoir 1949; Oakley 1974a; Barker and Allan 1976a, 1976b; Lipman-Blumen 1984; Collins and Gimenez 1990; Ahlander and Slaugh 1995). And there has been little research to assess their accuracy. Even more scarce is the kind of research that compares and contrasts the degree of job satisfaction of housewives and wage earners.[4]

Although many of my informants recognized that recent socioeconomic changes have had a diminishing effect on the value of their work, they nevertheless took pride in their role as mother and sitt al-bayt and frequently pointed out their importance in the household.[5] Their contributions as homemaker, good cook, good mother, and thrifty shopper were appreciated and highly valued by their households and by their husbands, neighbors, and networks.

These women enjoyed their relative autonomy in organizing their work and collaborating with neighbors or friends of their choosing.

3. For a summary of findings in the West, see Oakley 1974a: 92–95. See also Vaneck 1974; Brody 1975; Goldschmidt-Clermont 1982; Gerson 1993.

4. The negative attitude toward domestic work is at least partly derived from the prevalence and "legitimacy" of market values that tend to trivialize nonmarket contributions.

5. Other researchers have stressed the high value and status attached to being a sitt al-bayt in Egypt (Hammam 1979; Ibrahim 1980; MacLeod 1991, 1996; Singerman 1994).

MacLeod (1991) found that women office workers resented their loss of autonomy, having to punch a timeclock and engage in work that went unappreciated. Hammam (1979) has documented female workers' unfavorable assessment of their factory work in comparison to their roles as housewives. Both studies confirmed that many women preferred the idea of quitting their jobs and staying home, if they could afford to do so. Many white-collar women in my study proudly asserted that they were sittat al-bayt and *muwazzafat* (government office workers), and all gave priority to their domestic roles and contributions.

Domestic Work in the Neighborhoods

All married women considered housework their responsibility, regardless of whether or not they were engaged in cash-earning activities.[6] Women's daily conversation, both at work and at home, often centered on the details of how to perform household tasks. They were eager and interested to learn new ways and gather helpful information. Women known to be talented sittat al-bayt enjoyed special status and often were consulted on special occasions, particularly with regard to furniture arrangement and cooking.

Most families lived in small dwellings and cleaning did not involve much effort. Washing clothes and cooking were ranked as the most laborious jobs. My informants all said they prepared three meals a day; however, most households ate one cooked meal around midafternoon and had tea, some bread, and perhaps some cooked beans (ful) in the morning. Those who were hungry at night might find some bread or other leftovers for dinner. This pattern of eating enabled them to skip one meal a day, which for a large family meant considerable savings.

The main meal often consisted of either rice or pasta, one cooked vegetable, and plenty of bread. Only large households cooked every day; the majority cooked every other day, which saved women a great deal of time. Except on Fridays and holidays, people rarely ate together because most members of the households had different school hours or work schedules and tended to help themselves when they were hungry.

---

6. I have used domestic work and housework as umbrella concepts to refer to cooking, cleaning, shopping, and child care. These divisions are derived from the way the informants perceived their domestic work.

Cooked food was often stored under the bed—even when there was a refrigerator—to keep it at room temperature, making it possible to serve it without heating it up. Although this may not be the most hygienic method of keeping food fresh (particularly on hot days), it saved the cost and effort of reheating food.[7]

One or two weekdays in each household are known as wash days, *yawm al-ghasil.* Women organize their housework so that on those days they do little else. This was the most laborious domestic task, despite the fact that every household had a very simple Egyptian-made electric washing tumbler. Women had to carry water up to their flats and sometimes carry the dirty water down. All women grated bars of subsidized or other cheap soap into powder instead of using laundry detergent, which was much more expensive. Generally, white clothes and children's garments were boiled first and then washed separately. Doing laundry for a family of six would take as long as six or seven hours, often twice a week, particularly if the children are young. Working women usually reserved the weekend for washing. All women except those who had access to a roof would ask to use a neighbor's clothesline, which is usually above their narrow balcony overlooking the alleyway. This tactic was used especially by working women to prove they attended to their housework.

Women regarded housework as an important part of their contribution to the household and jealously guarded this domain from their husbands. They delegated these tasks only to their daughters, usually the eldest. Women considered having a daughter a great blessing, not only because she could take over some of the housework responsibilities but also because a daughter is a lifelong support for mothers. Hence women who did not have daughters were deeply pitied. Delegating housework to daughters is not viewed exploitive, for there was a sincere and deep-seated belief that, come what may, a woman should learn to run a household, and the best time to practice is under her mother's supervision. Mothers sometimes realized that the demands they placed on their daughters took them away from their schoolwork, but this was justified by saying that in the future they would have to combine a job with running their homes.

Most women expressed strong opposition to their husbands or even their sons participating in any housework. They presented the sexual

7. For a discussion of some hygienic practices in these neighborhoods, see Hoodfar 1984.

division of labor as natural rather than socially produced, and claimed that men were naturally and inherently incapable of performing these tasks and relied on women to perform them. Men often agreed with this and told tales about their incompetence in housework to emphasize that the existing division was natural. Men were teased and laughed at if they showed interest in housework, and it was often women who initiated such jokes and teasing to reinforce the traditional division of labor. Those who occasionally helped their wives said they never admitted this publicly since they felt that it might compromise their masculinity in the eyes of the community.

Women's tenacious adherence to gendered work roles must be viewed in the context of their lives and not as senseless traditionalism. The general trend in these neighborhoods has been a diminishment in the range of services that women traditionally performed. For instance, until ten or fifteen years ago, older women baked bread at home because it was cheaper, but home-baked bread has become increasingly expensive. Furthermore, few households possessed a traditional oven. Whereas previously husbands ate at home or packed a lunch to bring to work to save money, of my sample, only one white-collar worker took his sandwich from home, and many husbands ate their main meal out. Often the husbands' suits and other more expensive items of clothing were sent out to be laundered because they would be ruined if washed in the traditional manner.

Many women were alert to the fact that these changes had made their husbands less dependent on their services, while they had become much more dependent on their husbands' cash contribution to accomplish their domestic duties. Washing machines, gas cookers, and mixers were essential equipment; when women did not have an income of their own and these items were not part of their trousseau, they had to be purchased with the husbands' money. Women often felt the changes had diminished their power in their conjugal relationships, and they resisted further erosion by preventing men from taking over any traditionally female domestic duties. When discussing men's contribution to the housework, Umm Wa'el objected strongly and said,

I would never have my husband touch anything around the house. I will see to all his needs. He only rarely eats at home, and I send his clothes to be laundered because I cannot wash suits or iron them. If I also expect him to make his own tea and help with tidying up, then why would he want me or pay for me? God has made women for home and men for the market. It is not wise to change this order.

The commitment to keep men out of the female domain was often maintained to the extent that whenever a man was left on his own in the neighborhoods, other women, either kin or neighbors, would volunteer to perform his housework and cook for him.

Despite their firm presentation of gender roles as natural, however, all the women showed great interest in the different gender roles in England (where I had resided prior to my fieldwork). I was bombarded with questions about whether men scrubbed the floor or cooked. Did they also wash the dishes? Did they really change the diapers? Did they hold and carry very young babies in public? Some women, especially the more educated, were skeptical, finding it difficult to believe that some Western men were expected to do these domestic tasks. They challenged me, asking why was it that they never saw men doing these tasks in the Western films that are shown on television.[8] However, despite their skepticism, at every gathering where husbands were present, the women made me describe how men are expected to change diapers and do other housework. Then all the women would imagine, with great humor, Egyptian men doing the same tasks and would continuously remind their husbands of what their fate would have been had they been born in the West where manhood evidently meant nothing.

The widespread hostility and overt animosity toward employed women expressed by nonwaged wives stemmed partially from the conception that these women reinforced the diminishment of the importance of the homemaker's role. Though nonwaged women wished for their daughters to have jobs, they accused wage-earning women of not attending to their homes and children. Beneath this ambivalence lay more complex feelings of loss regarding a situation traditionally presented as a given. One young unmarried woman expressed her view in these words.

I dislike working women because by going to work they make our men lazy and irresponsible. All men now look to marry working women and women like me cannot find husbands.

Cash-earning wives, who unanimously saw housework and child care as their first priority, were conscious of the criticisms and strove to demonstrate their care for the home, performing their domestic tasks even more rigorously than many wives who stayed home. Furthermore,

8. TV is their main window on the outside world. It plays an important role in the formation of their view of the world beyond their immediate environment.

much the same as other women, they did not raise any objection to the sexual division of labor, which they saw as natural. Some wage-earning women had rejected their husbands' offers of help. Others said that they did not mind that their husbands occasionally helped them by setting the table or looking after the children while they were busy, but they made it clear that this must be absolutely voluntary, since these are female responsibilities. Umm Fu'ad gave me the details of her first marital problem.

Prior to my marriage my husband had been working in the Gulf, where he had a modern flat to himself and had learned to cook and do a little housework. After our marriage he always wanted to help me, particularly since often I arrived home after him. I did not like it because men in the kitchen look like women, but I said nothing. But he was so careless that he continued to do this in the presence of the neighbors and my brothers. My family and others started to be sarcastic about it and I had to be strict and tell my husband not to go into the kitchen, and if he wants to help occasionally he must make sure no one else is around.

Another wage-earning wife expressed her ideas in the following words.

If I am not well, or if the children are sick, and I need help, of course I appreciate his help, but I am perfectly capable of attending to my housework. If ever I felt I could not do both, I would give up my job and stay home. After all, a woman's prime responsibility is her home and not the job.

Far from questioning the basis of the sexual division of labor, women actively participated in reinforcing it by appealing to tradition and Islam. This contradicted the strong and unconventional desire that all women expressed that they or their daughters participate in the labor market and secure a personal income. In the face of social change, which had devalued their economic functions in the household, women were desperately trying to protect what opportunities they had and at the same time secure new ones in the labor market. Women's adherence to traditional ideology stemmed from the realization that any positive change would come about slowly at best. Changing socioeconomic conditions had generally failed to provide new cash-earning opportunities for women of low-income groups who were further disadvantaged by widespread illiteracy, a lack of formal training, a lack of marketable skills, and a lack of capital. Therefore, women had a vested interest in protecting the domains they still dominated.

This attitude is by no means peculiar to low-income Cairene women. Many of the middle-class Egyptian women whom I came to know saw the organization of child care and housework as their responsibility and employed a maid to perform these tasks. They paid the maid's wages from their own salaries, while insisting that their husbands pay for all other household expenses. In other words, they, too, saw an advantage in keeping the traditional division of responsibility.[9] In her study of housewives in the United Kingdom, Ann Oakley (1974a: 153–161) found that many working-class wives did not like their husbands to participate in the housework. Although Oakley attributes this to the effective internalization of the sexual division of labor, the women's comments suggest that they saw domestic work as their main contribution to the family's welfare and did not want to see it eroded by male intrusion.[10]

Gainfully employed women, even those in secure jobs, felt much the same as nonearning wives with regard to their husbands' participation in housework. It was this particular contribution of domestic labor that legitimized their demands on his income. They felt that sharing their traditional responsibilities would justify their husbands making parallel demands regarding support of the family. Furthermore, by publicly declaring that they saw the home as their prime responsibility, they hoped to avoid the criticism of the neighbors and avoid damaging the strong feeling of solidarity among the women in the lower-income neighborhoods.

Studies of other societies, including Western societies, have indicated that despite great social change and the emergence of a feminist consciousness, many married women engage in the labor market principally to support a home-centered lifestyle (Pahl 1984; MacLeod 1991). They feel less involved with their jobs and place family and housework responsibilities before employment. The determinants of such attitudes are broader than socialization and ideology. In the absence of much opportunity in other domains, the material and psychological gains that women may acquire from the traditional division of labor within the family can militate against a change of attitudes. This creates a vicious circle, re-creating and reinforcing circumstances that make it difficult to bring about a major change in the way women are incorporated into the labor market and the public life of the wider society.[11]

9. This is often based on the understanding that men never fully share their income with the family, a point validated by much research (Dwyer and Bruce 1988; Pahl 1989). Therefore, they should at least be held responsible for their Islamic duty to provide for the family.

10. For more discussion about the importance of contribution to power relations between conjugal partners, see Lipman-Blumen 1984: chaps. 3, 4.

11. Statistical data for many countries demonstrate that women universally are more heavily represented at the bottom of the labor hierarchy (Scott 1986; Hoodfar 1995b).

Child-rearing

Child care, particularly the care of younger children, was almost entirely women's responsibility. Both men and women viewed this as natural and an extension of women's biological function. Older women saw their reproductive capacity and nurturing ability as a source of pride as well as the main reason men should be responsible for providing for them. It was considered that God had given different abilities to the different sexes to make them interdependent. Umm Shadia, an elderly woman who was influential in her neighborhood, expressed her view.

Men may work and earn money. They may become the *malik* [king]. But they can never give birth and breastfeed their children. For this reason they will have to rely and depend on their women to the end of the world. In return, God has made them provide for their women.

Younger women, particularly those with more education, while seeing child care as a female responsibility, were less enthusiastic in this respect (Hoodfar 1995a). They did not see their reproductive ability as a source of pride, and some viewed it as an unfortunate law of nature. Nahed, a teacher engaged to be married, explained the consequence of her biological ability.

I would have tried to go to university and get a good job, but it all seemed to be a waste of time, since I am going to be married and have children. In the end, I would have to change diapers and breastfeed. I could not be the boss. Therefore, it is better to be a teacher with lots of holidays and shorter hours of work.

Formal education and the modern value system have facilitated the extension of the role of women in the labor market without changing the fundamental ideology of the sexual division of labor. Furthermore, the emphasis and value placed on achievements in the job market and economic sphere have coincided with the devaluation and trivialization of women's work—whether housework or child care. The most educated women often saw themselves as disadvantaged in the labor market, handicapped by their "physiological function," with little chance of escape from their wife/mother roles. No educated woman saw her child-rearing effort as a contribution to society or indicated that the labor market should take account of a woman's motherhood responsibilities.

Regardless of how positive or resentful women felt about child care, they all viewed it as their most important responsibility and invested much of their time and resources in child-rearing to the best of their ability. Furthermore, they saw themselves as accountable to their husbands and the community regarding this responsibility. All women had complex support networks of kin or friends who helped out with child care (Hoodfar 1995a). The most legitimate sources of support were elder daughters and grandmothers; the role of fathers in child care was limited to disciplining the children, particularly sons, once they were older.

Both men and women pointed out that child care had evolved into a much more demanding task in the modern social system, because of changing standards and living conditions. In the past, no mother would have had to worry about her children being run over by a car or a train. There was no danger of falling from the balcony, particularly for those who lived in the rural areas. There were no worries about schooling, which was becoming a full-time worry for all low-income Egyptian parents, who were preoccupied with finding a nearby government school that would accept the children and organizing the necessary papers and medical certificates. The greatest pressure was finding the money to pay for private tutorials; children learned little in the overcrowded schools where often more than fifty or sixty pupils attended classes in shifts of three hours a day.

Young mothers who were first-generation rural migrants found it particularly difficult to perform their maternal responsibilities. This was partly because the knowledge and experience they had accumulated as daughters in the village seemed to be of little relevance in the city and because they often did not have the social network of friends and kin who could give them help and support. They felt particularly handicapped when dealing with public hospital and health center procedures. A popular strategy for these mothers was to ally themselves with one or more women, often older ones, and ask for help and advice. To return these favors they often performed chores or helped the older women in whatever way they could. Salwa, who was nineteen years old and had come to Cairo with her husband three years previously, shopped almost daily for Umm Rose and helped her prepare the vegetables. On one occasion when we were talking about child care, she said,

When I came to live here from our village I was lost and did not know any place. It was my first time out of the village and I did not know anyone here. Several times my daughter was so sick that she almost died and I did not know what to do. It was Umm Rose who took me to the hospital and talked to the doctors and saved my child. I do not know about vaccination and where and when. I have left her birth certificate [which is also her vaccination record] with Umm Rose. When the time comes she takes me there or will ask another neighbor to take me with her. . . . Doing some of her chores—especially since she is growing old—is the only way I can repay her.

Men showed a high degree of awareness of the problems and time involved in child care and often openly admitted that they could never cope with children the way their wives could. Abu Hani, a blue-collar, public sector employee who also worked in the afternoon as a servant, said,

My wife could get a job in the factory the same as me, but we had children and no one to look after them. I thought that what comfort her wages would bring to our life would be counterbalanced with the worries that many things could happen to our children. Therefore, I took up another job in order for my wife to be a full-time mother.

Acknowledgment of the efforts of child care, however, did not translate into willingness of the fathers to take more part in it. Most husbands sympathized with their wives, and others were glad to believe that nature had left child care to women.

Mahmoud was having an argument with his wife, Mona, when I arrived one day at their home. The youngest son had fallen down the stairs and injured himself while his mother was not at home, and Mahmoud, who had been home at the time of the accident, was angry and accused his wife of not attending to her responsibilities. When I suggested that since he was home at the time he should have had an eye on the child, since his wife was out shopping for food, he said to me,

Whether I am home or not, it is her responsibility to look after her children. She gave birth to them and nature has made her and not I responsible for the children. All she can expect from me is to feed them, and I do.

Only one of the white-collar female informants raised objections to the absence of men from the child care sphere. Child care appeared to be the main legitimate reason for many men to disapprove of their wives joining the labor market. When women were employed outside of the home, it was absolutely their responsibility to organize child care and pay for it. Many unskilled women left the labor market when they married or when they had children,[12] except those working in their own neighborhoods, where they could combine the two (see chapter 4).

12. In contrast, white-collar women often earned more money and had better maternity rights and options that enabled them to organize a family network or paid child care.

Shopping

Shopping as a routine task has gained prominence with the expansion of the cash economy. Research in the United States suggests that in the 1970s families spent as long as one full working day per week on shopping and related travel, compared with two hours a week in the 1920s (Vaneck 1974). In the West shopping is often studied as part of housework and is always associated with women. However, responsibility for the shopping can differ sharply from one society to the next. In Egypt, men traditionally performed the bulk of family shopping; recently women are assuming more responsibility for this chore.

The media in industrial societies, and increasingly in the developing countries, associate women negatively as promoters of a culture of consumerism (Bartos 1988: 235–253; Jacobs 1988). Rarely do we hear or read, particularly in the literature on household economies, of the fact that efficient shopping can save households a great deal of money.[13] Women and some men in the neighborhoods were able to stretch their limited cash resources and improve their standard of living by keeping track of prices and bargains.

In urban Cairo, shopping has always been a daily household chore. Historically, in the old neighborhoods, there was a clear division of labor in low-income households that determined who shopped for which items (Nadim el-Messiri 1975). Women bought the vegetables from the local market, and men bought fruit and meat. This division is still reflected at the local market, where the vegetable vendors are generally women and men sell fruit and meat. Less routine purchases such as children's clothing and furniture were not designated tasks.

The old ways, however, are losing ground to an emerging style of shopping. In view of the unpredictable distribution of rationed and subsidized goods and volatile pricing in the free market, efficient shopping now requires effective channels of information, flexible time, and immediate access to cash. As men were becoming more restricted by working hours and distant work locales, women were taking over more shopping responsibilities.

Many women welcomed this change, as it gave them more say in household expenditures. However, some women had mixed feelings be-

---

13. Moreover, diverse channels of distribution of goods and services and methods of pricing make shopping strategies highly variable from society to society.

cause their husbands, who had become completely divorced from shopping, had little sense of the high inflation rate and accused their wives of mismanagement. Other men refused to increase their wives' housekeeping allowances for some years despite rising prices and their own higher wages. Many women pointed out that since they were doing most of the shopping and other daily tasks, men had become even more removed from the daily activity of the family, and this sometimes weakened their commitment to the household. Despite some reservations, however, all women saw this change in the division of shopping responsibilities as inevitable.

THE POLITICAL ECONOMY OF SHOPPING IN CAIRO

To provide an accurate picture, one needs to divide the period 1983–1994 into two different eras. During the first, 1983–1989, although basic need subsidies were declining, there existed a substantial difference in the prices of rationed items in the government cooperatives and in the free market. During the second, 1990–1994, subsidies declined substantially and many items were only available at free market prices.

Shopping Strategies, 1983–1989. There is no doubt that subsidies of basic items had an important impact on the standard of living of low-income households (Khouri-Dagher 1986, 1996). The urban bias prevalent in Egypt, as in other developing countries, made this impact even more tangible for urban low-income households (Korayem 1981; Mohie El-Din 1982; el-Sokkari 1984). Subsidized goods were distributed through several channels. Many items (e.g., rice, sugar, oil, beans, lentils, and tea) were available in fixed quantities, using a ration card at registered local *tamwin* (grocery stores). Other, less-subsidized items were distributed through a public sector network of government-run cooperatives spread erratically throughout Cairo (Ismail et al. 1982a, 1982b; Khouri-Dagher 1986, 1996). However, since 1988 many of these items, notably lentils, are no longer available at subsidized prices.

The astronomical rise in the demand for foodstuffs has caused constant shortages, despite government efforts and increased subsidies. During the 1980s, long lines for additional subsidized items became a feature of Cairo life, particularly for poorer households who could not afford to go to the free market. Because of the discrepancy between subsidized and free market prices, missing out on items from the co-op meant going without or substituting with inferior items for many households. Table 18 shows the substantial price differential between subsidized and free market goods: oil, for example, was nineteen times more expensive in the free market.

The importance of shopping efficiently and making use of subsidies becomes clearer when we consider that in the 1980s, food accounted for one- to two-thirds of the total budget of low-income urban households (though with rapid rent increases since the mid-1980s, these proportions have changed, especially for younger households that at the time of setting up their own homes had to rent at the new prices). My data for the 1983–1988 period suggest that among very poor households more than one-third of the total food budget was spent through government channels.[14] Subsidization of basic food items, particularly bread, had ensured a minimum calorie intake for all, which was a remarkable achievement for the Egyptian government. In fact, a national nutrition survey conducted in 1978 revealed no cases of severe malnutrition in Egypt.[15] This was a remarkable record considering per capita income and the fact that more than 60 percent of foodstuffs consumed, including wheat, rice, and broad beans, is imported.[16] However, removal of subsidies has hit hard for the poorest of the households who cannot afford the prices of the free market and are forced to cut their food budgets, already meager. It is not surprising that the removal of subsidies is the primary reason for my research population's critical views of the government. The poor had come to see affordable food—particularly items such as beans and lentils that were staples of their diet—as a basic right, a right that the present government has denied them for no legitimate reason they can see.

As free market prices became more inflated, the impact of subsidies on the standard of living of the poor became more pronounced. At least initially, this reaffirmed the preference of unskilled women for the

14. Macro-level data indicated that more than a quarter of the food budget of low-income households was spent through government channels (Khouri-Dagher 1986).

15. Khouri-Dagher (1986: 40) has calculated that, on average, 66 percent of total calorie intake among low-income Cairenes came from rationed food, bread, flour, and other partly subsidized foods distributed through government co-ops.

16. Only about 3.6 percent of the national territory is arable land. Due to population expansion, Egypt has become increasingly dependent on the world market to satisfy its food needs.

Table 18 *Food Prices in Three Distribution Channels, Winter 1988*

Per Capita Quantity (monthly)		Prices (piasters/kg)		
		Subsidized	*Co-op*	*Free Market*
Sugar	750 g	10	35	60
Oil	450 g	10	30	190
Tea	40 g	138	–	1,000
Rice	600 g	14	30	*
Lentils	**	–	35	185
Meat	***	–	275	550–600

Source: Personal field work, suggested by a framework used by Khouri-Dagher (1986).

* Only imported rice was available in the market and only rarely in low-income neighborhoods. However, some people would sell their extra rice for slightly more than the rationed price in times of desperate need for cash. Others borrowed from each other when they ran short.

** Lentils were not rationed, although when available, fixed quantities at a subsidized price would be given to each household.

*** When available, subsidized meat was distributed in quantities of only one kilo for each household. However, in middle-class neighborhoods the portions were much larger.

informal market since it would allow them to take advantage of the subsidies. A neighbor had found Zaynab a job in a small clothing factory that was 45 minutes away by bus. Here she would learn to use a sewing machine that could come in handy for her later. Though initially excited about it, she finally decided against taking the job. She said,

By selling soaked beans in the market, I can also look after my two little boys without having to take them to my parents, who themselves are too poor to feed my kids. I can also run to the government shop and buy cheap food when it is available, since we can never afford to buy these foods at free market prices.[17] While I am in the neighborhood, I can also queue for people who can't themselves wait in line, and make some money that way.

17. Channeling subsidized goods to the household costs women considerable time and energy, a significant detail often ignored when assessing the cost of subsidies. These pricing situations made it economically justifiable for many women to limit their cash-earning activities and invest their time in efficient shopping. It is ironic that the liberalization of economic policies has had a considerable influence on keeping women outside the labor market or pushing them into the low-paying activities of the informal economy.

For instance, if the person buys a tray of eggs, they will give me a few for having waited in line.

Efficient shopping can save as much as one-third of a low-income household's daily budget. Price levels and where to get the best and cheapest things were a continuous topic of conversation among women, a point other researchers have also noted (MacLeod 1991; Singerman 1995). Women's networks and mutual support were crucial with respect to shopping. Most basic items such as rice, oil, eggs, sugar, cheese, meat, and fish were in great demand but usually unaffordable at free market prices. In the past they were only sporadically sold in the cooperative shops, and when available, the entire stock sold out within a few hours. Effective, speedy communication concerning the availability of these goods was essential. Women spread the news to their friends and queued or sent their children to line up for one another. When there was a shortage of available cash they would lend money to each other. When the items were sold in larger quantities than one household could afford, women would negotiate and form a group to buy and share them.

Shopping Strategies, 1990–1994. As the government proceeded with its gradual removal of subsidies against a background of high inflation in the free market for food, clothing, and other items, cash-saving activity became essential for preserving a household's standard of living. As the gap between co-op and free market prices narrowed, shopping queues became shorter. However, it has also meant much more competition for those few items that are still available at lower prices in limited quantities. These daily competitions sometimes produced ill will between neighbors.

To demonstrate the importance of securing access to those few items still available in small quantities at the more subsidized rate, take the example of bread, a basic item that was essential to all households. During 1992, subsidized bread was only baked and sold for 2 and 5 piasters at certain hours of the day; after that, people had to buy bread at the free market price of 10 piasters (albeit for a slightly bigger loaf of bread). If we consider that on average a family of five consumed about fifteen to twenty pieces of bread each day, there would be a minimum difference of one Egyptian pound a day, which is substantial considering that the ten poorest households in my sample had a monthly food budget of less than 50 pounds. This budget already represents an increase of at least 15 to 20 pounds as compared with 1985–1986.

In 1988, the price of beef in the market was 6 to 7 pounds per kilo versus 2.75 pounds subsidized. Most families consumed between one and two kilograms of meat a month, but if they could not buy the subsidized meat, they often went without. In 1994, with the cost of red meat at 14 to 18 pounds per kilo, even the better-off households in the neighborhood rarely consumed meat except for special occasions such as the Muslim New Year. Those who could afford it might consume chicken, and some type of cheap fish a couple of times a month. Others go without. In 1992, when I visited Umm Wa'el and some of her neighbors, they teased me by saying that now I could go and live there forever since the market prices have turned everyone in the neighborhood into vegetarians (see chapter 1). They complained that even the few items such as rice and sugar that are still available in small quantities with their ration cards are often not in tamwin shops. Others, knowing my research interest in family life, told me if I lived in the neighborhood today, my research would be more interesting because I could write about frequent fights between husbands and wives over housekeeping money since men either do not have or do not want to give money to their wives, who have to feed hungry children regardless.

This situation had encouraged some of the younger wives to try to find cash-generating activities, but their domestic responsibilities and their lack of marketable skills and capital forced them to engage in activities such as making ice cream and jelly to sell to the children or retailing vegetables, making the already high competition among the vendors in the local suqs even stiffer. In fact, the price list that I made of vegetables in the local suqs in the summer of 1994 shows that the prices of items that women normally sell have increased the least, which often indicates their low rate of return. As many already said, now they pay so much more to buy these items from the wholesale suq.[18]

Shopping for household needs has become much more time-consuming in the low-income neighborhoods. Women, and sometimes men, may shop several times a day. Most items are bought in small quantities as the need arises. There were significant reasons for this pattern of frequent shopping besides frenzied market conditions and not having enough cash. Few households stored any food items besides those

18. For instance, *girgir* and parsley are sold at 0.05 Egyptian pounds a bunch, which is the same price as in 1988; the difference, however, is that the bunches are up to 25 percent smaller. In contrast, in August 1988 local grapes (one of the cheapest common fruits) sold for between 0.60 to 0.90 pounds per kilo, while in August 1994 the price was between 3 and 4 pounds per kilo. However, the male retailers I talked to said the wholesale prices have risen from one and a half to two times for summer produce.

bought on the ration cards, which were identical for all households. This manner of shopping was time-consuming and energy-consuming, as well as more costly. However, in the context of the prevailing lifestyle, it was a rational approach. The households in these neighborhoods interacted widely with their neighbors and had preserved and cherished the old ideas of sharing and giving; one often heard the phrase "*Ihna kullina wahid*" (We are all one unit). It was expected that everyone share what they had, and never turn away a request if it could be granted. However, this style of life was not easily affordable. By keeping stocks of food at home identical to those of the neighbors, households cut their losses while maintaining the essential social network that was their main support. Women holding regular jobs outside the community were to some extent exceptions to this generalization. They might have more food stocks at home, but since their time was limited and they were not available during the day, their neighborly exchanges were also limited. Attention to the details of life patterns and social context can often help explain seemingly irrational behavior and choices.

Cash-saving Labor

To improve their standard of living, urban households are engaged in a whole range of economic activities outside the cash market that are clearly beyond the broadest definition of housework and are sometimes referred to as "informal economy." In both the First and the Third worlds, these activities represent a substantial amount that is not accounted for in the gross national product (Gershuny and Thomas 1984; Pahl 1984; Portes, Castells, and Benton 1989; Anderson, Bechhofer, and Gershuny 1994).[19] Economic opportunities, the state of the national economy, and wage levels have an important influence on the extent to which individuals and households may engage in these activities.[20] Moreover, sexual division of labor within the household and differential gender opportunities in the labor market have a signifi-

19. The arguments for the inclusion of the value of housework and cash-saving labor in the calculation of GNP are interwoven.

20. Pahl (1984), in his study of the Isle of Shepy (U.K.), found that social welfare policies encouraged men to engage in home-improvement projects and request unemployment benefits. Women engaged in part-time jobs and reduced some of their subsistence projects. For examples from other industrialized nations, see Redclift and Mingione 1985; Mingione 1994.

cant impact on the extent to which individuals may contribute to their households.

Both male and female informants engaged in cash-saving economic activities whenever they could. However, it appears that the development of commoditization in Egypt has had differential effects on the subsistence activities of male and female informants. Women reported that in the past they made jam, pickles, and dried vegetables, when they were in season and cheap, and saved them for later use. This practice had stopped because the resultant savings had become negligible; instead, they bought preserved items from the cooperative shops. Many women, however, still raised chickens, rabbits, geese, pigeons, and occasionally sheep for their own consumption, and infrequently to sell to neighbors. They fed these animals on household refuse, which cost them nothing, and raising animals usually meant that the household could afford to eat meat more often. Raising animals, usually poultry, for subsistence was widely practiced in Cairo, especially in the newly urbanized, low-income neighborhoods. In the early 1980s it was estimated that one-seventh of the eggs consumed in the city were home produced (Khouri-Dagher 1986); however, the scarcity of space has increasingly curtailed poultry raising.

Many of the neighborhoods of Greater Cairo did not (and still do not) have water. Households bought water daily from dealers traveling door-to-door, or carried it home from the public taps (Nadim 1980). Carrying water was a task universally performed by women, although usually the water dealers were men. Two out of the three neighborhoods in the study did not have water when I began my research, and all the women carried the water home daily rather than purchase it. In a different neighborhood in Cairo, Manshiet Nasser, Frederic Shorter (1985: 21) estimated that the monthly cost of water to an average household was 19.2 pounds. Women's contribution to the household budget in this manner was therefore quite substantial, even when we take into account price differences between neighborhoods.[21] By 1987, a second neighborhood in this study was connected to city water, usually only at night due to the water shortage in Cairo, and only those households who could afford to pay the dues enjoyed running water. Many could not, and so they either continued to carry water from the public tap or relied on their richer neighbors to give it to them. Nonetheless, most people, particularly women, praised the government effort to give them

21. The farther a neighborhood was from sources of drinking water, the more expensive water delivery was.

water. Gradually, by 1992, only a small number of houses in this neighborhood were not connected to the city water system.

Traditionally, men in Cairo had little chance of contributing to the household other than financially. This, however, changed in recent years. Men spent time painting and repairing the apartment, a job hired out to a specialist in the past. Many owned buildings they had built themselves with minimal paid labor. If the tasks were greater than what they could accomplish in their free time, they sometimes took leave from their jobs to attend to them. This new trend in urban Egypt, however, ran contrary to the traditional mores that obliged individuals to respect the boundaries of other people's livelihoods. This ethos had been an effective means of redistribution of wealth and job opportunity among urbanites. This tradition was so deeply felt that many of the male informants were compelled to justify their activities. Abu Said, a blue-collar worker in the public sector, was painting their home when he explained,

I wanted to ask a *naqqash* [painter] to come and paint the flat because it was very dirty, but it was estimated that would cost me 120 pounds. I could not afford it. Besides I only earn 35 pounds a week from both my jobs. Thus I applied for leave from my jobs and I am doing it myself. This way I save a lot, and my children will live in a clean and neat flat.

The considerable savings derived from undertaking these unconventional tasks was considered a legitimate justification. Hamid was an unskilled worker in the public sector with a second job as a doorman and a successful former migrant who had managed to build a flat for his family. He proudly explained how he had managed to improve their housing conditions.

I took three weeks of my yearly holiday and with the help of my two eldest sons finished building the first room. Of course, for some parts we had to employ skilled people, but we did whatever we could because it is so expensive to hire skilled workers. They demanded five or six times more than I earn in one day. Once the first room was finished my family moved here and I gradually built a second room and a kitchen. Now I am working on the second floor whenever I have time and the money to buy some materials. I reckon in a year or two I can finish the second floor too.[22]

22. In fact, by 1994, he had almost completed the third floor. The ground floor was given to his elder daughter and her husband to accelerate her marriage and the third floor was reserved for his eldest son on his marriage. He thought he might even start a fourth floor for the second son who has now, to the great joy of his parents, entered Cairo University.

Whether these activities are regarded as an extension of the informal economy (Pahl 1988), subsistence work, or, as I have categorized them, cash-saving labor, they are the outcome of the same economic rationale. In allocating their available labor power, households try to maximize their gains. However, it is important to note that these new trends in Egypt have affected men and women differently. Due to the matrix of prices women have lost certain ground, such as food processing, to the cash market, while men have gained opportunities to contribute to their households in forms other than cash. This situation has brought about new imbalances in the extent to which men and women can contribute to their households, which in turn may have implications for men's and women's interdependent roles and responsibilities.

Dealing with Public Institutions

The process of industrialization and modernization is concurrent with urbanization and the development of communal consumption of goods and services, which are essential for the progressive reproduction of industrial society (Castells 1977; Schmink 1984; Pfeifer 1993). The state controls, either fully or partially, the production and distribution of collective amenities, health, education, housing, and infrastructure. The extent to which any state may intervene in the process of production and consumption is affected by its dominant ideology, the level of development of its productive forces, accessibility to material resources, and ability and authority to enforce its decisions. Because of its postindependence welfare ideology, the Egyptian state has considerable control over consumption and distribution of a wide range of goods and services. Like most other developing nations, Egypt has had a long-term policy favoring urban areas, which has increased the considerable rural-urban income gap (Korayem 1981; Richards and Waterbury 1990: 277–287). The bureaucracy in Egypt has expanded with the extension of state control; however, lack of sufficient resources and the inefficiency common to many other developing countries have made any transaction with the state a laborious and time-consuming task. Dealing with official institutions in Egypt meant long hours, often day after day, in the corridors of government buildings, filling in forms, collecting signatures, and paying bribes (Singerman 1995).

As complicated as this was, low-income households could not afford to overlook the benefits the state offered. Since men were often busy earning money, increasingly women tended to develop networks and expertise to deal with the institutions. Their missions varied from taking the children to the public hospital to getting a ration card—a lengthy procedure (Khouri-Dagher 1986: 9–12)—registering children at school, dealing with housing institutes or the tax office, and applying for the passports and paperwork needed for their husbands to migrate (Hoodfar 1995b).

Performing these tasks ran contrary to the role most women were trained to perform. A woman was socialized to believe that her place was at home, not in the public domain, and her role was to attend to her children and husband. Because a woman's chastity was crucial to the honor of her family and her chances of marrying respectably, in her early youth, she would be prevented from going out unaccompanied in public beyond the immediate neighborhood. Consequently, many young women were fearful of leaving their neighborhoods on their own and preferred to go with friends. Many men prized young women who knew (or more commonly pretended that they knew) nothing of the world beyond the four walls of their homes and who were incapable of performing any task traditionally outside the female domain.[23]

Nahed, an intelligent eighteen-year-old in her last year of high school, went shopping with a friend who was preparing to get married. Nahed explained that although she never had any money to buy things, she loved to wander around the nice shops and had learned a lot about what to buy, where, and the cheapest prices. Therefore, her friends often sought her advice. That day, she was very late in returning home and her parents were extremely worried. She looked very upset when she arrived, and as the parents started to question her, she burst into tears and explained that she had got lost and went from one bus route to the next. Her father suddenly calmed down and sent her to wash her face. In her absence, with a smile on his face, he explained to me,

We should have never permitted her to go with her friends because she is not like other girls, she only knows the bus that takes her to school and back. Society is corrupt and the only way to protect young women is to keep them at home. We make sure Nahed does not go anywhere without her mother or brother; therefore, it is not her fault that she lost her way home.

Nahed later said to me,

23. On numerous occasions I witnessed young, capable women act hopeless and ignorant in front of their parents and very often laugh about it later when they talked to me or close friends.

You know, we had gone shopping and went for an ice cream afterward. So we were late, but we all [the four shoppers] decided to say the same thing to our parents. Our parents and most men are old-fashioned and like stupid women. They like to think their daughters, even when educated, are socially stupid and incapable. They force us to act stupid. . . . If you don't believe me, you can come and talk to all my friends from school and they all will tell you the same thing.

The traditional ideology and practice of sexual division of labor, which make any task beyond the physical boundaries of the home a man's responsibility, are increasingly in conflict with the pattern of daily life in a modern society that has created new domains, institutional and otherwise, that must be dealt with. Since men were principally engaged in meeting the family's financial needs, women were forced to assume other responsibilities. The performance of these tasks by women, however, has not been matched by a change in attitudes and ideology. Thus women performed these tasks under the auspices of their husbands and received no credit or acknowledgment for them.

The exceptions were the wives of migrants, who in the absence of their husbands had been encouraged to see themselves as heads of household and publicly demand credit for their contribution. They had achieved a new adulthood and their self-perception had changed. This had a considerable impact on the way they related to their broader community, husbands, and children. The words of Umm Ahmad typify this new attitude.

I was brought up to be a "woman," but nowadays everyone has to be a "man." I learned the hard way, but I'm raising my daughters to be "men" so that they can take care of themselves and not be dependent on others.

Summary

The standard of living of urban households, particularly those with limited cash resources, is affected by nonmonetary contributions such as domestic work, cash-saving activities, and the appropriation of state provisions. The omission of nonmonetary factors from the household or national economy represents a considerable underestimation of the standard of living and fogs our understanding of the household's survival strategies and economic and social choices. However, when these contributions are taken into account, many supposedly irrational choices make perfect economic sense. Following the traditional division of labor, which is reinforced by the modern ideology of the male as breadwinner, domestic work and child care have remained women's domains in the neighborhoods, though women were conscious that their domestic work is increasingly undervalued in comparison to cash contributions. Despite its apparent static image, the new commercial economy has had a profound impact on women's domestic and other nonmonetary contributions. Many tasks and services traditionally performed by women have been transferred to the cash market, making women more dependent on their husbands' income. Many women were aware that this has had a negative impact on their position in the household. In contrast, interaction with formal institutions is traditionally a male domain, but men's engagement in cash-raising activities has caused women to assume the responsibility for channeling public goods to the household. As the nature of women's domestic responsibilities, the unfavorable terms of the labor market, and their limited salable skills discouraged women from participating in the labor market and acknowledging their contributions to the household pool, they sought to preserve their domestic domain from male encroachment by promoting the traditional gender ideology. This attitude, I argue, stemmed not merely from traditionalism but from women's need to protect their interests, especially the legitimacy of financial support from their husbands and their uncontested right to their own wages. However, this strategy can result in reproducing the existing sexual division of labor and the gender ideology that has disadvantaged women in the context of the commercialized economy.

CHAPTER 7

Expenditure and Consumption Patterns

Survival and coping strategies should be primarily about the different ways in which a household negotiates its incorporation into the life of its community. Despite the fact that consumption is an important means by which people reaffirm their socioeconomic status in their community (Douglas and Isherwood 1978; Bloch and Parry 1989; McCracken 1990; Warde 1994), studies of survival strategies have often concentrated on income-earning activities and neglected consumption patterns. The significance of household income lies in the fact that it is a primary determinant of household consumption. Among low-income households, in urban and increasingly commercialized contexts, where cash supply is limited and unpredictable, consumption strategies gain special importance since they have direct influence on people's well-being.

Consumption is one of the frontiers at which "the culture is fought over and licked into shape" (Douglas and Isherwood 1978: 57), and participation in this process is part of community life. In fact, the real hindrance of having a low income is that it restricts people from such participation.[1] At the extreme, this exclusion may bring a society to the verge of breakdown, both politically and socially. Most societies have

1. As early as 1977 a memorandum that was submitted by the Supplementary Benefit Commission to the Royal Commission on Distribution of Income and Wealth, U.K., defined income as "a means of access to a social system. The significance of low-income is that it restricts such access and below a certain level it may virtually exclude people from participating fully in the life of the community of which they are members" (quoted in Douglas and Isherwood 1978: 90).

evolved cultural practices to prevent such an eventuality, for instance, by encouraging those who have more to provide a greater share for communal consumption.

In modern, complex societies it is usually the state that regulates the economy and furthers political stability by expanding the degree of national incorporation into a shared social system. Material culture and consumption is an effective channel through which to achieve shared values and experience. Hence many states deploy a variety of welfare policies to facilitate a minimum consumption level. For instance, state social security and supplementary benefit policies in many industrialized countries are designed to prevent the exclusion of underprivileged segments of the population beyond a minimum limit. In Egypt, heavy subsidization of basic food items, oil, and public transportation had similarly been designed to ensure minimum consumption for all members of the society.[2]

Other aspects of consumption deserve closer examination. In market-based societies, consumption (particularly of nationally produced items) achieves balanced economic expansion and develops the internal market. This is particularly important for developing nations that, in the early stages of industrialization, have little chance of exploiting the international market beyond the export of primary goods. To encourage manufacturing and to protect domestically produced goods, the state may subsidize their cost, protect the domestic market from foreign goods, or facilitate consumption by establishing the necessary infrastructure. For instance, the spread of electricity encourages the purchase and use of electric equipment such as televisions or washing machines. Despite their relegation to residual categories by economists, cultural factors feature prominently both in the expansion of the economy and in the development of the national market. Although frequently overlooked, the cultural values and practices of a society can facilitate or discourage increased consumption or the adoption of new lifestyles.[3]

2. In fact, the gradual removal of these subsidies has resulted in the widespread attraction of oppositional Islamic movements because they preach communal values and basic provisions for the economically least privileged (Sullivan 1992, 1994).

3. Gell (1986) found that a conservative attitude and lack of interest in the consumption of goods beyond the prescribed or acceptable limit prevented Mura Gondas of India from translating their economic success into their daily life. In contrast, Stirratt, in his 1989 study of a recently prosperous Sri Lankan fishing community, found that they invested their wealth in constructing garages and electrical items despite the lack of electricity and roads.

When a culture is adaptive and receptive to new ideas or has an inherent capacity for incorporation and indigenization of foreign ideas, the economy has fertile terrain in which to grow. "Some societies take to consumerism without hesitation and experience no difficulties elaborating a previously given set of status symbols and personality-marking possessions with goods previously unavailable or unknown" (Gell 1986: 113). Others may only very slowly and gradually respond to socioeconomic changes (Appadurai 1986; Bloch and Parry 1989). Still others may adopt a pattern of consumption that does not stimulate the economy.[4] The accumulation of gold, especially by women, was the preferred form of wealth in many Middle Eastern cultures. Widespread consumption patterns of this sort would be disastrous for the economy as it removes a substantial part of a nation's capital from productive circulation. In short, different cultures respond differently to consumption opportunities. Cultural traits conducive to a market economy should be viewed as additional resources for societies pursuing such development.

Low-income Egyptians have eagerly welcomed many of the products of modern technology and adapted their lifestyles to incorporate their consumption. In many instances, they have used both material and nonmaterial resources to finance their new pattern of consumption, which is also their major source of saving in the form of durable household goods.[5] This new consumption pattern has increased prosperity and stimulated the local and national economies.[6] The back streets of old Cairo, with hundreds of different kinds of workshops, illustrate the initiative and innovation of local production, much of which is stimulated by the new mode of consumption (Ayata 1986; Meyer 1987; Stauth 1991; Singerman 1995, 1996b).

The Egyptian low-income consumption pattern has not evolved in a vacuum. It is strongly influenced by Egyptians' desires to be part of their rapidly "modernizing" culture and modes of life and to secure their long-term material well-being. In this chapter, I review household

4. For instance, as in the case of the Iban and the collection of Chinese porcelain (Freeman 1970).

5. For instance, Egypt, like most other developing countries, has very limited formal credit facilities that rarely extend to the low-income strata. However, local entrepreneurs developed a credit system that relies on a customer's reputation and face-to-face relationships in the neighborhood as a guarantee against debt.

6. Although this indicates many Egyptian low-income households live beyond their means, most of the products they use are nationally produced, which is not the case with the middle classes. Given a healthy economic situation, this should have a positive impact on the economy and the rate of employment.

expenditure patterns and factors influencing the matrix of household consumption. I will discuss and examine the strategies my informants adopted not only to survive biologically and to ensure their long-term security but also to promote their incorporation in the life of their society. I also examine how male and female informants perceived their differential consumption preferences.

Patterns of Expenditure

Studies of household/individual allocation of income have often borrowed economists' concepts and categories such as consumption (primary and luxury), saving, and investment. These categories, however, are rarely useful for the study of income allocation because their boundaries are arbitrarily decided. For instance, educational expenditure is considered an investment and dietary expenditure is considered consumption, although both items are channeled to build human capital. In this study I found that daily living practices made saving money virtually impossible; durable consumer goods were obtained primarily as secure investments and seen as savings for future needs and other investments. In effect, people saved through investing in household goods, which also enabled households to enjoy their utility in actual and prestige terms.

Although saving is often treated as a residual category and refers to income put aside for future use, I found that saving, albeit in the form of assets, is a top priority. As a saving strategy, households spent their anticipated income accumulating assets (durable goods) before the money was even earned. Saving clubs were formed with friends or colleagues with the intention of purchasing items as soon as money was accumulated. The money was always spent, though sometimes on something other than what was originally intended. Migrants who saved money while working in the Gulf quickly invested their remittances in durable goods, housing, or a business, often before their actual return to Egypt.

The conventional division of consumption into essential and luxury cannot be employed, as in practice the definition and boundaries of these categories are fluid. Such divisions are also highly class and culture bound and carry strong moral judgments. Further, though widely accepted, they cannot provide variables for cross-cultural studies: an essential item in one society may be considered a luxury in another, depending on the level of "development" and ecological needs.[7] In brief, the neat categories applied by economists are more a source of confusion than clarity, at least in the case of this study. Hence, with reference to my data, I have distinguished two categories of expenditure: routine and recurrent items such as food, education, and rent; and the accumulation of assets in the form of household durable goods and possibly housing.

Aside from income level, the social and material position that households envisaged for themselves influenced the allocation of their expenditure. A further significant factor was the power relation between husband and wife, and to a lesser degree the influence of children and other members of the household. Expenditures and the allocation of the households' resources, whether regarding food, school expenses, or household goods, were often the source of disagreement among husbands and wives or parents and children. As cash contribution becomes increasingly important, men, who most commonly control the money, emerge with more power and authority than traditionally ascribed to them. Resentful of this situation, women's reactions vary from passive acceptance to arguing, manipulating their husbands, or joining the labor market to earn money of their own.

Recurrent Expenditures

Most household income was allocated to meet recurrent needs (food, clothing, education, rent and energy bills, medical costs, and small daily expenses). The level of consumption of each of these items was carefully weighed against acceptable minimum neighborhood standards and the consumption level of households of comparable social standing. All households tried to minimize these costs to allow the accumulation of assets. Some households (particularly those in which the husbands were government employees) allocated the most secure part of their cash income to meet basic needs, and all other income from

7. Despite these criticisms, such distinctions are essential for countries wishing to pursue an effective income redistribution policy. Nevertheless, definition of the consumption categories should include the historical and political framework, per capita income, and national habits and customs.

overtime work, second jobs, or other activities went to expanding their collection of assets.

FOOD

The informants considered a rich diet an important element of a good life. However, with the exception of the very poor, there was little variance in the dietary practices of different income-level households. Beyond the locally acceptable minimum expenditure on food, priority tended to be given to other items such as education or household goods. There was no marked difference between the diet of the households where wives had independent cash income and those without. Food expenditure was seen as the prime responsibility of the husband, and except for the very poor households and those with a guest husband, cash-earning wives rarely spent their wages on food, as discussed in chapter 5.

Most people had two meals a day. The main meal consisted of either rice or pasta and one kind of vegetable, normally cooked in thick tomato sauce and served with a large quantity of bread. Ideally, meat, either chicken or beef, was eaten once a week, while wealthier households often supplemented their diet with cheap fish and eggs several times a week. Poorer households rarely consumed meat and ate more fish; for special occasions, they might cook one of their home-raised chickens.[8] Meat was the most prestigious item in the diet and was portioned out to household members, usually according to their status within the home, by the most senior woman of the house. For example, sons, and those older daughters who contributed either by performing housework or with cash, received a bigger portion of meat.

In recent years, declining subsidies and ever-rising prices have further curbed the consumption of meat and more expensive vegetables, although most households allocated a higher percentage of their income for food.[9] This shortage of food had become a source of bitter complaint for women and a source of spousal arguments. Most women ac-

8. Sixty percent of the households of the core sample rarely served eggs, cheese, or fruit.

9. In Cairo, fresh and fairly inexpensive vegetables have been an important part of the daily diet, and though they are still more affordable than many other items, price hikes in the last decade have curbed their consumption. For example, in the early years of fieldwork (1983–1988) salad used to be an inexpensive part of every household's diet during the long summer season but is now considered a luxury and prepared only on Fridays or to guests.

knowledged that husbands who ate out as a rule consumed more meat, and this was often justified by pointing out that hard work requires more energy, or, as Mona put it,

One man's appetite can be satisfied by eating half a cooked chicken, which costs around 1.5 pounds, but the whole family would need two chickens, which is clearly not affordable for most of us.

Others passively accepted this as a fact of life. Umm Sharif put it this way.

It is his money. If he does not put the family first and does not do what all other good husbands and fathers do, what can I do? I cannot fight and have arguments with him every day.

Younger wives who had more problematic relationships with their husbands were less forgiving or accepting of this situation. Being acutely conscious that the claim to food was probably the most legitimate request of a wife from her husband, they used every opportunity to point out, in different ways, that their husbands ate meat every day while the rest of their families did not eat meat even once a month. Such an accusation was intended to communicate that their husbands were selfish and irresponsible rather than to criticize eating habits. Sometimes a husband, by acknowledging his wife's claims and admitting his extravagances (often falsely), made her feel even more humiliated as she did not have the power to force him to change. This attitude among husbands contributed partially to the wives' rationale for adopting a passive attitude. Traditionally, men worked in their own neighborhoods and were very sensitive about their reputations, which affected their income-earning opportunities. Wives could therefore take their complaints to an influential member of the neighborhood and ask him or her to speak with the husband; in this way women could exert social pressure on their husbands to conform to socially accepted practices (Nadim el-Messiri 1975, 1977). As men began working away from their homes and neighborhoods, women have lost this recourse.

There are other dimensions to food consumption that communicate the degree of knowledge, aspiration, and ability with which a particular household associates itself with modern culture and middle-class taste. For instance, in the past Egyptians consumed whole grain bread, but recently white French rolls have become popular. Since bread of this sort is associated with modernity, it carries more prestige. Many young educated men and their younger children refuse to eat other kinds of bread at home, and as there was no marked difference in price, many families have switched to white bread despite the fact that most were aware that brown bread is more nutritious. Since this change was associated with modernity, the women tended to score prestige by publicizing it. The following conversation illustrates this. On a hot afternoon when many neighbors had gathered in Umm Fatma's flat to escape from the heat, Umm Wa'el complained about her family.

I spent the whole morning cleaning and chopping mulukhiya leaves and made a lovely soup. When I served the lunch, Mahmud and Wa'el [her husband and son] would not eat because there was only baladi bread. I know that they prefer *fino* [French rolls], but mulukhiya tastes better with the traditional bread. But would father and son have it? No way. I had to run to the bakery to buy some fino.

Modern convenience foods such as canned fish and frozen vegetables are highly appreciated, particularly those imported or produced in the private sector. Consumption of these foods, promoted through television and radio advertisements, is associated with modernity and sophistication. Although these foods are often more expensive than the fresh items in the local market, women occasionally indulged in luxury food items and told their peers at every possible opportunity.

This kind of infrequent expenditure remained a novelty, a token demonstration of people's receptiveness to modernity and "progress." The informants recognized that they were motivated by the social meaning of their expenditure rather than by the actual use value of the product. On one occasion, when I was watching television with women neighbors, an advertisement for frozen vegetables came on and Nadia said,

A few months ago I bought a packet of frozen okra and cooked it. [Other women confirmed this.] It was so nice and easy. It also tasted good. But the problem is that it cost three and a half times more than the fresh okra I buy from the local market. It is a pity that one cannot afford to buy it all the time.

At this point other women gave me examples of their experience with modern convenience foods. A younger woman told me,

It is not that we do not want to buy modern food and cook and serve it in a fashionable way on a set table, just like one sees on television or the way your rich middle-class friends serve food [jokingly pointing to me]. It is generally the financial problem that prevents us.

Women, particularly younger and more educated ones, showed a high degree of receptivity to trying modern food items and attempted to purchase them with as little financial loss to their households as possible. The importance of this occasional consumption remained in its symbolic communicative value. By using their very modest access to forms of economic expression, women communicate their eagerness to be incorporated in what they perceive as modern Egyptian consumer culture.

CLOTHING

Clothing is an important consumer good in most societies, but in Egypt attire is especially significant because it visibly defines what social strata people come from, or identify themselves with (see Wikan 1985; Rugh 1986). The mode and quality of one's clothes are carefully observed and judged (Rugh 1979, 1986; Early 1993). For instance, a woman or a man who wears the traditional gallabiya is expressing her or his adherence to baladi culture. Other, subtler features, such as the quality and the detail of cloth and design, can indicate one's financial and geographic background. Since baladi culture is identified with backwardness and a lack of sophistication, most urban Egyptians, particularly the younger generation, prefer not to dress in this traditional manner. Conversely, European-style clothing defines a person as modern and progressive and carries prestige (see also Early 1993: 67–79).

Until the mid-1970s, the educated and the middle classes tended to dress in the European style. I was reminded several times that the law has made it compulsory for men in government, in the public sector, or at universities to dress in this manner.[10] During the last decade a new style of clothing, referred to as Islamic, has gained popularity especially among more educated and working women of the lower middle classes (Hoodfar 1991; MacLeod 1991). This Islamic style for women consists of a long dress that borrows more from the European than the Middle Eastern tradition and a head cover that is very different from traditional headgear. This mode of dressing avoids the connotation of

10. Although women's return to the veil aroused much interest, especially in the Occident, few scholars have paid attention to the legal restriction applied to men's clothing. Despite the fact that extreme heat makes Western-style clothing less suitable for much of the year, male students and government officials are legally obliged to wear European-style clothing.

backwardness implicit in the traditional style of dressing and indicates the modernity of women who wear it, while at the same time it reflects that the wearer behaves in accordance with indigenous values and mores and is not Westernized.

Although many observers have attached a strong religious dimension to this mode of dressing, I found a powerful social and economic reasoning at work, *besides personal religious conviction* (Hoodfar 1991). For one thing, it indicated a deviation from the Eurocentric elite and other Westernized social groups. As well, it carried the notion of modernity without compromising the traditional and Islamic norms and values of modesty. This was particularly advantageous for young women using overcrowded public transportation, particularly in the very early and late hours of the day, who in the past often reported that they were either molested or harshly judged by male pedestrians for appearing unescorted in the streets at inappropriate hours (Hammam 1979; Hoodfar 1991). The economic advantage lies in the fact that these women were not expected to have many different sets of clothing to appear smartly dressed. And finally, since these women appear to follow the Islamic code, they can establish much more egalitarian relations with their male colleagues or clients without being accused of seduction (an accusation that is often used to control or halt female behavior; see Hoodfar 1991). However, by 1994 the economic advantage was rapidly evaporating as the production of Islamic clothes has become commercialized and a number of boutiques specializing in Islamic clothing have opened in Cairo. "Islamic fashion" has become a preoccupation of many who can afford the time and cost. Similarly the social respect and prestige that the veil had allowed women (especially as far as it saved them from being molested in public or becoming the subject of malicious gossip) was fading fast as the majority of young women are now veiled.

In the *haya sha'biya*, the folk or popular neighborhood, there was also a sharp distinction between what was worn at home and in the neighborhood and what people wore outside the immediate neighborhood or for special occasions such as weddings (Nadim el-Messiri 1975). There was strong social pressure to conform to the dominant style of dress in the neighborhood, to reduce visible social differences. However, on leaving the neighborhood people were expected to change clothing to demonstrate their social and ideological position vis-à-vis the wider society.

Women usually dress in gallabiyas made of cheap cotton that, until recently, was obtained at a subsidized rate and sewn by the local tailor

at very low cost.[11] Women with a number of gallabiyas as well as European-style clothing made sure their peers had detailed accounts of their
wardrobe and its cost but often wore their oldest piece of clothing.
Children were generally dressed in either gallabiyas or pajama tops made
of subsidized cotton, but since it has become harder to obtain cheap
fabric over the last few years, many households have started buying
ready-made children's clothes. Most men dressed in the European style,
but the gallabiya was commonly worn at home and around the neighborhood.

While the clothing of their household members was a constant preoccupation of women, men were either indifferent or concerned only
with their own attire. This is because, whereas a woman's social standing is defined within her neighborhood and is affected by the household
as a whole, a man's social position is primarily defined in his working
environment and is rarely affected by other members of his household.
This often caused friction between couples when allocating their budget. Although clothing, like food, was considered the male provider's
responsibility, women with an independent income were willing to
spend part of their money on clothing for themselves and their children.
Despite variance in the aggregate level of family income, clothing probably represents the most pronounced difference between households
with cash-earning women and those without.

Mothers were very concerned about how their daughters of marriage age were dressed, for this had a direct impact on their marriage
chances. Many mothers overlooked their own needs to properly outfit
their daughters. Fathers, by contrast, did not attach much value to their
daughters' clothing and were less willing to spend money, particularly for the more expensive European styles. As Abu Ahmad explained to me after a rather bitter argument with his wife over money
for a dress for their daughter, who was going to attend a relative's wedding:

Why can't she wear a gallabiya like her mother? Why should I pay the money
I do not have for a dress—so that a modern educated man who has nothing
in his pocket can come to ask for her hand and expect me to pay for the
wedding and furnish his flat too?

11. The cost of sewing a gallabiya varied from 75 piasters to about 2 pounds in 1986.
Now these prices have doubled and tripled. Nonetheless, all the women preferred to buy
ready-made gallabiyas, but they often sewed them themselves because this was much
cheaper.

After he left the house, Umm Ahmad agreed with her husband that modern educated men are less willing to pay for the mahr and expect more contributions from the bride's family. But she added,

It is the Islamic duty of any father to marry off his daughters respectfully. I want my daughter to find a good hardworking man, educated or not. . . . I do not want her to beg for money for her children, like I have to do. If we don't dress her nicely, we won't find a respectable suitor who is prepared to work hard for his wedding and setting up a home.[12]

Fathers, however, were more willing to spend on their sons' clothing, despite the even greater cost, not just because it was prestigious to have well-dressed sons but also because it improved their sons' chances of finding better jobs. Most daughters resented this differential treatment but rarely raised objections, since they said it would not change the situation and might cost them the support and solidarity they could expect from their brothers particularly in regard to finding them a suitor.

Despite the importance women placed on clothing, there was a gap between the way men and women—particularly nonearning wives and their husbands—dressed. Men tended to be much better dressed than women, and even in the baladi style they still spent much more than women did. Even in households where the wife was financial manager, she felt obliged to allocate more money for her husband's clothing than for her own, though the sons were not automatically so favored.

EDUCATION

Education is a major expense in families with school-aged children. Theoretically, education is free and compulsory, but the phenomenal rate of population growth in Cairo has hampered the initially well-organized educational system. As schools have become overcrowded and inefficient, additional private tutoring has become a norm in Cairo (Herrera 1992; Singerman 1995; Kamphoefner 1996). Private lessons have also become a means by which poorly paid teachers supplement their incomes. In effect, schooling has become partly privatized; pupils are expected to go to private lessons (given at the school to a group of students referred to as *magmu'a*) or take tutorials at the

12. Many Egyptians accept, as an Islamic principle, that a husband is expected to support his wife in the style to which she was accustomed in her father's house. This means, for example, that a well-dressed fiancée would expect her husband to continue to provide her with the means to maintain her appearance.

teacher's house. All school-aged children in the sample, except those few whose mothers were educated, whether in primary, secondary, or high school, had some private lessons.[13]

The beginning of the school term was one of the most difficult times for households. To buy the required uniforms, school bags, stationery, and other supplies for all the children presented a major monetary challenge, despite the efforts of most households to save and budget year-round for the beginning of school. Although women and sometimes men generally entered into gamʿiya with neighbors to raise the sum for schooling expenses and private lessons, most households had to borrow some money from their better-off friends to cover the costs of starting the school year.

The beginning of school season precipitated increased family tensions, especially among siblings, who each argued for a larger allowance. The situation was exacerbated by the favoring of one child over another. Each child was judged by his or her ability and anticipated future social role and responsibilities. Children assessed as intelligent received a larger share of the educational budget. Contrary to much of the literature on Egypt, households in the neighborhoods were not small autocracies where an individual's position and degree of influence were rigidly fixed. There was considerable flexibility and room for contestation.[14] Therefore, each child tried to argue his or her case to secure a bigger share of the resources.[15]

Though most people gave special value to education (see also Kamphoefner 1996), the willingness to invest in children's education beyond primary school was closely tied to the level of return, in terms of

13. The children of educated mothers were all in the early years of primary school, and their mothers did not expect to help the children once they were in high school. Most educated mothers hoped to send their children to a private school when they were older, but few managed.

14. A considerable amount of arguments, disagreements, and sometimes physical violence occurred between the family members, each trying to secure a better share of resources for herself or himself (see also Singerman 1995). The existence of open conflict and arguments indicates that individual members did see room for maneuver and that the hierarchies of power within the households were not as fixed as the literature on Egyptian society indicates (e.g., Wikan 1980).

15. On all occasions when I raised this issue with parents, they explained to me that children, though all loved, are like the fingers of a hand: each is different and each has different abilities. Therefore, it is not fair to the most intelligent children to be deprived of resources that would enable them to study, in favor of those who may be good at something else. In effect it was efficient management of resources that they were concerned with, rather than fairness. When I discussed the matters with the children, they rarely raised any objection to these justifications and many repeated "Allah does not create us the same; we are all different."

future job opportunity. As a result of change in wage structures, boys were viewed as better off learning technical skills (see chapter 3), allowing most households to allocate more funds for their daughters' education toward secure, if low-paying, jobs (since girls' future husbands would theoretically bear primary financial responsibility for the household). This assessment of the labor market helps to explain the much faster rate of increase in female attendance in secondary and higher education.

Children always put their demands regarding school expenses to their mothers, even when the arrangement was that fathers would pay for all educational expenses. Mothers in turn conveyed these demands to the fathers. When these were denied, for whatever reason, mothers were torn between the children's demands and the fathers' denial. At times, to solve the problem and to prevent further friction in the household, they would try to cover these expenses with housekeeping money, their own money, or even money borrowed from friends. It is in such situations that mothers win the support and loyalty of their children, an opportunity denied fathers whose financial contributions are viewed as their duty and responsibility, regardless of the degree of sacrifice involved.

All wage-earning women contributed substantially to educational expenses, though without exception they considered this to be their husbands' responsibility. The fathers, knowing education was a priority that their wives would pay for if necessary, tried to resist contribution as much as possible. All the children above fourteen years of age said that though their fathers were responsible for educational costs, it was easier to talk with their mothers and ask them to convey their needs. In fact, many children perceived their mothers as more perceptive and aware of problems and felt that mothers should be the financial managers. One fourteen-year-old son said,

It is not that my mum gives me money easier. No, to the contrary, I can always get money for a drink or pocket money much easier from my father than my mother. But fathers have no sense of priority: they give money for going to a movie but not to buy my school books. But women, it is in their nature that they know what is good for the family and how to spend money. My father does not even know how to haggle and bargain to get a good price, but my mother almost drives the vendor crazy to get two piasters off. . . . Men should earn money and women should manage it.

I asked if he would give his wages to his wife when he is married. He replied,

I will marry a clever woman like my mother and then give her everything and tell her all about my wages. I will buy her presents, too. My father never does that except for some fruit that mostly we and not my mother eat.

Rent and Other Miscellaneous Routine Expenditures

Egypt's austere economic policies since the late 1970s have had a manifold inflationary impact on rent and energy bills. During the socialist era, rent control laws were effectively enforced and landlords could not easily evict a tenant or raise the rent. Although the same principle still applies for long-standing tenants, the liberal economy has been more lenient toward landlords, allowing them to levy much higher rents.[16] This has created a wide discrepancy between the rent paid by established households and the rent paid by more recent ones—who may find themselves paying more than half their stable income for rent. To give an example, Azza was twenty-four-years old and had been married one year. Her husband earned 90 pounds a month as a bookkeeper. They rented a small one-bedroom flat near her mother for 45 pounds a month, half of which was paid five years in advance. They had borrowed the money from a bank and were paying interest on it. In contrast, Azza's mother paid only 7 pounds a month for an identical flat that she had been renting for fifteen years. Although Azza was a white-collar government employee, her husband had to work overtime and accept other odd jobs to meet the family's needs.

High rents force young couples to move to informal housing on the outskirts of Cairo, where rents are cheaper. As discussed in chapter 4, this creates enormous problems for young women in terms of child care, particularly if they are employed outside their neighborhoods. To counter this situation, many employed women and their children stayed with their parents on weekdays and went home only on weekends.[17] Other employed mothers would leave their children with their grandmothers, visit them midweek, and then pick them up on Thursday afternoon only to bring them back on Saturday morning. Older couples were very sympathetic to the problems of younger couples and tried to

16. See Springberg 1991 for further debate on owner-tenant relations.
17. The weekend in Muslim countries is Friday only, but in some it may also include Thursdays for civil servants and white-collar workers.

help out. Every family dreamed that one day they would manage to buy a small piece of land and build a multistoried apartment building to house their children. This would prevent the children from scattering around the city just when their aging parents needed them nearby. A few families in the neighborhood had invested their earnings from migration and built several flats atop one another, which generally housed married sons and occasionally daughters.[18] Whenever the housing issue came up, all parents pointed to those few families who had succeeded in realizing this dream. Since the cost of building materials was rising rapidly, those who owned land—even if it was so far away from Cairo that they could not yet build and live on it—would invest whatever cash they could spare in building materials for future use.

There were other irregular but recurrent expenses such as gifts and medical treatment for which households had to budget.[19] The amounts of such expenditures often correlated with the social image the household projected for itself rather than with their income. For instance, part of the claim to modernity and sophistication involved the use of the private medical system (Hoodfar 1984, 1995a; Oldham 1984). Whereas adults rarely saw private physicians and commonly consulted with pharmacists and bought the recommended medications, children, especially boys, were usually taken to private clinics. Boys received better treatment for two major reasons. First, because most mothers felt men were more willing to spend money for their sons; second, because mothers commonly believed that little boys are weaker than girls and are much more likely to contract serious illnesses. There are other reasons as well, which Umm Naglah pointed out as I walked her back from her visit to the local private clinic.

I don't think it was necessary to visit the doctor because he only has a cold, but I worry that if he gets worse or something happened to him, Abu Naglah would accuse me of being negligent of his son, and create an argument. . . . Men feel daughters belong to their mothers while at home and then marry and leave the family, but sons are supposed to help the family in the future.

Very few households budgeted for medical expenditures; when the need arose, most families had to divert funds from other needs or, most commonly, borrow from better-off friends.

18. It is generally the responsibility of the groom to provide housing. Therefore, parents feel they should help their sons before helping their sons-in-law, though mothers often prefer to have their daughters live near them.

19. For a discussion of the Egyptian public health system, see Gallagher 1990.

Accumulation of Assets

There was an apparent eagerness on the part of the households, particularly the women, to allocate as large a portion of the budget as possible for the acquisition of household goods, many of which are categorized as luxury goods. The desire for consumption of these "luxury" goods, which until the 1980s was the prerogative of the middle classes, had fueled much criticism of the low-income social group by the middle classes, social critics, and sometimes scholars. Such criticism arises from a conventional assumption on the part of scholars concerned with problems of poverty and survival strategies that expenditure patterns represent a hierarchy of need, descending from primary and physiological needs toward fulfillment of secondary, nonessential, and luxury wants as income level permits. Deviations from this pattern have been viewed critically as distorted priorities, particularly if the population in question belongs to the low-income social group, which is expected to be concerned only with primary needs.[20]

Such a view stems from a narrow, economist's approach to the material needs of social persons, as well as to the meaning of consumption (Lewis 1966; Appadurai 1986; McCracken 1990; Warde 1994). People as social beings need to reproduce themselves not only physically on a day-to-day and generational basis but also as members of their evolving cultures. Ethnographic and sociological literature has demonstrated time and again that consumption is a social act and its material or psychic utility often may be of secondary importance (Douglas and Isherwood 1978; Appadurai 1986; Warde 1994).

At the outset of my research, I had intended to document the allocation of resources within the household, particularly with respect to the husbands and wives and daughters and sons. However, after a few months of living in the neighborhoods, my daily interaction with my neighbors and friends brought to my attention a new aspect of a household's daily concerns: its consumption strategies. All households, especially the women informants, had a sequence of items in mind and devised different strategies to obtain them. Men were encouraged to seek extra employment and women engaged in any possible cash-earning activity to finance the accumulation of these items. This pattern of ex-

---

20. In the sociological and anthropological literature, these views were particularly expressed in the culture of poverty perspectives (see Lewis 1959, 1966; Wikan 1980).

Table 19 *Inventory of Modern Electric Household Goods*

Item*	Years of Ownership				Without	Total
	1–3	4–7	8–10	11+		
Cooker	14	21	12	5	7	50
Refrigerator	12	17	6	3	21	59
Television	26	26	13	1	4	59
Washing machine	16	26	10	1	6	59
Fan	21	15	7	–	16	59
Cassette player	14	15	20	–	15	59

* For this table I have selected mainly electric appliances and items that had recently gained popularity. Many other items, such as beds, benches, and wardrobes, were traditionally considered essential and were therefore owned by all households.

penditure and preoccupation with acquiring new items was very recent, the result of new socioeconomic conditions.

Traditionally, women's dowries included all the necessary household items, which for low-income urbanites consisted of cooking vessels, bedding, and possibly a bench, a wardrobe, and a few other small items. The dowry was often funded in part by the mahr, which the groom pays before marriage, and partly by the bride's parents. In the past, lower-income households might replace these items when necessary but rarely bought any other furniture (Nadim el-Messiri 1975; Rugh 1979). The history of the households' inventory, which I collected in 1986 (see table 19), suggests a significant shift in the composition of household durable items over a recent ten-year period (1975–1986). Items such as televisions and electric washing tumblers (very simple washing machines) only a decade earlier were categorized as luxury items and used exclusively by the middle class. By the mid-1980s, however, they were considered basic items, and the dowry of even the poorest brides in the urban neighborhoods was expected to include at least some of them.

There was a multitude of motives behind the acquisition of modern appliances. They were obtained primarily as a means of saving through the accumulation of durable goods—and as a kind of insurance against hard times. Almost all informants listed their priorities as better housing, establishing a business (for those without a permanent or secure job), and only then improving their day-to-day living conditions by investing in modern appliances and better clothing and diet.

Achieving the first two priorities required a substantial amount of capital. Without any possibility of a loan from financial institutions, long-term saving strategies were essential. However, in these low-income neighborhoods, the chronic cash shortage and the sharing spirit made saving money practically impossible. There was always a neighbor without funds whose sick child needed immediate medical care, or a niece or nephew in desperate need of cash to prevent jeopardizing his or her wedding, or the sudden death of a friend or neighbor who left nothing behind for the family. The importance of the social network and the great value placed on sharing and helping each other meant any small savings disappeared as neighbors responded to each others' day-to-day emergencies. These loans were rarely repaid in lump sums, and repayment usually took a long time, particularly when substantial amounts were involved.

This being the case, the best saving strategy was to invest whatever funds were available, or were to become available, on goods that retained their value, while their utility could be freely shared with friends and neighbors. All neighbors were welcome to watch the color television or put meat in the refrigerator or ask for some ice. Generosity of this sort brought status and power to a household, but no one expected anyone to sell a possession to pay a neighbor's emergency expense. And if a family fell on hard times, all these items could be easily converted into cash, with little of their value lost because of the high inflation rate in Egypt. Given these circumstances, the collection of such durable goods was the most viable savings strategy.

I went to visit Umm Habiba in her new flat, which had two small rooms and a small balcony but no kitchen—a great improvement over just one room in a house shared with five other households. She was excited and extremely happy.

Everybody thought that with five children, I would never be able to move to a better residence. When, against my husband's wishes, I bought the television and the radio and all the other things on installment, everybody thought I was in the wrong. But when, through a friend, I became aware that this flat was becoming vacant I talked to the landlord and reached an agreement with him on a sum of key money. Then I talked to my husband and he agreed to apply for a 200-pound loan, I sold every item, and we raised the 1,000 pounds to pay the landlord. I know I have to start to buy the appliances again, but everybody agrees that the most important thing is the flat. I know in a few years I can replace the items in the same way I bought them the first time.

Umm Fatma, admiring the cleverness of her neighbor Umm Ahmad, said,

Now they have four rooms to live in, but it did not come easy. I witnessed Umm Ahmad twice fill her home with all the household appliances and have to sell them all to build a new room. They are nine people and need the space, but the only way they could raise the money was as she did.

Lack of access to any other source of credit also encouraged the households to obtain items on installment (see Financing Methods, below) and then sell them for cash. Umm Saaid bought a new television for 180 pounds on installment. Three months later, when her husband was to migrate to Saudi Arabia, she sold the television (on which she was still paying installments) for 135 pounds and her gold bracelet—the only thing she had in her own name—for 80 pounds, to fund the initial costs. She told me that in anticipation of migration expenses they had decided to buy a television on installment that they could later sell for cash, because they did not have any friend able to loan them the necessary money. In this way, households who had no chance of using formal institutions such as banks and did not have a social network able to lend cash could use their only capital—their established membership in good standing in the neighborhood. With reputation as collateral, items could be purchased on installment from the local shops (which tended to be slightly more expensive than elsewhere).

Both the men and the women had a clear notion of their priorities: better housing, investment toward a more secure source of income, and improvement of home conditions—all of which incidentally correspond with those of the middle classes. In contrast to many middle-class and wealthier households, however, the low-income strata must employ different strategies to achieve these goals. While some households' aspirations were not fulfilled (due to lack of means), they did strive to satisfy their less immediate needs. Thus a poor household that lived in one room might still have a television or a modern stove.

Different socioeconomic conditions induce different strategies by different classes or social groups to alleviate insecurities about the future. While some cultural and economic conditions may encourage a tendency to save cash as a security and survival strategy, in another context, it may be more economical to spend, albeit in a particular manner. Low-income Egyptians, motivated by safeguarding their future and social mobility, have opted for spending as much of their income as possible on acquiring assets in the form of household goods that retain their value.

Besides the accumulation of assets as a means of saving, there are other factors that explain the eagerness to acquire modern appliances.

In contrast to conventional economic assumptions, the acquisition of these appliances had little to do with their time-saving features. Consumer goods have significance that goes far beyond the commercial value or utility that manufacturers and producers intend. They symbolically communicate cultural meanings that the wider community has assigned to them (Douglas and Isherwood 1978; Appadurai 1986; McCracken 1990; Warde 1994). In the neighborhoods, household goods carried high status and were symbols of modernity, statements of "progress" and the willingness to accept and try new ways. They were tangible proof that the household was in line with current social changes, a means by which the poor challenged their exclusion from the changing social system. Such acquisitions were a demonstration that the household had the impetus for upward mobility, a trait highly valued in Egyptian society. Households doing well are much admired, envied, and respected; since emulation of socially respected and ambitious individuals is highly regarded in Egyptian culture, households were encouraged to upgrade their own positions in the neighborhood.

The eagerness to acquire modern household appliances is not to be interpreted as total acceptance of the consumer habits that these goods may advocate. Such innovations were incorporated in daily life only to the extent that they did not disrupt the continuity of valued social practices. For instance, it was common for women to place their electric washing tumblers on the balcony or even in the alleyway, and converse with their neighbors while washing clothes. And, although by 1988 almost all the households had a television set, women preferred to watch their favorite programs together and discuss them.

I was talking to Mabruka in her flat when she suddenly interrupted to ask me the time. "Quarter past seven," I answered. She called out to her six-year-old daughter to go upstairs and call Umm Fatma and Umm Abir to come down quickly, because the *tamsiliya* (soap opera) was to begin soon on TV. Then she turned to me and said,

We like to watch the serials together because then we can discuss them. It is more fun this way because it gives us a chance to relax together. A few years ago only I had television, so we always gathered in my flat. But now that all of us have television we often rotate and go to different homes. . . . We feel especially lucky to be able to enjoy the serials together because our ·husbands do not come home until much later.

On a different occasion, when I was going to the market with Mona, she met her close friend and neighbor.

Ya Nadia, where were you last night? There was such a lovely, romantic film on and I really wanted to watch it with you but your light was off.

After Nadia left us, Mona turned to me:

I love television. It is the only leisure I have since Mahmud [her husband] never takes us out. But I like to watch the films with my friends to enjoy them best. Without them it is never the same. When we watch films together we make remarks and talk about them. All women enjoy the films more when they are together. . . . Poor Umm Sabah [another neighbor of hers] can rarely join us because her husband comes home so early. He is a lazy . . . good-for-nothing man who does not like working.

Similarly, despite the fact that most households owned a gas stove, it was used only occasionally, because gas stoves, unlike kerosene burners, are not portable.[21] Much of the cooking was done on small portable kerosene or gas burners, allowing the women to change the location of their cooking. They might cook on the balcony, or in the common corridor, while chatting with friends, for example, or in the room while watching television or entertaining guests.

  I met Umm Azza as she hurried toward one of the alleyways in her neighborhood. I asked why she was in such a rush. She asked me to accompany her and continued to walk while she explained.

I gave the babbur to be repaired and when I sent Merfat [her daughter] to collect it, they told her it was not ready. I cannot do without it at all. They promised it will be ready in a day.

I reminded her that she had a gas stove. She said,

Yes, but I cannot carry the gas cooker into the room when I watch television, and anyway, the flat is too small and it gets very hot if I do all my cooking inside. Umm Ahmad [her neighbor] and I always place our babbur in the corridor and do our cooking together. This way our flats do not get hot or messy with the vegetable shells, and we can chat.

Although women welcomed the new appliances as an improvement, they rejected practices that would curtail social interaction. At times the men—particularly the more educated and better-off husbands— did try to minimize their wives' interaction with other women through acquisition of such appliances, and by encouraging an afrangi (Western) style of domestic organization.

---

21. There was also the problem of obtaining bottled gas. Further, they tried to keep their stoves in the best condition for possible resale.

Financing Methods

Considering the minimal income of most of the households, it is surprising that they managed to acquire a number of relatively expensive items. A survey I conducted suggests that households generally adopted a combination of methods. The wealthier households joined saving clubs with their neighbors, colleagues, or friends (see chapter 8 for details) with the intention of buying specific goods as soon as money came into their possession. The advantage in this collective method of saving lay in the fact that while the money was accumulating neither the club members nor needy neighbors or friends could make a claim on it.[22]

Obtaining durable goods on installment was the most common method of financing. The local retailers did not hesitate to sell to local people with whom they had face-to-face relations, and communal knowledge of every sale worked as a guarantee against failure to make payments.[23] Low-income consumers seized the opportunity to obtain goods by committing to a gradual payment schedule. Although useful for those households without a social network, this system discouraged them from making an effort to weave themselves into one. The installment terms were adapted to suit the conditions of those with small and unpredictable incomes. A few households obtained a television set at 2 pounds a week. Although it was recognized that goods were more expensive under this system, often the financial loss was minimized by the very high inflation rate. Zaynab, who sold broad beans in the local vegetable market, managed to obtain a television, a fan, and a small gas burner in two years. She said,

The money goes whether I buy these items or not. Abu Ahmad [the local retailer in hardware] suggested I take the goods and pay him 1 pound every other day, and he does not mind if sometimes I did not have enough to pay. He is a good man. The television he gave me last year for 130 pounds is now 150, because things become more expensive every day. If you do not buy today, tomorrow you have to pay more.

22. Only a small number of people, mainly the white-collar government workers in the neighborhood, had a bank account that was primarily used to cash their paychecks.

23. Both the purchaser and the local dealer made sure that the community was aware of the purchase. The purchaser wanted to advertise the new gain and how much the item cost both for the prestige and in case it was necessary to resell the item in the future. The retailer's intention was to prevent the buyer from trying to get out of the debt and at the same time encourage the rest of the community to buy more items.

Remittances from household members working in the Gulf were another major source of financing the purchase of household items.[24] The money was either sent every few months or would be transferred on the migrants' return, to be invested in durable goods with as little delay as possible. For more successful migrants, it became standard practice to buy a small piece of land on the outskirts of Cairo as soon as they had saved enough for a down payment and to pay the balance on installment.

Decision Making

This discussion of the acquisition of household goods should not be taken as an indicator that all members of a household had the same interest or commitment toward such accumulation, or agreed on what its composition should be. There were wide discrepancies between what men and women preferred to acquire first. I asked thirty-five women in my core sample to list the first three items they would purchase, and then asked them to name what they thought their husbands' first priority would be. As table 20 indicates, while women's top priorities were a gas stove and an electric washing tumbler, they thought the men would go for a television and cassette recorder. Women agreed that men had little interest in equipping their homes, especially the kitchen, since they spent so little time there. Instead, men tended to prefer to invest in items that they directly benefited from or those that had more market demand and could therefore be sold quickly.

Since husbands, as the main cash contributors, often retained financial control, they could influence expenditure patterns more strongly. In fact, the aggregate national data (table 21) on the consumption of electric household goods closely correlates with what my female informants perceived as mens' priorities. My own data on household inventory, however, correlated more closely with female preferences; this may

24. International migration had been the platform from which much criticism of consumption has been launched (Ibrahim 1982; Saad el-Din and Abdel-Fadil 1983). It was assumed that remittances went to conspicuous consumption, and little went to investment, particularly "productive" investment. I found no major difference in the pattern of expenditure of migrant and other households (Hoodfar 1996a). Fergany's (1987) nationally representative study confirmed my observation. All informants, migrants or not, preferred foreign-made electric goods, but the difference in price encouraged them to buy Egyptian goods whenever they had the option.

Table 20 *Priority of Purchase of Household Items*

	Items	Frequency
Wives' priorities		
First choice	Washing machine	35
Second choice	Gas stove	28
Third choice	Television	27
Husbands' priorities, according to their wives		
First choice	Television	35
Second choice	Cassette recorder	24
Third choice	Refrigerator	21

Table 21 *Annual Consumption of Electric Household Appliances (in thousands)*

Item	1978	1979	1980–1981	1981–1982	1982–1983
Television	525	435	556	864	1,011
Radio/ Cassette recorder	568	609	748	709	897
Refrigerator	151	210	243	375	475
Fan	264	445	281	557	397
Washing machine	241	285	274	279	321
Gas stove	122	156	142	151	145

Source: CAPMAS, Consumption of Goods in the ARE (Egypt), 1982/1983; December 1984 (Arabic), quoted in Khouri-Dagher 1986: 11.

be because of the larger proportion of waged women in my core group relative to the national figure. Moreover, there were many migrant households among the informants, which meant that many wives had easier access to cash. Both these factors influenced the amount of control women had over decisions of cash allocation in their households.

Women showed a strong desire to upgrade their standard of living through acquisition of household goods; achievement of this aim was among the most frequent reasons women gave for wishing to have paid employment. MacLeod (1991), in her study of working women in Cairo, found that many young women, at least theoretically, planned to quit their jobs after they bought all the appliances they considered necessary. All cash earning women said spending on household durable goods is the best way to contribute to family income. When they had the option, they allocated a large part of their income to the acquisition of household goods. Many women had sold their gold to buy an electric washing tumbler or a gas cooker.[25] The older, nonearning wives felt disadvantaged because they had not acquired such goods when setting up their households as part of their marriage arrangements. The meager income of their households and the objections of their husbands made such purchases unlikely. These two factors contributed to the eagerness of many wives for their husbands to migrate and enable them to improve their material lives.

There were ways to influence the pattern of expenditure or combat a husband's unwillingness to invest in household items. Brides-to-be, through their mothers and families, tended to demand much larger sums as mahr, which would be invested in household goods prior to the wedding (see chapter 2). Married women openly discussed different strategies for manipulating their husbands and sometimes planned together how to go about encouraging a particular husband to buy certain items. Women who were considered successful strategists were deeply respected and frequently consulted. This kind of manipulation was not considered, either by the husbands or others, as crafty, malicious, or deceitful; on the contrary, it served to benefit the entire household. To illustrate this point let me describe one of many instances in which I was an unsolicited part of the plot. I was invited to spend an afternoon with Umm Wa'el. Her husband was a junior white-collar worker who despite his two jobs paid little attention to his family's needs and had not increased the housekeeping allowance for three years, which had made Umm Wa'el very bitter. Before her husband left for work, she mentioned to him that we might go to visit his sister who lived nearby. However, we did not go and spent the afternoon and early evening chatting with other women from her balcony. When her husband returned, she welcomed him with a cup of tea and then said she had a very bad headache.

Husband: Why?

Umm Wa'el: Because Wa'el and Walid wanted to go to their aunt's to watch television and because I did not take them they were in a bad mood

25. It is customary that women receive at least one piece of gold at their marriage. Some women had also inherited from their mothers or had bought a small ring or earring from their own savings.

and cried. [In fact, the issue never came up and the boys were happily play-ing in the alleyway.] I had to spend the time entertaining them rather than attending to my guest.

> *Husband:* Why didn't you take them to my sister's?

> *Umm Wa'el:* I like your sister very much and I will always go to help her with her children but I will not go there in the evenings.

> *Husband:* Why not?

> *Umm Wa'el:* Because although she is very kind-hearted some-times, unintentionally she says things that break my heart.

> *Husband (impatiently):* What do you mean?

> *Umm Wa'el:* On the last occasion we were there, after we had said good-bye and came downstairs, she shouted from the top floor that I must go there more evenings and take the children to watch television be-cause we do not have one. I know she was being kind, but what would the neighbors think? All those who arrived in the city yesterday have a television set and we—with an educated and modern man—do not have one. We are very poor! Now you know why I do not want to go there in the evening.

Her husband had often tried to impress me with his education and modernity, especially by putting baladi and peasant people down, and felt uncomfortable with me witnessing this conversation—exactly what his wife had hoped for. We continued to talk about the advantages and disadvantages of television for a while, and then I left. Within a week, her husband agreed to buy a television on installment and all the neigh-bors congratulated her on her success.

In contrast with the harsh judgments on husbands who were believed to be skimping on routine expenses, men's unwillingness to accumulate household goods was tolerated, mainly because it was not viewed as an essential male responsibility. Women were expected to mastermind and manipulate their husbands to work harder, and to save through accumulation of assets to improve the household's lot. Both men and women admired those women who managed to influence their hus-bands to the benefit of the household. As an older male informant said,

The man with a clever wife will go far. I was so poor when I married my wife and spent all my money on smoking hash and having fun with other men. My wife cleverly used to take the money from me. One day she would say she is sick, the next day the child was sick and she needed money to buy medicine. The week after, my mother was visiting, so she needed to buy more and better food. I gave her the money and felt she was greedy and sometimes I would not treat her very kindly. After five years she told me, "Abu Hassan, I now have saved 300 pounds from your money and we can sell my gold and buy a piece of land." I could not believe my ears. At that time that was a lot of money. I could not believe that one day I would be able to buy a piece of land, but she had already even found the land. But she is an honest woman and did not want to buy the land in her name. We bought this piece of land, which at the time was so far from what was then Cairo, I wondered whether it was of any use. But she said Cairo will grow and she wanted a roof of her own. I listened to her and from that time on, I worked very hard and gave my money to her and we gradually built this house. Hamdullah—thanks to God—now we have a house and we can leave something for our children when we go.

Many of my informants had variations on this theme of how men can earn money but it is women who know how to use it.[26]

Summary

Consumption is an important means through which people (and communities) reproduce themselves both biologically and socially. Thus strategies designed to promote consumption while balancing physiological and social needs form a vital aspect of low-income households' survival strategies. Although consumption conventionally is regarded as the antonym of saving, this does not always hold true. While in some socioeconomic contexts it is more advantageous to minimize spending and save cash as a means of future security, cultural and economic conditions in Cairo encourage low-income households to invest cash income (actual and anticipated) in durable household goods. This trend has attracted much criticism on the part of the middle classes and social critics who misunderstood the tendency of the poor to consume beyond their incomes, which arises not from their lack of consideration for the future or unforeseen needs but from concern for such eventualities. After all, they know through experience that in times of hardship, they can rely only on themselves.

Moreover, in a rush of condemnation of mass consumption in Egypt, scholars and social critics have failed to credit the nation for its vitality and enthusiastic approach to the consumption of modern goods. Egyptians have incorporated a whole range of new ideas and objects, some of which bear no relation to traditional patterns of life, into the modern Egyptian context. In this manner they have indicated their approval of what industrialization has to offer, while in the process they have

26. For similar findings and discussion, see Wikan 1985.

also innovatively "Egyptianized" the usage of these foreign items. The Egyptian eagerness for new goods and consumption patterns should be viewed as a positive stimulant for the national economy, particularly since it is the low-income Egyptians and not the middle classes or export market who buy nationally produced household goods.

Household consumption patterns provide a window through which to observe the interplay between individual self-interest and collective interest, which may not always be in harmony. While women advocated more communal expenditures, men, who for the most part work and spend much of their time outside the neighborhoods and away from their families, tended to be more influenced by their own needs. I have argued that such tendencies were not innate and biological but rather the result of the differential position of men and women in the household structure as well as in the wider society.

CHAPTER 8

Social Networks and Informal Associations

Studies of societies in many parts of the world have documented the vitality of neighborhood and community networks for urban low-income groups (Stack 1974; Lomnitz 1977, 1987; March and Taqqu 1986; Grieco 1987; Greenhalgh 1988; Becker 1990; Mansbridge 1990; Gonzalez de la Rocha 1994; Singerman 1995). Small and often unpredictable incomes and the inaccessibility of support from formal institutions such as banks have made it necessary for people to search for supplementary means of survival and security. Reciprocal networks and informal associations in the low-income neighborhoods of Cairo have evolved as parallel economic structures that also offer moral support and ensure better standards of living for their participants (Singerman 1995). Without undermining the importance of these sites as culturally rich worlds, here I focus primarily on those functions that specifically help households fulfill their material needs and contribute to their survival strategies.

Reciprocity is a specific mode of exchange of goods and services that includes emotional support and that should be distinguished from market exchange (Fiske 1991). An important characteristic of the reciprocal flow of goods and services is that it presupposes continuity beyond a single transaction. For this reason reciprocal exchanges usually take place within stable communities, whether they be communities of kin, neighbors, friends, or a cultural group (Hall and Wellman 1985; March and Taqqu 1986; Singerman 1995). However, even in stable groups, reciprocity does not take place arbitrarily between individuals or families.

People carefully assess the costs and benefits of material and nonmaterial exchanges when deciding with whom they will engage in such exchanges. In this process they may create, change, or simply reinforce the existing culturally recognized and legitimate social institutions regulating reciprocal relationships. Therefore, as it has been pointed out, it would be misleading to view these reciprocal exchanges in modern industrial cities as some lingering remnant from romantic or obsolete ceremonies of the past (Lomnitz 1977: 203).

Reciprocal exchanges can take place both horizontally, that is, between people and households with the same standard of living and social position, and vertically, between households and individuals of higher and lower socioeconomic levels. The exchanges in horizontal networks are often for similar goods and services, while vertical networks typically provide opportunities for the exchange of different types of goods and services. For instance, a more affluent and influential housewife may use her influence to find a job for a poorer member of her network in exchange for personal services or political support. These social contacts and exchanges also contribute to the creation and maintenance of social cohesion.[1]

In urban Cairo, these networks also formed the basis of many other informal associations through which the less powerful helped one another. The most important and more readily identifiable of these associations were the gamᶜiyat, saving clubs or rotating credit associations, which were, in fact, an effective parallel banking system (Singerman 1995, 1996b), and the gift exchanges, which take place on occasions such as the birth of a child, an engagement, or a wedding. In practice, these gifts, which are often in the form of cash, make it easier for new parents or new couples to cope financially. According to some of my older informants, there were many more of these effective informal economic and social associations in the neighborhoods of Cairo in the past. They lamented that recent population movements in and around Cairo have resulted in culturally diverse neighborhoods of people with different regional origins who do not always share the same customs, and this has weakened some of these informal associations.

A prominent feature of the social networks and the informal associations in the neighborhoods of Cairo was the centrality of the role

---

1. Other researchers in the Middle East and elsewhere have pointed out the importance of these networks in promoting social cohesion, for instance, Aswad 1974; Joseph 1983, 1987, 1993.

of women, a feature that has been observed in several cross-cultural studies (Velez-Ibañez 1983; March and Taqqu 1986; Joseph 1987; Singerman 1995). This has been partly due to the nature of ascribed gender roles, which brought women into frequent contact with each other and with kin in the course of performing their responsibilities. In contrast, men were often away at work, sometimes out of the country. Only those in stable occupations had the opportunity to interact with the same colleagues over long periods and establish long-term reciprocal relationships.[2] Women formed effective horizontal and vertical networks in their neighborhoods and sometimes with their colleagues. Many of the informal associations such as saving clubs, though they often included male members, were run by women. This has brought status and power to the women and their families. Moreover, women were very aware that their access to effective networks gave them power in their marital relations, and they often referred to this.[3]

The Saving Associations

The rotating credit associations called gamʿiyat were probably the most significant neighborhood networks in urban Cairo. In fact, Diane Singerman (1995), who studied a commercial neighborhood in the heart of old Cairo, has referred to these associations as a parallel banking system through which huge amounts of money exchanges hands while escaping state control. In a gamʿiya a group of people join together, usually under the leadership of an elderly woman, and contribute a fixed sum of money at fixed time intervals. At each interval the money is given to one of the members. The amount of each installment may vary greatly from one saving association to another. For in-

2. However, even among the men with stable jobs, only older men, and then rarely, formed similar kinds of associations with their workmates. That is because, in contrast to women, men often interact with one another as individuals and do not usually talk about their family situations with one another except if they are close kin. Moreover, they are expected to give the impression that they are in control. Therefore, in times of crisis they could not expect the same support women could from one another.

3. My findings, following Joseph (1983, 1993), Maher (1976), Hamalian (1974), Singerman (1995), and Early (1993), contest the old notion that Middle Eastern women do not create instrumental or nonkin networks (Rosenfeld 1960; Wikan 1980). Women create solidarity with other women for economic and social purposes and support one another in their goals to improve their personal and their household's socioeconomic positions.

stance, among my informants it ranged from as little as 25 piasters to as much as 100 pounds.[4] These associations are so much part of day-to-day life that even children, particularly girls, as young as eight and nine years old formed gamʿiyat with their very small amounts of pocket money so that they could buy more expensive sweets or a pen. In this manner, women were trained to plan and budget from a very young age.

People joined these associations with the goal of raising the cash they needed without having to borrow from a bank or from other individuals. Having contacts with women who had reputations as effective and influential gamʿiya leaders was instrumental for families. For as soon as a gamʿiya leader knew of a friend or neighbor who was facing a financial crisis, she would immediately form a gamʿiya with the intention of giving the first allotment to that person.[5] The following incident made me realize the centrality of saving clubs for the people of low-income households who are excluded from the more formal credit and banking system by their poverty. Umm Nasser was killed in a car accident on her way home from the local hospital. Her family was of very modest means and her son, Nasser, who had only just found a job after some months of unemployment, did not have the money for the funeral. Umm Samir, another elderly woman in the neighborhood, immediately organized a gamʿiya with twenty other people and raised 300 pounds to be given to Nasser. Nasser, who was deeply shocked by the accident, later told me,

I am forever grateful to Umm Samir. I did not have any money that month, and I have no rich relative to whom I could go for such a large sum. But she enabled me to give a decent funeral to my mother who suffered a hard life to bring me and my sisters up. I could never walk in this neighborhood if I had failed to do so. . . . It is one thing to repay 15 pounds every two weeks but quite a different story to try to borrow 300 pounds.

There were many other similar occasions. One woman told me,

Without gamʿiyat we could never get anywhere. The rich have no problem to raise cash, but we are all poor. If we did not have gamʿiyat to help one another, we all would be lost.

4. According to Singerman (1995), among wealthier and more traditional business people, each single contribution may be as high as 1,000 pounds. They use this method especially to help one another in hard economic times.

5. The sum for such a gamʿiya was usually decided by the amount of money needed by the person/household in crisis and the amount considered affordable by households invited to join the gamʿiya.

Whether the man or the woman of a household joined a gamʿiya was a reflection of who managed the household's financial matters. However, women were generally considered to be better suited. A woman might be a member of several gamʿiyat at the same time. For instance, with a very small sum, she would join one to buy small household utensils. She might join another one with the intention of raising money for the beginning of the school term. She might join another with the intention of buying part of a daughter's dowry and trousseau. One woman who had four daughters told me that she had belonged to gamʿiyat for her daughters' trousseaus for the last twelve years, since her eldest daughter was seven.

We do not have very much money, and if we do not plan years ahead, we cannot marry our daughters decently. I want to be able to give them a better start than I had.

An important but often unstated function of the saving clubs was to eliminate the need to borrow from members of one's own network. In fact, asking for loans was very rare, particularly from outside the immediate family and the inner circle of close friends, who tended to be of the same social and economic standing.[6] Saving clubs enabled friends and acquaintances to help one another while minimizing the risk of irregular payments or defaulting on debts. Involvement of many people in the transaction made the latter so costly that it almost never happened. On many occasions, when several of my friends in the neighborhoods feared that they might not be able to make their payment because of unexpected circumstances, they immediately organized a smaller gamʿiya where they could receive the first installment and honor their commitment to the first gamʿiya. Safeguarding one's reputation for honoring gamʿiya commitments was so vital to households that even on occasions when wives had joined them without the approval of their husbands and could not meet their commitment, their husbands would pay, although not always without frequently reminding their wives that they had to bail them out. One friend's husband, who was not pleased about having to help his wife with a payment of 12 pounds, told me,

I am annoyed because I knew that she couldn't save 20 pounds a month to pay to the gamʿiya, but she did not listen to me because she knew that I

6. A loan from one's family was not borrowed with the intention of paying it back as soon as possible; rather it was to be repaid if ever the donor or his dependents were in need.

would bail her out. I can't let her reputation and mine suffer because a default in a payment means people would not trust us again and no leader would accept us in their gamʿiya if we ever need to join one.

Communal Marital and Childbirth Contributions

Setting up a household was a costly process, especially for low-income groups. The situation was heightened by the strong desire on the part of almost all parents to get their children off to a better start than they themselves had. The lack of financial resources often meant a delay in marriage, a situation young people felt ambivalent about. Once a marriage was agreed on, the bride's family would organize a party to which most of the neighborhood, friends, and acquaintances were invited, a long-standing custom in old Cairo. Traditionally, a huge tent would be set up in the street. However, since the streets and even the back alleyways are now crowded with cars and motorcycles and special permission is required from the police, few people in Cairo bother to set up such a tent. During these parties, many neighbors contributed small amounts of cash that one or two people, usually close relatives of the bride, collected, making careful mental notes of who contributed how much. The cash gathered in this way often exceeded the cost of the party and would be invested in buying the necessary items for the new household. Such a ceremony may be repeated three times for each marriage—on the day of engagement, on the day of religious and legal registration of the marriage, and on the actual wedding day.

The friends' and relatives' contributions would be returned to their families at similar occasions. The returned gifts, however, were not expected to be identical; every household was expected to participate in the exchange according to its means. The advantage of this institution was that the often-lengthy delay between receiving and returning the contributions allowed the family of the bride to cope with the financial burden a wedding imposes. Furthermore, since richer households were expected to contribute more, this institution served as a means of reinforcing social cohesiveness, strengthening the vertical as well as the horizontal social ties of household members, and reinforcing the feeling of belonging to a community. These celebrations also provided social entertainment for women and children, who rarely left their neighborhoods for leisure. In the past, close relatives of the groom-to-be would also contribute to the cost of the wedding. Although such traditions are reported to still be practiced in the older quarters to some degree (Singerman 1995), I witnessed very little contribution on the part of the groom's family in the newly urbanized neighborhoods, a situation that has developed as a result of parents' lack of financial means and young men's decision to postpone marriage until they have saved some money.[7]

A similar gift exchange, though on a much smaller scale, takes place on the occasion of the birth of the first few children of a family. Friends and neighbors visit the mother soon after the birth, bearing a gift, usually of money,[8] which among poor households might be as little as 2 pounds. These gifts are returned on appropriate future occasions. Women, especially, would try to return such gifts as soon as possible to avoid being indebted to their friends, because, as Umm Azza told me, "If one misses the occasion to reciprocate a friend's favor without legitimate reasons, people will start to gossip and say you are mean and just take and take." In this manner, low-income households help one another cope with the financial crises engendered by new phases in the family cycle.

Neighborly Networks

Neighborly relations and neighborhood leadership, dominated by women, have historically played a very prominent role in Cairo (Mahfouz 1966; Nadim el-Messiri 1975; el-Messiri 1978a). In the last few decades, socioeconomic changes and employment opportunities have removed men from their neighborhoods for most of the day, while gender roles and responsibilities tie women more closely to their neighborhoods even when they too are employed elsewhere. In the newly urbanized residential areas of Cairo, women's presence is even more

7. Although, religiously and ideally, parents should marry off both their male and female children, the marriage of sons costs many times more than that of daughters since the groom is to pay for much of the cost of setting up the new household. Also, since marrying off girls decently is more closely tied to the honor of the family, parents focus more in this regard on daughters rather than on sons.

8. For Egyptian birth rituals, see the anthropological film by Fadwa el-Guindi, *El Sebou* (1986). See also Early 1993: 99–102.

prominent, for these neighborhoods lack artisan workshops or other trade activities prevalent in old Cairo which provide job opportunities for men.[9]

Physical proximity was the primary determinant in the intensity of women's interactions, because the primary function of these neighborhood relations was to provide support with day-to-day chores and problems. Women often recounted reasons why good neighbors are better than relatives. They repeated the Arabic proverb "The neighbor who is near is better than brothers who are far away." Beyond emotional support, they relied on one another for services, borrowing household goods and clothing, giving each other advice, and mobilizing networks to find jobs for their husbands and children.

Generally women's neighborly networks were differentiated at several levels, ranging from the most significant and intense, the inner circle made up of a few friends, to much wider networks in which the frequency and nature of interaction varied greatly. The friends of the inner circle usually shared similar standards of living and similar values, aspirations, and hopes for the future. They usually lived in the same building or within a few blocks of each other. They spent much time together and often performed their domestic tasks in each other's company. They especially helped each other with queuing up to shop for subsidized goods, sharing information about cheap places to shop, and child care.

These inner circles of friends were very important for the basic daily survival of the households. At times of crisis they took each other's children to the hospital or took over each other's household responsibilities. Umm Fatma and Umm Ahmad (my own immediate neighbors) had been neighbors for ten years. During the last two years, Umm Ahmad was very sick and was hospitalized on many occasions, sometimes for as long as two months. Umm Fatma shopped, cooked, and looked after Umm Ahmad's three children and her husband during these periods. At least twice a week she also cooked food and sent it to the hospital for Umm Ahmad. One day when I was helping her with the cooking she told me,

9. This situation is not unique to Cairo. Joseph (1983), studying an urban neighborhood in Lebanon, recorded 1,300 individual visits in one week among a sample of 65 households. All but a few of these visits were carried out by women and mostly within the same neighborhood (p. 6). Just as in Cairo, she found that the norm was for women to join one or more visiting circles and develop links of solidarity with one another (see also Hamalian 1974; Joseph 1978, 1993; Fernea 1975; Eickelman 1984; Early 1993; Singerman 1995).

It is not easy to run two households, but the fact that they live across from us helps, and anyway what could I do, she is my close friend. If we do not help one another in times of hardship, who would? Can you think what would have become of her family if everything was left to her husband who has to work and earn their bread? He probably would have to marry a second wife because there was no one else to look after the family. [Jokingly:] You know men love to have excuses like that to find themselves another woman. So we women should help and support one another. Anyway, today Umm Ahmad is sick, perhaps tomorrow it will be my turn, who knows.

There was also a considerable degree of sharing within these close circles. All sorts of household goods, including more precious items such as electric washing tumblers, mixers, and television sets, were lent and borrowed. Those who had refrigerators offered to store their friends' meat and gave them ice. People would turn their flat over to friends for a wedding or birthday celebration. Women also lent small amounts of cash from their housekeeping money to tide one another over, usually for a day or two.

Among younger married women, these relationships could become quite emotionally intense, but as their children—especially their daughters—grew older they directed their emotions more toward their children and sometimes their husbands. The segregated social and economic activities of husbands and wives limited the possibilities for the development of friendship between them. The marital relationship, based on respect and the fulfillment of respective conjugal duties, was expected to develop into friendship only after years of living together, and often a common interest in the future of their children as they grew older was an important vehicle for the creation of closer ties. Older women thought that this pattern of relationship was healthy because it made women more independent of their husbands in their early years of marriage.

In these circles, women often used fictive kinship terms to address each other, and the children would refer to them accordingly, for instance, as *khalti* (my mother's sister). As many of them carefully avoided using any words or phrases suggesting that their relationship was not one of kinship, it could take quite some time for an outsider like myself to distinguish between friends and kin. Very often, in an attempt to solidify their relationships and ensure a higher degree of stability, women who were very close to one another planned and matched marriages between their children or other close kin, for despite the fact that all households had their most intense relationships with friends and neighbors and not with their kinspeople, they were still very conscious that kinship ties were independent of variables such as proximity and compatibility. Kinship ties went beyond "individual whims," as one of my older informants explained.

Besides these tight circles of close neighbors, there were wider networks based on generalized neighborly relations. Here people exchanged information and perhaps services but few material or monetary items. For instance, women might look after children, shop, or carry water for each other in an emergency situation. Men might help with housing repair or take a neighbor's child to the hospital at night if no adult male household member was available. These actions were conceived of as neighborly consideration, and people did not have to know each other well to offer such services. These were the moral duties of each neighbor toward the other, the responsibilities of an individual to the community, and a hadith (a saying traced back to the Prophet Muhammad) or Qur'anic verse was often quoted in support of this attitude.

These neighborly duties superseded friendship, and personal antagonisms rarely prevented people from offering this kind of support. Mahmud had had disagreements and had been on bad terms with his next-door neighbor, Abu Ahmad, for the last three years, and I had heard about how much they disliked each other ever since I moved into the neighborhood. One night, a year after Abu Ahmad had migrated to Saudi Arabia, his son fell very ill. Mahmud took the child to the hospital in the middle of night and stayed with him all night. He also gave a loan of 15 pounds to Abu Ahmad's wife to help her to cope with the extra expenses until she received money from her husband. When we were discussing the event later, I asked if he had patched up his differences with Abu Ahmad and his family. He told me,

I do not like Abu Ahmad's attitude and find it difficult to be his friend. But of course, that will never discourage me from performing my neighborly duty. Here is a family whose male is away in the foreign land trying to earn a living for them. How could I deny my help to a woman who has no man around. God would never forgive me. I thank God a thousand times that I have a job here and can attend to my family's needs.

On a different occasion, Nadia carried six-year-old Wa'el, who had fallen down some stairs and was crying, to her house. She washed his wound, calmed him down, and gave him something to eat. All the while, she was talking to me and denouncing his mother, who I knew she did not like, as an irresponsible and terrible mother. I commented that as she was so tenderly attending this child, I assumed the two women had become friends. She replied,

Friends! No, we are more like enemies, but that has nothing to do with the child. God would not forgive me if I left the child crying in the street when his licentious mother is not around.

Sometimes this neighborly support could mean the end of hostility or generate the beginning of a closer relationship. Being supportive of and available to neighbors earned people a good name and high status. A good reputation, over and above status, would translate into material reward in the long run, by, for instance, being admitted to the gamʿiyat that would help in times of economic crisis.

I never came across the kind of hostility that Unni Wikan (1980) described for the back streets of Cairo. If anything, I was surprised at the extent of cooperation and consideration built into the cultural and moral values—though people often failed to acknowledge these qualities, they made the poverty and the insecurity of their lives bearable. After living in the neighborhoods for some time, I realized that the women usually aired their complaints about each other very quickly and that, in particular, neighbors who lived next to one another sometimes argued loudly over very petty issues.[10] These, however, rarely resulted in an end to their relationships. Quite the contrary, given the close physical proximity in these densely populated quarters and the intensity of voluntary and nonvoluntary interactions, such a strategy worked as a safety valve preventing people from becoming too frustrated with one another. It also established and reestablished the boundaries of neighbors' expectations of one another.

It was also true that people's expectations of their neighbors, particularly women's, were so high that they often failed to credit them for the help they actually offered. For instance, Umm Mona, whose husband had been a migrant for the last ten years, often stated that her life was difficult because she had no one to give her a hand in times of need. Once I asked whether the neighbors were helpful and she replied, "They are all *ulad kalb* [dog's children, implying they are mean] and only think of themselves. In the old days people relied on their neighbors, but now it is different. . . . Times have changed."

---

10. Despite many arguments, long shouting matches, and even threats of violence, which often developed over children, there was a remarkable lack of physical violence, contrary to Wikan's (1980) observations. In the nine months I continuously lived in one neighborhood, only two physical fights came to my attention. One was between a landlady and her tenant over rent, and the second was between a woman and a man who continually drove his truck in the alleyways without consideration for the children who played there. Young boys of twelve to fifteen would sometimes fight, usually over football, but nobody, including them, took it seriously.

Two other women neighbors who were present agreed with her. Only when I reminded her that her next-door neighbor helped her fix her window a few weeks ago and that her other neighbor often minded her children when she went on errands did she tell me how her eight-year-old son had been lost during the early part of the school term and the whole neighborhood had mobilized, checking every hospital and police station to find him. She thought a few seconds and said, "Yes, but not all of them are nice, and in my case it is different because everybody knows that my husband is away and that I am a lonely woman and people feel obliged to help me."

Most people's expectations were based on the ideal of very stable neighborhoods where relationships span generations and unstated but strongly observed rules of reciprocity govern. However, even in the old neighborhoods of Cairo where this ideal supposedly did exist, homogeneity and familiarity were under continuous assault from increased population movement (Singerman 1995; Hassan 1996). This process had modified the rules of reciprocity, in spite of the fact that the old standard of neighborly relations persisted.

Men's Networks

Men often developed networks with workmates, and their primary exchanges consisted of information about jobs and employment opportunities. This was valued even by public employees who had secure jobs since without contacts it was impossible to find second or odd jobs, the income from which played an important role in their lives. Men sometimes also helped each other with services, but such networking rarely involved direct material transactions, such as borrowing money, which were considered to be risky to a friendship. However, those with stable employment said they might ask their friends to form a gamʿiya to help them out if the need arose.

While those with permanent employment stayed in touch with their networks through the workplace, others such as construction or casual workers—whose networks were even more crucial for finding employment—often met in teahouses. Traditionally, in old Cairo, men would meet at the local teahouse since their neighborhood was also the site of their economic activities. However, this was rarely the case in newly urbanized areas. This meant that men, even when they were unemployed, spent much time outside their neighborhoods.

I came to realize the centrality of the teahouses for male networking and employment opportunities only after several of my friends in the neighborhoods drew my attention to them. I visited Zaynab, whose husband, a construction worker, had been unemployed for more than two months. The family was under great financial stress because the money she earned from selling soaked beans in the local market was barely enough to buy food. I asked whether he had found any work and she replied,

No, and may God help us because I do not see how he can find a job in the future either. He has no friends because we have not had enough money for him to go to the teahouses. . . . That is where men find jobs. People would know of the employment possibilities and would take their friends. It costs 30 or 50 piasters a day, which is not much when he has a job, but I only earn about 70 piasters out of which we [Zaynab, her husband, and her two young sons] have to eat and pay the rent.

It was not unusual to hear people from the middle classes complain that the poor spent their time in the teahouses rather than working and thus it was no wonder they remained poor. But my data suggest that those who went to teahouses regularly were rarely unemployed for any number of days. It was the very poor men who could not afford to go to the teahouses who had difficulty finding employment.

As a female researcher, I had little chance to observe men's interactions since they often took place outside the neighborhoods and in the teahouses, which were generally male domains. Men almost never entertained their friends at home unless they also happened to be neighbors.[11] With the exception of young unmarried men, men usually described their relationships in functional rather than affectional terms. Men's relationships with other men, in contrast to women's friendships, did not extend to ties with other household members.

Vertical and Bureaucratic Networks

Vertical networks are made up of those contacts established between members of higher or lower social and economic groups. Bureaucratic networks refer to those connections people mobilized to resolve or regulate their dealings with the state and the labor market.

11. Family members might know of the men's close friends but see them only on occasions such as weddings or funerals.

These networks are considered very valuable assets and play an important role in survival strategies. My informants devoted considerable time and energy to ensuring the continuity of established links and cultivating new ones. These networks are considered key to successfully negotiating one's way through Egyptian civic life, particularly for finding jobs or solving bureaucratic problems. They sometimes carry more weight than having the necessary credentials or legal rights, and are viewed as indispensable channels of social mobility.

During the early period of my fieldwork, when I was living with Hamid's family, a notice was delivered regarding the connection of their premises to the city water line. As Hamid could not afford to take any time off from work, his wife usually took care of dealing with official business. Since they did not know anyone who worked in the "water office," they asked their neighbors. The next afternoon, Hamid's wife and one of the neighbors went to visit the neighbor's connection, a junior clerk, who promised to help. Since they only needed to sign a form, I could not comprehend why this mobilization of networks was necessary. Umm Hani explained to me,

If I go not knowing anybody they will not deal with me and send me from one office to the next and will ask me to return day after day. But if I know someone who knows the rules and knows the people, the whole thing may not take more than a few hours. Here nobody helps you if you do not have connections.

Apparently this attitude prevailed, not just among the poor and illiterate who might have been unfamiliar with the procedures, but among the middle classes. Bureaucratic regulations were sometimes ambiguous or the officer in charge was not quite sure of the regulation. Furthermore, personal loyalty was still stronger than more obscure national loyalty. Networks could expedite bureaucratic processes, no doubt occasionally at a cost to less influential clients, but they were most often used to enforce one's legal rights.

Sadia, a white-collar worker, repeatedly expressed her gratitude to the influential man who helped her to get a job with the government. When I reminded her that following her graduation from high school she was legally entitled to such a job, she said,

To have a legal entitlement to a job is not the same as having a job. If it was not for the kind man, I would have had to wait many months or even years before I was offered a job. But he knew many people and interceded

on my behalf and told them that my family depends on the income, so they
gave me the job.

It was rare that these favors were performed for explicitly negotiated
bribes. Neither were these relationships necessarily of the classical pa-
tron-client type, since in many cases they took place between members
of equal or only slightly differentiated social strata. The principle of
nonmonetary reciprocity in these relationships was strongly observed,
and favors were returned at the earliest opportunity. Until then, they
remained a debt to be paid. In cultural terms, indebtedness is not an
acceptable state, and this attitude made the functioning of the chain
of these interactions run more smoothly. Those who failed to reciprocate could not expect further favors and their poor reputation became
an obstacle in attempts to form new networks.

Within a vertical network, the nature of the exchange is necessarily
uneven. Reciprocating for bureaucratic intervention, for example, may
take the form of personal services or gifts on occasions such as weddings or births. Sadia regularly visited the man who had helped her to
find her job nine years previously, and gave wedding presents to his
children. Umm Zaynab had frequently made her personal services available during family crises to the family who had helped her to rent her
flat. Those who had not yet had the opportunity to return favors would
publicly and frequently acknowledge their debts. In this way they spread
the word of the creditor's generosity, benefiting the latter's reputation
and social status. Through this strategy, people could retain their network despite delays in reciprocation.

Such ties could take priority over immediate economic advantages.
Hassan had been working for five years, during which time his employer
had helped his brother find a job in Saudi Arabia. He had also given
Hassan advances on his salary when his father was ill, and when he
wanted to get married. He occasionally used his influence to intercede
on Hassan's behalf in solving bureaucratic problems such as sorting out
his exemption from military service and dealing with his ration cards.
However, Hassan's wages had remained lower than the wages of his
counterparts in other workshops. Through a neighbor, he was offered
another job with an income 50 percent higher, but he refused this offer,
choosing instead to find indirect ways of persuading his employer to
increase his salary. He explained that his employer was a good man and
always helped him solve his problems, either by advancing his salary or
by mobilizing his networks. He thought it would be shortsighted if he

sacrificed such an important connection just for money. He said, "In our society people without connections get nowhere. He has offered me and my family this very needed link and I will not jeopardize it for money."

Men used their networks for securing jobs for themselves and their children, solving their bureaucratic problems, and receiving salary advances. Women's networks were much more multipurpose. They used their networks for collecting information on matters such as children's education, investments in household goods, and finding the right partner for their marriageable daughters and sometimes their sons, as well as for arbitrating family problems (Nadim el-Messiri 1977; Joseph 1983, 1987, 1993; Early 1993; Singerman 1995). Women often preferred to cultivate bureaucratic links within their neighborhoods, making the connections easier to maintain. However, maintaining links with relatives of higher social strata, even if they lived outside the neighborhood, was also considered important, and women especially cultivated relations with these families by visiting them on formal occasions and making their personal services available whenever they were required. Women's networks were viewed as the family's networks and were also more likely to be used to help close friends. Such willingness to share resulted in wider access to vertical and bureaucratic networks.

Kin Networks

The literature on Middle Eastern societies depicts strong norms of patrilocality (Stirling 1965; Tillion 1966; Abu-Lughod 1986; Altorki 1986; Joseph 1987; Early 1993; Tucker 1993b). It is assumed that Middle Eastern women break with their own families when they marry and that, in part, it is the desire to avoid a traumatic transition that encourages women to favor consanguineal marriages (Stirling 1965; Tillion 1966; Taylor 1984; Kressel 1986; Holy 1990). My field data, however, suggest that residence and kin interaction patterns were influenced by a variety of factors. I found the imposition of categories such as matrilocal and patrilocal unhelpful, obsolete, and simplistic for understanding the intricate patterns of interaction in complex and changing societies. The tendency to generalize under the influence of these terms has had a discouraging impact on the depiction of the varieties of practices observed by different cultural entities or classes within the

Middle East, particularly among Muslim communities (Rugh 1984; Cronin 1987; Joseph 1987, 1993).

Furthermore, many of these classifications stem from the dominant ideological perspective, or from examining the practices of the dominant class (Cronin 1987; Thompson 1987), which may be quite different from the practices of the majority, who may have followed, ignored, or temporarily observed residency norms (Good 1987; Thompson 1987). Moreover, residency rules do not necessarily reflect relations of authority and dominance but should be understood in the context of cultural practice and the options available to individual households. My study and other recent studies of Middle Eastern societies suggest that cultural norms and practices are often flexible and adaptable, and people continually make choices that reflect changing situations.

Though my friends and informants always explained that paternal relatives were the most significant extended family members, they frequently qualified this by explaining that in their cases, for one reason or another, their fathers' relatives were not so significant in their own lives. A few women said that the most important relatives were those who were kinder and more supportive. My observations, however, suggest that more than an arbitrary rule governs which relatives people chose to interact with most frequently. Although the rules of patriarchal kin relations were rarely contested, in practice only the better-off households adhered to them. The general pattern among the poorer households, and in cases where a man married a woman from a wealthier household than his own, was not only a more intense interaction with the woman's kin but also a strong preference to establish residence near her family if possible.

Women's relationships with their brothers were often of affection and respect but maintained a ritualized aspect, particularly after brothers married.[12] Nevertheless, women valued their relationships with their brothers and were careful not to damage them by making excessive demands. Women rarely established close ties with their brothers' wives or their husband's sisters, who were regarded as competition for his resources. This was because, culturally, a sister had a legitimate claim to her brothers' support, both financially and otherwise. The extreme value of kin networks, especially the relationship of a woman with her brothers, derived from the cultural legitimacy of a brother's support for a woman experiencing marital problems, which extended beyond

12. For further discussion about brother-sister relationships, see Joseph 1994.

anything friendship could offer. Cultural norms define the home of a brother, parents, or close relatives as a legitimate refuge for a woman in time of need, and only blood ties provide this type of protection and support.

I heard from my neighbor that Umm Sabah, a friend I often spent time with, was upset because her husband had refused to give her any housekeeping money for the last three days as punishment. So I went to visit her and later we were joined by Mona, who for the second time that month had a black mark on her face. When I asked what happened she told me that her husband, upset over the children, had slapped her face in anger the night before. It was rare for men to be physically violent toward their wives, though some men frequently threatened violence. Most marital disagreements resulted in yelling matches, usually ending with the man leaving the house and spending several hours at a neighbor's house. If a woman felt in danger, however, she would immediately open the door or windows and stand near them so the neighbors would hear her and intervene.[13] Once, at the end of a long conversation, Umm Sabah told me,

Women like Mona and me, who do not have parents or brothers or sisters or other relatives to interfere on our behalf or provide us with refuge when our husbands are being unreasonable, are *ghalbanin* [meaning here "people without kin support"]. They [the husbands] know that we have no one to turn to and no one will come to beat them up in retaliation for what they do to us. They know we would have to live with them at whatever cost since we have no money or kin. . . . Our only refuge is God.

In fact, among my sample only three wives, who had no kin support or income, were mistreated and physically abused by their husbands. Three other women who had incomes but no real kin support often complained about their husbands' lack of financial participation but were not, to my knowledge, subjected to physical violence. Despite the discrepancy of power and authority between husbands and wives, it appears that Egyptian low-income women are less often subjected to physical violence than what is reported of their counterparts in some Latin American countries (Beneria and Roldan 1987; Gonzalez de la

13. I found that women considered a husband's physical violence legitimate only if a wife had been suspected of having a flirtatious attitude toward other men. In such instances, when a woman's alleged behavior was common knowledge, the neighbors might be slow to intervene. Many women took this abuse as a sign of a husband's love and desire not to lose his wife.

Rocha 1994), thanks to the support of their male kin and the lower consumption of alcohol. Having said that physical abuse was not common, I must mention that psychological abuse was frequent, and implicit if sometimes unspoken. Men often threatened to divorce their wives and take the children away during arguments and teasing exchanges, thus reminding them of the husband's authority and keeping them in line.

My field observations suggest that the families' patterns of interaction with their kin are primarily influenced by two factors: geographic proximity and level of income. Generally, households long established in the neighborhoods tended to have relatives living in their neighborhood or within easy reach. However, as neighborhoods became more densely populated and rents inflated, it became more difficult for recently arrived households to find space for their relatives. Geographic dispersal reduced the frequency of supportive interaction between kin, though they still kept in touch and helped one another in times of crisis.

Young wives showed a strong preference for establishing residence near their mothers and sometimes forwent economic advantages to do so. This tendency was strongest among women working outside their homes, who needed their mother's help with child care. Women would mobilize their support networks to collect information about housing availability and prices, to help their close relatives move nearby. Women who lost their close contacts with family due to housing problems lamented it deeply. Umm Mona, who moved to her flat from a neighborhood in old Cairo three years previous, regretfully told me,

I have more room in this flat, but I was happier in my one room in the old place. It took me a long time to get used to this place and find new close friends. Before we moved here we lived near my sister. We often helped each other with child care and shopping, and we took each other's children to the hospital. When I had my first three children, she came and cooked and cleaned, looked after my children, and attended to the guests and my husband. She would go home before her husband returned from work. I had no worries and could rest and take it easy for the first forty days after the births. But when my last child was born she could only come for two days because her children had to go to school and there was nobody to attend to her husband. Though my neighbors were very kind and helped, I was still new and did not have very many close friends here to help me with daily chores. I had to get back on my feet and carry water and wash my children's clothes before I had fully recovered and since then I have backaches. It is a blessing for a woman to have her sisters or mother around.

Poorer families in the neighborhoods tended to have more involvement with maternal relatives, particularly with sisters and mothers. Though husbands might not participate much in these interactions, they were usually well informed about such comings and goings and often had reciprocal relations with their wives' brothers-in-law and sometimes with her brothers which included helping each other find jobs or with home repairs. I knew of a couple of occasions when they lent each other small amounts of money (under 100 pounds), though this was generally discouraged by their wives, who feared that it would lead to disagreements that might jeopardize family relations.

In contrast, the interaction of poorer families with paternal kin was minimal, even when they lived in the same neighborhood. Many male informants had not seen their brothers for many years despite the fact that they lived in Cairo. Some men reported that they occasionally met with their brothers at their workplaces or in a teahouse. Many men, independently of their wives or children, kept in touch with sisters who lived in Cairo. If a man's mother lived reasonably nearby, then he would keep in touch with her and there would be periodic visits between the mother and the son's family.

Men's lack of contact with their own relatives, particularly with brothers, stemmed at least partly from their resistance to customary financial obligations. Traditionally, men have had important financial obligations to parents, to brothers and their families, and to sisters, and were expected to help unconditionally in times of financial crisis. Such help was not necessarily considered a loan, but a duty that the receiver was expected to reciprocate if the situation was reversed and financial means allowed. In fact, according to traditions and Egyptian law, a man was financially responsible for his parents should they lack the means to support themselves, and for his brother's children should his brother die. Many men who had left the villages for the city were able to break away from the burden of these traditional obligations and attempt to establish new forms of social support where they could define the terms of mutual obligation themselves.

Women, in contrast, have no financial obligation to their natal families, particularly after they marry and leave their parents' home. Instead they benefit from interaction based on mutual support, and often can control the extent to which they have contact or gift exchanges with their own families to suit their needs and circumstances.

The pattern of kin interaction was very different among households who originally came from wealthier backgrounds. The financial support of the stem families played an important role from the inception of these households. Since hypergamy (marrying into a higher economic class) was the norm for women, the husbands' families tended to be wealthier. Five such families among the sample had provided flats for their sons on marriage,[14] and two other younger couples lived in extended households with their in-laws.

Inheritance was viewed as an important means of keeping the family together, and many people openly admitted to this. Hagg was the father of four children. His two sons were married and lived on the second and third floors of the old building he owned. One afternoon, Hagg and one of his sons went to help a poor elderly man go to the hospital, and when he returned home, we asked him about the old man's health. He told us the situation was serious and the doctors were not optimistic, and then he made the following comment: "Praise to God that I had enough wealth to be able to keep my children around me." Directing the following words to me, he continued,

This poor man has three children, and his two sons who are unemployed most of the time have not come to see him for eight months. Partly because they have no money to help him, partly because there is no incentive to bring them back. His daughter brings food or helps him a bit, but she has no money of her own and five children to care for.

On a different occasion, Umm Shadia, who owned property, told me that intelligent parents use their wealth to keep their children around them and united. She pointed out that her four daughters should inherit as much as her sons because they attended her most and gave her the most support with her housework and with running her home-based business. Though this went against the Muslim law of inheritance, her children raised no objection to it; it remains to be seen whether her wishes will be put into practice.[15]

More interaction with a husband's family did not exclude a woman's interaction with her kin but modified it. Young women demonstrated a preference for establishing independent sources of support for daily chores and child care with their own families. Those who did not have relatives living nearby mobilized their neighborly support network. However, they often had a hierarchical exchange of services with their mothers-in-law. For instance, they felt obliged to reciprocate for gifts

14. Successful migration of the parents had provided them with the necessary resources.

15. According to Islamic law, daughters inherit only half as much as sons.

or child support they received from their mothers-in-law by helping them with the shopping or the housework.

Family networking among the wealthier households was generally in terms of helping each other with bureaucratic tasks, acquiring more expensive subsidized items, or migration by providing information or financial support. These groups of families often had members in various government offices who, though in junior clerical posts, nonetheless could intercede on a family member's behalf when the need arose.

Households that had started out very poor and had gradually improved their economic lot had not changed their pattern of interaction. Abu Ahmad had been poor for many years, and finally he migrated and saved enough money to buy a small piece of land and build his own house. He had not seen his brother for many years. After ten years, when his brother's children came to see him on the occasion of the new year, he was not very hospitable. When his wife mildly criticized him for his behavior, he said to her,

You may have forgotten, but when we were very poor and many nights our children did not have even enough bread to eat, they never came to see us. My brother never sent his children to see their uncle then. Now I do not need him. He needs me because tomorrow his daughter will be getting married, his son needs capital, and so on. I know him well. I have enough for my own children, not for his children.

On a different occasion Abu Azza was very angry when I arrived. I asked what was wrong, and he blurted out,

My brother from the village came to visit us and has brought as a gift some bread and very little cheese despite the fact he is a rich man. He never offered to help me when I was unemployed for almost a year. But now that his children have been accepted at the university in Cairo he wants to come and use my home as his base and my wife as his cook. But even now he cannot be generous enough to bring a proper gift after years of absence.

Later Abu Azza sent a message to his brother implying that he was not welcome in his home.

Although the kin interaction among my sample was frequent enough for me to distinguish the two major patterns I have described here, it is important to remember that the differences should be viewed more on a continuum rather than as two clear-cut categories. Personal characteristics and the circumstances of individual households were other important factors that modified these interactions. People did not interact with one another only because they were brothers and sisters or only because there were certain ascribed cultural rules that had to be followed. Many chose to interact with certain of their siblings and relatives as opposed to others. Yet others continued to interact with certain relatives despite the fact that they did not get along well. Moreover, the focus of this research, though broadly defined, was less on psychic (emotional) and more on actual and potential material support. In reality, moral support and compassion are also important factors in determining people's interaction with kin or others.

Summary

The key to both survival and the improvement of living conditions for lower-income groups in Cairo lay in their innovative and effective use of social as well as material resources. They have preserved and adapted reciprocal exchange systems to increase their level of security against an unstable labor market and unpredictable crises. As a rule, households networked on several levels. These networks were formed and disbanded according to economic and social factors including standards of living, values, and geographic proximity. The neighborhoods have also preserved and adapted some of the traditional informal associations, such as saving clubs (gamᶜiyat) and wedding or childbirth funds. The gamᶜiyat are rotating credit associations that function on the basis of mutual trust, and they were the single most important channel for raising money, saving, and helping members of the network without much cost or risk to individuals. These revitalized local practices may provide a basis for culturally and socially appropriate development policies.

Economic and social conditions in urban Cairo have encouraged a new pattern of interaction for many lower-income families. In contrast to accepted ideology and Islamic tenets that attribute a special value to paternal kin relations, most households interact more intensely with women's kin networks. This pattern, which has developed in response to the high costs of men's traditional economic obligations to their stem families, has afforded women more protection vis-à-vis their husbands. Women's networks were multipurpose and extended to all members of the households. In contrast, male networks were personal and primarily concerned with employment. Women were very conscious of their importance in cultivating social networks, and this increased their confidence and their status at home. In particular, women who had reputations as good gamʿiya organizers enjoyed special status in the neighborhoods and their friendship was sought after.

CHAPTER 9

Fertility and Sexual Politics

In 1983 when I first embarked on this research project, I did not intend to examine fertility and sexuality. When I was asked to comment on these issues, I would first reiterate that I was interested in the household as an economic unit and not as a biological one. Only then would I reply based on my observations in the neighborhoods. Later, however, as Egyptian and international organizations working in the field of child health began to examine the implications of daily practices and women's views on their reproductive behavior and on children's health, I was encouraged to devote part of my work to this area, as a separate project (see Hoodfar 1984, 1986, 1995a). This separate project and several women's discussions on the role of children and sexual relations in their lives made me more aware of the intricacy and importance of sexuality and fertility for the household's, especially women's, economic as well as emotional well-being.

There were other reasons behind my hesitation to touch on the subject of sexuality and fertility in the neighborhoods. At the time, the question of female circumcision (infibulation), which is practiced in Egypt, had once again become a hotly debated issue among Western European and North American feminists, some of whom at times treated the subject as their front line against patriarchy. Through an international student network, I had become very aware of the North African feminists' and nationalists' bitter criticism of these Western "activists." They believed that Western feminists, even when their concern was genuine, were playing a role in perpetuating racism and anti-

Arab sentiment through ignorance of the complexity of the issues surrounding female circumcision.[1] Their unwise intervention under the banner "sisterhood is global" stemmed from their self-righteous and neocolonial attitude that prevented them from either seeing the agency of women or contextualizing the matter and searching for culturally appropriate means of improving the situation for the women in question.[2] These Western feminists' interventions created such apprehension and division around female circumcision that, in practice, local initiatives and culturally appropriate channels for addressing the issue were blocked.[3] I recall that a Sudanese friend visiting Manchester University told me with a great deal of sadness that this unwise intervention had led to female circumcision being viewed as an act of nationalism and that anyone, particularly secular people, who dared to criticize it was construed as an agent of Western imperialism. She and many others were convinced that the "outsiders" on this front had done more harm than good. Being so keenly aware of the sensitivity of these issues, I, though Muslim and Iranian, was an outsider and made a conscious effort to leave the subject alone.

However, once I became enmeshed in the daily life of my research community, I realized that the division between the domains of biology and economics is an artificial one, and that to overlook the significance of reproductive and cultural factors regarding sexuality in light of their impact on women's economic reality would be to overlook the ways in which sexuality and fertility play a role in daily survival strategies. Thus I briefly explore here the role that fertility and sexuality plays in domestic politics and in the survival strategies of individuals and their households.[4] I hope this work can be a vehicle for the voices of the women

1. See AAWORD 1983; Toubia 1985, 1988; Davis 1989. For a critical reflection on the subject, see Gunning 1991; for more recent responses to genital mutilation, see Toubia 1993, 1995.

2. For debates on the issue of "Western" and Third World feminists, see Mohanty et al. 1991; Lazreg 1994.

3. For instance, at least for the Muslim population, female infibulation could be presented as anti-Islamic as it has not been part of Islamic practices and it is not practiced in the Arab peninsula, and certainly neither the wives of the prophet nor his daughter were circumcised. See also the statement in AAWORD 1983 and Toubia 1995.

4. This is not meant to cover the entire debate on the issue of female infibulation, which today has evolved into a vast area of inquiry (Toubia 1985, 1993, 1995; Gunning 1991; Gordon 1992). Rather, it is an attempt to document some of my own observations and understanding of the subject of fertility primarily from women's point of view. I address the issue of female circumcision only to the extent that the women saw it as relevant to their fertility and sexual lives.

in the neighborhoods, and perhaps contribute to the understanding of the complexity of issues of fertility, of female circumcision as a social institution as well as a health issue, and of family planning.

Fertility

The desire to have children is considered the most important reason for the interdependence of men and women. In fact, a marriage is considered secure only after several children have been born within it. Procreation is particularly important to women, who see themselves as the primary agents of reproduction and fear "barrenness"; most women hope to conceive very early in marriage (Inhorn 1996). Many women boasted that they conceived on their wedding night, demonstrating their excellent health and also taking credit for proving their husbands' manhood and health to the community. Some of the more educated newly married women or brides-to-be said that ideally couples should wait one or two years before having their first child; however, none wanted to use contraceptives for fear of jeopardizing her fertility. Some of the younger women in my sample said they became anxious when they had not become pregnant by the third month of their marriage, and sought the advice of either a physician or a traditional *daya* (midwife). Apart from the fear of barrenness, young brides were also under enormous pressure from neighbors and relatives who were constantly speculating about the ability of both wife and husband to conceive.[5]

The women valued their fertility and drew privileges from it in many different ways. They believed a clever woman was one who made her husband appreciate this ability of hers, particularly during pregnancy when he should demonstrate his appreciation by taking special care of her. Husbands are under enormous social pressure to fulfill the desires of their pregnant wives. They are expected to be kind and loving, to never use physical force against their wives, and to prevent situations that may upset them. Women, particularly those who did not aspire to be afrangi, recognize their fertility as potentially empowering and as

5. When a woman does not conceive, it is automatically assumed that the fault is hers, and only after she has gone through all kinds of medical examinations does the husband agree to see a doctor.

a way to gain certain advantages as well as fulfill their own desire for children.

Women often talked and joked about how the first two or three pregnancies gave them a golden chance to eat well and demand attention from others, particularly their husbands. Umm Shadia, a knowledgeable elderly woman, explained to me,

Fertility is one function that God has granted women only. Men may learn to cook, to wash, and so on, but they can never give birth to a child or care for him or her. For this, men must always rely on their women. Therefore, it is justifiable for women to use this unique opportunity to gain some advantages for themselves.

Once the first child is born and the fertility of both husband and wife has been proven, women—particularly those who are more educated and work outside their neighborhoods—may consider the use of contraception. Although legally children are their father's responsibility and it is he who has custody and guardianship over them, traditionally women have controlled reproduction; they have been the primary perpetuators of the knowledge, beliefs, and practices relating to matters of fertility, and this has been generally accepted by men.[6] Since most modern contraceptive devices are directed at women, they continue to assume primary responsibility in this regard. Men may, however, express their preference for more or fewer children to their wives but generally do not participate in such decisions.[7] Increasingly, however, legal issues connected with modern medicine and the regulation of its accessibility are extending men's control into this sphere, as most physicians and pharmacists are men. Moreover, regulations such as the requirement of a husband's consent to obtain an abortion, and in the past for the use of some contraceptive devices such as the IUD, are other channels extending male control in this domain.

Men's legal authority concerning women's fertility stood in sharp contrast to the traditional ideology in the neighborhood and at times made couples' lives complicated. While discussing family planning matters with a couple I knew well, they told me the story of their fifth child,

6. Although Islam has sanctioned the use of contraceptives, the most widely reported practice in most parts of the Middle East has been withdrawal (coitus interruptus), which makes men the responsible party in the prevention of conception, the major religious limitation being the permission of the wife (Musallam 1983; Omran 1992).

7. Of course, exercising this traditional control must be qualified. Should he be unhappy with her decision, he has the option of finding a second wife or even divorcing her.

which aptly illustrates how problems can arise. The couple did not want any more children, and when they learned that the wife had conceived, they both agreed that she should terminate the pregnancy. She arranged to have an abortion, which was justified given the state of her health and the size of their family. On the day of the appointment, the couple went together to the hospital. When an official there asked the husband to sign the documents giving his consent, he assumed that in so doing he would be admitting to forcing his wife to have an abortion. He insisted that the abortion was his wife's idea, but when he could not persuade the official to proceed without his signature he angrily left the hospital. He simply could not understand, even four years later as he was telling me about it, what role he could possibly play in this matter beyond accompanying his wife and lending his support. His wife returned home disappointed and tried several traditional abortion methods that caused her to bleed for several months but failed to end the pregnancy. Her youngest son was born.

Many women who did not want to use contraceptives but who were facing pressure from medical practitioners or neighbors to practice family planning used the legitimacy of a husband's authority, claiming that their husbands objected and that to act without a husband's permission would jeopardize their marriage. When Umm Sabah, who already had five children, the oldest of which was only ten, became pregnant, neighbors and friends were blatantly unpleasant. They accused her of being shortsighted and not thinking of her children's future, particularly since she was informed about contraception.[8] The objection, of course, was actually because the family was very poor, living in a single room without kitchen space and sharing toilet facilities with several other households. Umm Sabah blamed her husband who she said objected to her using contraceptives. Most of the neighbor women remained unconvinced, on the grounds that her husband could not have really stopped her from taking the pill. Still, her public statement remained a legitimate one and some of the blame was directed at her husband. In fact, the husband was not happy about the prospect of yet another child, but Umm Sabah told me he was an irresponsible lazy man and only God knew what would happen to her in her old age,[9] for a husband

8. On several occasions she had helped several of her neighbors by taking them to family planning clinics.

9. The accusation of laziness and irresponsibility was fueled by his failure to try to find a permanent second job.

who does not work hard in his youth would not be better in his old age. Her solution was to have at least three sons to make sure that when she was old she would not be left in the street like her aunt had been—a widow with two married daughters who could not look after her.

Given that women tended to be younger than their husbands, widowhood was the destiny of most, the majority of whom had little or no material resources. The desire to secure their old age played a very important role in the way women viewed their fertility. Although ideologically the preference for a small family is gaining great popularity, the poorest members of the neighborhood tended to have the largest families, usually a result of trying for more sons. As Umm Samir, the mother of three sons and one daughter explained to me, it was not that sons were better; in fact most women felt that daughters were easier to raise.

But a family needs protection and daughters cannot give protection. They may give love and care, but that is all. As you know Abu Samir earns very little and he is often not well enough to resume his work. My sons give us money, pay our rent, buy us medicine. Moreover, the sons protect their sisters should their husbands be unkind to them.

For many women, their children, particularly their sons, were their most valuable resource. Some women were very clear that if they had an old-age pension they too would opt for smaller families.

Contrary to my expectation, I found that although men wanted to have at least one son, it was primarily women who were preoccupied with producing sons. Younger women usually presented their preference for sons as fulfillment of their marriage obligations to their husbands. Many women said that not having male children is disastrous since every husband wants to have sons who will carry on his name. Hence, in the eyes of the community, a marriage that had not produced a son was incomplete because the need of the husband had not yet been fulfilled.

Most men said they would prefer to have both girls and boys but would like to have at least one son. Significantly, they rarely failed to add that whatever God blessed them with would please them. In fact, I heard some fathers declare that "daughters are more caring and faithful to their parents than sons." Other fathers told me that if they were rich and could marry their children well, they would prefer to have many daughters, but poor men were better off with sons, who tended to be able to look after themselves and, God willing, look after their parents too. An increasing appreciation of daughters, partly a reflection of changing attitudes in the society at large, was also engendered by stronger bonds between daughters and their parents as women marry later and spend many more years in their father's house than in the past.

Older women, however, were more outspoken about their preference for sons. They referred to their fear of widowhood and to actual cases in which women would have been left in the streets had it not been for their sons. For this reason, although many women in my sample said three children with a combination of boys and a girl was ideal, many of them continued to have more children. Some women said that if they had only girls, social pressures forced them to continue to have more children until they had one or two sons. However, my observation indicated that much of the pressure came from the other women rather than from their husbands. These pressures might take the form of advice from friends, especially older friends and relatives, or the actions of foes who would use any opportunity to publicly denigrate women who did not have sons.

Once, Umm Nadia and Umm Ahmad got into a yelling match, with other women trying to calm them down. Umm Ahmad shouted from her balcony that if Umm Nadia was a good woman, God would have blessed her with sons, as she herself had been. Later I joined Umm Nadia and found her crying and extremely upset. She told me,

I wanted to have only two children. And my husband and I are very happy with our two daughters, hamdullah. My husband is working for the government [meaning they have an old-age pension]. We do not need sons to feed us. I have resisted getting pregnant for six years, but I can no longer put up with the public abuse because I have no sons. We wanted to have fewer children and have them educated to become muwazzafat [government employees] and then marry and be independent, but people do not let us live our lives.

Umm Nadia now has four children, three daughters and one son.

Another woman in the neighborhood who had eight daughters said,

My husband has resigned himself to the fact that God is not giving us a son. Many times I started to use contraceptives, but other women, both friends and enemies, put so much pressure on me that I stopped using contraceptives on my own accord. And yet each time I had another girl.

Given the realities of women's lives, they are active players in perpetuating the preference for sons.[10] However, this preference should not be understood as a lack of love and affection for daughters. There

10. The reality that most women would have children of both sexes makes them less sensitive to the plight of women who do not have sons.

was strong conviction among all women that it was their daughters who would give them lifelong support. Several women said, "There is no woman lonelier than the one without a daughter." A woman considered lucky would bear a female child first who could then help with housework and child-rearing. Both fathers and mothers were convinced that bringing up daughters was much easier than raising boys, who want to run in the street "as soon as they can crawl" and cause problems with neighbors. But parents felt that they remained continuously responsible and concerned for their daughters, even after they marry and have children of their own. If a daughter's marriage is problematic or dissolves, responsibility for her reverts to her parents. One father who was particularly fond of his two daughters told me, "Girls are little angels who are, in our society, treated like slaves." What was evident, regardless of how people felt about their daughters, was that girls were considered to have more affectionate relationships with their parents.

Young women, especially those who did not have harmonious marriages, constantly worried about the prospect of being deserted or divorced in favor of another woman. Most women were realistic in assessing their husbands' inability to support two families, even if men wanted and intended to fulfill their legal and religious obligations to the first family. Women then regarded having several children as the best guarantor of a secure marriage by tying men to their homes, if not to their wives. Umm Batta was considered a hardworking and pleasant woman and was loved by the neighbors. A few months after I moved into the neighborhood, it became known that her husband had married a second wife and started a new family. Gradually he stopped coming home to Umm Batta and rarely paid the daily expenses. She had to start selling vegetables in the local market and also began a home-based business, preparing food for sale. But her income remained meager and she was continuously worried about the future of her two daughters.

The circle of neighbors always blamed her for not being astute in producing a family fast enough to keep her husband busy and forcing him to work hard. Sahar, a young neighbor who had given birth to four children in five years of marriage, told me in reference to Umm Batta,

She wanted to be afrangi and have only two children. So her husband started to chase other women, many of whom will marry any man even if they already have three other wives. His new wife—whom I have not met— must be clever since she already has three children [she has had at least one more since then] and has managed to stop him from even coming to say hello to his daughters here. [This was an exaggeration. He did, though infrequently, visit his daughters.]

Talking to me while we were cleaning broad beans for her food business, Umm Batta indicated that she was still bitter about her sad married life.

I do not know who to believe. Maybe it was my fault. Maybe if I had six children he wouldn't leave us. But who knows, maybe he would go anyway. Maybe this is my *nasib* [destiny].

Mona, hearing her comment, said,

But if you had six children, at least your sons would grow up and look after you in your old age. Who has heard of a mother who has six children being left in the street?

In contrast to Umm Batta, Halah's story was considered a success. She often took pride in explaining how she salvaged her marriage and her children's lives. Halah's marriage was not a happy one. She had married a "modern" and "educated" (with a high school diploma) man, as she put it, despite the wishes of her uncle, who was her guardian after her parents' death. She had to live with her husband's mother, he did not give her any housekeeping money for the first four years of their marriage, and he did not want any children. Nonetheless, she became pregnant and gave birth to her first son, making a promise to her husband that she would not get pregnant again. Having heard from a neighbor that if she took pills she would not get pregnant, she began to take an aspirin tablet every night. However, within a year and half she was pregnant again, in retrospect recognizing this occurred right after she stopped breastfeeding her first son. Her husband threatened to divorce her if she went ahead with the pregnancy, and without taking notice of her tears, he took her to a doctor to arrange for an abortion. It was only then that she realized she should have taken contraceptive pills and not aspirin (her second son is still occasionally referred to as "the son of aspirin" by family friends).[11] Halah, by evoking her mother-in-law's religious sentiment and by involving the rest of her husband's siblings, managed to convince him to keep the second child. Again, she made him a promise: if she became pregnant a third time, she would have an abortion. A couple of years later, Halah was pregnant again and could not convince her husband to keep the child. She had an abortion. Seven years later, she found out that her husband had married a widow

---

11. There were a few such cases in the neighborhood when women had become pregnant while taking aspirin for birth control. Since I began this research, access to information on contraception has gradually improved, especially through television advertisements.

in the adjacent neighborhood. For a few months, the two women frequently had public yelling matches, usually outside the new wife's door, each wife demanding that the husband divorce the other. During this time Halah managed to become pregnant again, deliberately plotting it, as she put it, and to her good fortune, she gave birth to twins. The second wife, hearing of the news, also became pregnant despite an apparent agreement with the husband that they would not have any children. The two wives continued to have periodic public clashes, and the husband kept threatening to divorce the two of them and marry a third woman.

In 1992, when I visited Halah and her neighbors and was catching up with the events that had occurred during my absence, particularly concerning Halah's marriage, I found out that in contrast to Umm Batta's situation, the women lauded Halah for being clever and acting fast. They were confident that when it came down to a decision, it was Halah's co-wife who would be abandoned by the husband.[12] That was because she has more children by him and the economic, social, and emotional cost of divorcing Halah would be greater.

In the context of limited employment and other financial opportunities, women view their fertility as the ultimate tool for securing their marriages and dealing with economic uncertainty. Given that population control and family planning have emerged as a priority for the Egyptian government, the success of family planning in Egypt among urban low-income groups not only depends on the dissemination of information and the provision of services, as important as these are, but also on improving women's status within marriage and providing them with educational and economic opportunities so they can have some degree of economic security.

Sexuality and Sexual Desire in Everyday Life

Having discussed fertility in the context of households and women's survival strategies, I wish to avoid leaving the impression that men and women treated their fertility and sexual desire mainly as

---

12. The women's assumption was statistically borne out. Egypt's national statistics on divorce indicate that the higher the number of children, the less likely the prospect of divorce (see UN 1992: 884).

tools of their economic well-being. Men and women viewed sexual desire as a God-given pleasure and believed its healthy expression would lead to a happy family life. Fertility and sexual desire are viewed as an important basis for men's and women's interdependence.

Umm Samir was an elderly woman who had taken special interest in my "exams" and wanted me to do well and to make my stay in Egypt worthwhile. Once while discussing sexual needs, she explained to me her philosophical approach to life.

It is this constant sexual desire that underlies the construction of human society and civilization. If we, like most other creatures, just needed food, then males and females would go about finding their food in forests and once every few years would copulate just like elephants. But besides food we have sexual needs, and God has sent us instruction on how best we enjoy and fulfill this aspect of our need, and we are blessed with children who are the fruit of our pleasures.

Sex and sexual needs were discussed openly in women's gatherings and were the most frequent topics of jokes and teasing. Young girls were often present during these exchanges, but quickly learned that though they might listen they could not comment or show appreciation for the jokes. Nevertheless, as an unmarried woman and despite my age, I frequently found myself in circles of giggling girls where it was made clear to me that not only did they follow the jokes very closely, but, in fact, the joking of the adult women was the most important source of their sexual knowledge.

Generally, sexual needs were recognized as natural for all men and women, but a great deal of effort was invested by parents to direct these needs toward marriage as the only socially acceptable channel for sexual fulfillment. Having sexual desires and being sexually desired by one's husband was considered a healthy state for a woman. I was told frequently by young married women that making love is the best form of communication between young couples; that it brings men and women romantically closer and solves many family problems. In fact, neighbors' sex lives were so much a part of casual conversation that they were the yardstick by which the stability of a young woman's marriage was measured. Young women spent considerable effort in the early years of their marriage to demonstrate that their husbands were indeed interested in them. When a young woman wanted to belittle another woman, she would spread gossip that so-and-so's husband was not interested in his wife and that the couple always slept separately. Young women who suspected that this type of gossip was circulating about them would frequently wash their hair in the morning and appear on the balcony and in the window with a towel on their head for people to see. On a few occasions, I heard young married women in the neighborhoods who had a falling-out accuse each other of falsely washing their hair to disguise their husband's lack of interest. At first the significance of this was not apparent to me. I later realized that since Muslims are supposed to have a complete rinse from head to toe after making love, the towel and the wet hair in the morning indicated to the public that the husband and wife are on good terms and have a healthy sex life.[13] Hence neighboring women accused each other of exaggerating the extent of their husbands' love.

Among their intimate friends, women discussed many of their sexual problems, including a husband's lack of interest or excessive interest, pain during intercourse, and a woman's own loss of sexual appetite; advice was sought from other women, particularly from the more experienced. One day when I went to see Umm Shadia all the neighbors were drinking tea, teasing Umm Hassan and giving her advice. I had heard before that her husband made excessive sexual demands. She, her husband, and their three children shared a small flat with another family of four. She found it embarrassing when her husband made sexual demands even in the afternoons when their children and neighbors would be coming and going. Some women concluded that it was better to have too much than too little attention from the husband. Others said that at least she knew that her husband loved her. One of her friends annoyed her, saying that she was not shrewd enough because if her husband was only half as interested in her, by now she would have made a beautiful home for herself and her children. Many women believed that a clever wife can manipulate a husband who enjoys sex to work harder and to provide a better material life for his wife and children. Other women advised her that she should see this as a source of power over her husband and not a problem. Yet others reminded her that she should not deprive him since there were other women who would gladly take her place.

Older and more traditional women, particularly if they were nearing

13. In fact, this was an added reason some of the working wives took the veil. Muhaggabat did not worry about setting their hair frequently or not washing it every day, which could cause neighbors and colleagues to wonder about a woman's relationship with her husband or her religiosity and moral commitment.

or close to menopause, had few qualms about publicly airing their views on the sexual needs of women, even in the presence of men. On one occasion, when I was returning home to the neighborhood, I boarded a taxi that was already carrying several passengers, one of whom was an elderly woman I saw frequently in the neighborhood. We overheard the driver and a male passenger seated in the front claim that women have lost their morals, remarrying right after divorce or widowhood and neglecting their children to attend to their new husbands. The old woman became very angry at this and interrupted their conversation.

Why shouldn't women marry? Don't young women have desires? Why should women deny themselves what God has made halal [permissible]? Why won't fathers to whom the children belong take care of their children? If the men were not so mean and would pay for their women and not divorce them, society wouldn't have all these problems with children running around unsupervised in the streets.

The men became very apologetic at this unexpected intervention and admitted that perhaps they had not looked at the problem from the women's point of view. They agreed that certainly all Muslims should enjoy the pleasure of marriage (see chapter 2, footnote 2).

Women were aware that Islam gave them the right to be sexually satisfied and that dissatisfaction in this regard is reasonable grounds for divorce with or without the husband's consent.[14] However, they also said that no woman would invoke this right if she already had children. They were equally aware that according to Islam, they should never deny their husbands' sexual demands without a good reason. Women who were not sexually satisfied presented their case in terms of their husbands' neglecting their Islamic duty, a sin that God would not forgive,[15] and discussed how to solve the problem of a sexually neglectful husband without the woman being obliged to initiate intercourse directly. Although a woman's sexual needs are acknowledged, it is considered a blow to her pride to indicate her interest directly, which would undermine her bargaining power vis-à-vis her husband. Therefore

14. This is an important reason young married men rarely migrate until they have two or three children, at which stage the economic needs of the family take precedence over the couple's sexual needs.

15. Women quoted a variation on theological views of desire and sexuality. In Islam, sexual desire is good since it is a taste of what heaven will bring believers. Although sexual pleasure is fleeting, the enjoyment of heaven is constant; thus believers should not deprive themselves of sexual pleasure because it encourages them to remember heaven (see Murata 1992: chaps. 5, 6).

women were advised to clean themselves and remove all their body hair,[16] to wear perfume and a nice nightgown, to be gentle and pleasant to their husbands, and to sleep close to them. If these measures were fruitless, women could resort to feeding a neglectful husband special foods or herbs that were supposed to energize men. One day, a frustrated friend asked me if I could talk to my educated friends at American University and get some good medicine that she could feed her husband without his knowledge. Seeing my surprise at her request, she said she was sure that doctors have medicine for sexually weak men and I just needed to ask them. Sometimes older women, if they were close to the couple, could take the initiative and hint indirectly to the husband that he was neglecting his wife's needs.

Men and women are thought to mature differently in regard to their sexual needs. As women grow older and their children reach puberty, they are expected to gradually withdraw from sex, particularly if their daughters are married and have begun having children of their own. It is considered shameful for women to give birth after their children are grown up, and certainly after they are married. These customs, enmeshed in cultural institutions and moral values, play a part in the reduction of fertility, although they are rarely framed this way (Patel 1994). Women who happen to get pregnant at this stage in their lives do their utmost to induce an abortion, usually by using traditional means. Nonetheless, not every woman manages to withdraw from sex; either her husband objects, or she would like to have more children, or her sexual appetite has not diminished. In any case, societal norms dictate that women cease to demonstrate an interest in sex after a certain point in their life cycles, even if they enjoy sex. Women who have reached menopause or have managed to convince their husbands to withdraw from sexual activity enjoy high prestige among other women and are frequently consulted on marital issues. Most women who were considered community leaders or who managed saving clubs were among this group, as is the case in many other cultures, particularly in Africa. The higher profile of these women was due, in part, to the proximity of daughters and daughters-in-law, who helped with the older women's domestic tasks and freed them to devote more time to socializing, community service, and networking.

The customary sexual norm for men, however, was very different. It was assumed that a healthy man would remain sexually active all his

---

16. Traditionally young married Egyptian women keep their bodies free of hair.

life. Men were expected to demonstrate great resistance to the with-drawal of their wives from sexual activity and threaten to remarry if the wife remained steadfast in her decision. Husbands declared that not having sex when their bodies desired it would cause severe pain and illness, and sometimes took this complaint to older women who were close to their family. Wives, in turn, would quickly publicize their hus-bands' resistance; older women would sometimes discuss the issue with their children, something men never did. However, in most cases, such resistance appeared to be more a matter of image management than of actual strife on the husband's part. Healthy men are expected to have sexual needs, and their masculinity and self-respect depend on this. Therefore, the husband's resistance to decreased sexual activity was often meant to confirm his masculinity more than anything else. The wife, in publicizing his complaints, would not only confirm his love and desire for her but also indicate that her decision to withdraw from sexual activity was based on her support of convention and the security of her marriage. Furthermore, by making her husband's objections known, she would confirm his virility and masculinity. Custom expects men to remain bitter about this issue.

This image management factor in terms of conjugal relations along with the unquestioned role of men as heads of household were impor-tant for maintaining respect as a family in the neighborhood. For in-stance, women were expected to be deferential to their husbands and treat them as the ultimate decision makers, something many women insisted on, notwithstanding my observations that in most cases indi-cated otherwise. For example, toward the end of my second year there, noticing the large gap between what women said about their husband's power at home and what actually took place in most homes, I decided to discuss the issues more systematically with the women, particularly with women who had been married for more than ten years. I was talk-ing to Umm Rose at a gathering of friends, and she was saying that a wife should always ask her husband for permission to go out, in accor-dance with the Qur'an. I asked her whether she would go out if her husband denied permission. Surprised, she answered, "He won't say no. Didn't I ask him?" The assumption was that a wife is supposed to ask and the husband is supposed to agree. Husbands, particularly those who were more traditional and less educated, were well aware of the unspoken rules and rarely objected to their wives' wishes. Hence there was little ground for women to question the wisdom of these inequi-table customs and rules. However, the growing number of wives whose husbands had decided to exercise the power nominally ascribed to them were left without much recourse and sometimes without much sympathy.

In another gathering I asked why women should respect their husbands so much. While everybody was trying to explain, Umm Shadia called for her companions to be quiet and said,

Because God has made men work very hard. They have to work in unpleasant jobs, leave home early and come home late. Their employer is not pleasant to them and if they don't find jobs to bring money home, their wives and children look down on them. It is true that women work too, but we work among our friends next to our children and have much more comfort than men.

Then with a twinkle in her eye, she looked at the younger women and added, "Even at night they cannot rest. If women are tired they can lay down and enjoy it, but our men have to work hard at it." At this point, the women laughingly told me that I should write for my professors at American University and in England that in Islam everything has its logic.

Enhancing Children's Sexuality: Why Circumcision?

Preoccupation with sexuality played a significant role in the everyday life of individuals: single people in search of partners; husbands and wives who wish to enrich their relationship with one another; and parents who have to ensure a healthy and secure life for their children. Although femininity and masculinity are viewed as natural phenomena in men and women, nonetheless it is assumed that children's sexuality can be enhanced through appropriate social and cultural practices. Thus an important responsibility of parents is to ensure that their children are socialized into proper gender roles and appropriate sexual desires. In this context, circumcision is viewed as a crucial channel through which the sexuality of boys and girls is enhanced, which in turn is a step toward ensuring a successful marriage and family life for them. Circumcision, or *tahur* (literally, an act of purification), is just such a vehicle. In fact, some parents were convinced that circumcision was the single most important factor in producing sexually healthy children, particularly daughters. It was considered the most important event in the lives of boys and girls between birth and marriage.

All boys in the neighborhood were circumcised by the time they reached the age of seven or eight. Men and women were aware that male tahur was not a universal practice despite its wide use in the Middle East. However, all Muslims were conscious that Islam requires boys to be circumcised to confirm their membership in the male Muslim community. Several fathers pointed out that overlooking this important *wagib* (duty) is considered a great sin. A few mentioned that even Americans have realized the health benefits of circumcision and many have their sons circumcised. In contrast to the discussions of female circumcision, however, there were no direct references to a connection between circumcision and fertility or masculinity; rather the stress was put on health issues and Islamic requirement.

Many people described the elaborate ceremonies and feasts traditionally held for boys' circumcisions, particularly eldest sons', which took place when boys were about eight or nine. Today, however, the situation is very different, and few people in Cairo throw such parties. In fact, among the families I lived with, boys whose birth was attended by a doctor (at the hospital or at home) were circumcised at birth; others underwent the operation within the first few years of life with a minimum of ceremony.[17] Several families with sons around the same age arranged to take the boys to a hospital, or sometimes to a *hakim* (a traditionally trained health practitioner). The boys were kept in bed, or at least indoors for a few days, and they would be given sweets and sometimes a new toy. A favorite meat dish, usually chicken, was prepared for them. Neighbors would visit and congratulate the family; one or two close friends might bring candy or pastries. People refrained from mentioning the boys' pain and discomfort. Fathers were actively involved in decisions regarding their sons' circumcision, particularly for boys older than two. On the whole, relative to girls' circumcision, the boys' circumcisions were nonevents.

All girl children in the neighborhoods were circumcised, usually between the ages of eight and twelve, to ensure femininity and fertility and as part of their preparation for marriage and motherhood. Al-

---

17. During the two and a half years I spent in the field, there were none of the elaborate parties I had been told about. Some of the women explained that if they had more money, they would have given the boys a party; they believed that the rich still held lavish circumcision parties and feasts.

though female circumcision has been prohibited and the Egyptian government launched a campaign against it in the sixties, all the women I
met in the neighborhoods, regardless of regional, educational, and family backgrounds, were circumcised (or at least claimed to be), and none
objected to or suggested not doing the same with their daughters.[18]
Most women were aware of the law, but they either did not take the
ban seriously or considered that such matters were none of the government's business. Nonetheless, it was commonly known that in many
cultures, especially in Western societies, women are not circumcised. To
justify female circumcision, women initially explained it to me as an
Islamic practice. When I reminded them that people in Iran or Saudi
Arabia and many other Muslim countries do not practice it, they then
suggested it was part of Egyptian culture. Occasionally, in support of
this view, the women added that Christian Copts also share this Egyptian tradition. It was common knowledge that there are different degrees of circumcision (infibulation) and that a more severe type, which
they did not approve of and referred to as Pharaonic, was practiced
among the Sudanese. As in the case of males, circumcision was considered purification, and the process involved removing all or part of the
clitoris to make women feminine and sexually more receptive to men
as well as to improve fertility.[19]

In discussing why women need to be circumcised, I was struck by
the way it was described to me: "It makes a woman clean, soft, and
feminine. It makes a woman desire a man and be receptive to his seed,
and it increases her chances of getting pregnant." Women frequently
stated that the clitoris, were it not removed, would continue to grow
and become like a penis, making women cold to men. Apparently, it
was for this reason that circumcision of women was often delayed until
the girls were older, for the clitoris might grow again and women would
have to undergo a second operation. In support of their belief, my female informants explained that upper-class women (who are not circumcised due to the influence of the West) often marry very late and

18. More educated women said that in the old days, when hygiene was poor, many
women had complications but added that nowadays few women face these problems
because of improved cleanliness during the procedure. They pointed out that if young
girls do experience infection after the operation, they are easily treated with injections of
penicillin or other antibiotics.

19. Although I received an invitation to accompany two girls who were to be circumcised to the home of the hakima, I refused on the grounds that it was un-Islamic and that
I could not bear to see the little girls suffer so much pain. The neighborhood women
thought that I was too sensitive.

frequently have unhappy marriages, sometimes resulting in divorce. They suggested that this was because uncircumcised women are too cold sexually and are not receptive to their husbands' sexual demands. Some women used my own case to prove their point. They remarked that at the age of twenty-seven my spinsterhood was attributable to the fact that my parents had chosen not to have me circumcised, and I had thus grown cold to men.[20]

As the only uncircumcised woman, I was often the subject of jokes and teasing. Frequently friends jokingly suggested that they organize a circumcision for me before my return to England so as to ensure my eventual marriage and pregnancy. In fact, I was taken by surprise when close to my departure from Cairo in 1986, one of the older neighborhood women who had become fond of me and treated me like her daughter took me aside. She suggested, seriously, that maybe I should consider having a circumcision if I was interested in family life, which she thought I must be since my research and studies dealt primarily with women, family life, and children. She said that, of course, if my own mother had been there she would have discussed it with her since no woman should organize her own circumcision. I politely refused, saying that no women in my family, or in our Iranian tradition, were circumcised and that all modern medical sciences (in which they had a great deal of trust) indicated that circumcision was bad for a woman's health and had a negative impact on reproductive health. She looked at me in disbelief and said that the doctors must have looked at the Sudanese type of circumcision, not at the Egyptian. She then asked me why Egypt has the largest population if circumcision is bad, and why it is that throughout the Arab world men want to marry Egyptian women.[21] My explanation that the cost of marriage was lower in Egypt

20. In fact, at the time I was not twenty-seven but thirty-three. I had discovered early in my fieldwork that at my age, the neighborhood women would find my choice to remain unmarried not just anomalous but suspicious. Therefore, in 1983 when in a guessing game they could not believe that I was more than twenty-four, I did not correct them. My apparent lack of interest in men was viewed as a lack of femininity, which only confirmed their views about uncircumcised women.

21. There is a strong assumption among Egyptian women, but also men, that Arab men are particularly fond of Egyptian women and prefer to marry them. With the advent of migration and more contact with the Arab world, many non-Egyptian Arab men have chosen to marry Egyptian women, often because the cost of marriage in their own countries is very high. Additionally, Egyptian movies, television soap operas, and music have given a certain cachet to Egyptian/Cairene women, who are assumed to be more assertive and outspoken.

than in Iraq, Kuwait, and Saudi Arabia was dismissed, as she pointed out that the cost of marriage in those places had gone up only recently, but the preference for Egyptian women goes back centuries. After a few seconds of silence, she told me that even the Egyptian men who go to Europe and marry Europeans with white skin and yellow hair divorce these wives after a while and marry Egyptian women because they make men happy (meaning sexually) and are very good mothers. Unfortunately, the news of my marriage, to a man who my friends in the neighborhoods decided was much older than I by looking at his photograph, later combined with the fact that I had no children after four years of marriage, only served to confirm their views (see also Sholkamy 1994; Inhorn 1996: 29–37).

Apparently, female circumcision in the past occasioned a celebration for women neighbors and relatives, and the circumcised girls were given small gifts. The celebrations are now much more modest and, like boys' circumcision parties, generally consist of visits from close friends and relatives of the mother who may or may not offer a little present to the circumcised girl. If the family's budget allows, the girl might receive a new dress or other item of clothing, or maybe a small piece of jewelry such as earrings. She rests for a week or so and is given nourishing food; chicken or pigeon is prepared if the family can afford it. Traditionally, girls bathed in the Nile River after circumcision; now, I was told, the girls throw the piece of flesh into the Nile (see also Early 1993: 102–106).

Fathers remained aloof during their daughters' circumcision, their role being limited primarily to paying the bills. As a young Muslim woman, it was not appropriate for me to discuss these issues with men. However, most women I spoke with said that their husbands had no opinion on the subject. On a couple of occasions men brought up the subject themselves, having heard that I was opposed to the practice as "un-Islamic." One man who had migrated to several Gulf countries and knew that the circumcision of women has nothing to do with Islam but is an African tradition told me that when he tried to convince his wife that perhaps the operation was unnecessary for their daughter, his wife accused him of being cheap and not wanting to pay the expenses. So he gave in and his daughter was circumcised.

Some of the men who were among the more educated persons of my sample explained to me that they were not sure of the wisdom of the practice but had been persuaded by their womenfolk that it would be a shame for daughters to grow up uninterested in men and have unhappy marriages. At least in two cases women also told the fathers who were reluctant to perform the circumcision that they would have to accept the responsibility if their daughters could not find suitors because everyone would know if their daughters were not circumcised. Fathers were reminded that there are few men who would want to marry an uncircumcised woman. This, of course, was an effective threat since no father wanted to jeopardize his daughter's chances of finding a good husband. As one woman who had just circumcised her daughter and knew of my reservations told me, "The fact is that men who have reservations about circumcision would marry circumcised women, but those who see circumcision as necessary for women would not marry uncircumcised women." Fertility and marriage are so important that few parents will risk allowing their daughters to go uncircumcised, lest it endanger her marriageability and chances of motherhood.

Moreover, circumcision, for boys and especially for girls, was an important event in other social and individual respects.[22] Contrary to my expectation based on my reading of the feminist literature,[23] I found women often shared their circumcision experiences and talked light-heartedly of the shock and pain they went through. In a way, this common experience of women was a rite of passage to the feminine world. None felt bitter about it, although all knew that many Muslim and non-Muslim women were not circumcised. A few women pointed out that both girls and boys have to experience pain and discomfort to appreciate sexual pleasure in adulthood.

My observations and the many discussions I had with women on the subject of female circumcision contradicted almost everything I had heard or read about the topic in England. I realized, despite the impression fostered in the literature and through feminist lectures I had attended, that men actually had a minimal direct role in female circumcision. Moreover, women's unreserved and open discussion about sexual pleasure clearly contradicted the common assumption about the loss of sexual interest and feeling among circumcised women, which included my entire sample.[24] What is significant is that women's perceptions of

22. See Lightfoot-Klein 1989 and Toubia 1993, 1995 for a thorough study of circumcision in Africa.

23. See, for instance, Hayes 1975; el-Sa'dawi 1980; Abdalla 1982.

24. Obviously, this study has not been a medical one. Neither has it been a comparative one with a control sample of uncircumcised women. I am relying only on what I have observed. However, I have come across at least one case study in Sudan that has confirmed that circumcised women do experience orgasm (Lightfoot-Klein 1989).

their situation contradict the widely held belief that circumcision is meant to control women's sexuality.[25] Those who practiced circumcision in these low-income communities of Cairo believed that circumcision makes women more sexually receptive to men and is an important catalyst for creating a healthy sexual relationship between a husband and wife.[26] Given the extremely wide gap between the women's perception of circumcision and the perceptions of those who advocate its abolition, it is not surprising that the campaign for the eradication of female circumcision has not been successful. Views of women who practice female circumcision and see it as an integral part of their lives have not been taken into consideration in devising strategies that would convince them to stop the practice for their own good. Unfortunately, neither the government nor its critics have used the legitimacy of Islam to discourage women from practicing female circumcision.

Summary

Although Egyptian culture generally is very child-centered and people desire and love children, the economic cost of raising children has brought about a theoretical appreciation of smaller families. However, in the context of limited employment and financial security, women viewed fertility as their ultimate tool for dealing with economic insecurity, particularly since they expect to be widowed at some stage of their lives. Therefore, many opted to have three or four sons who could take care of them in their old age. Moreover, it was believed, and national statistics support this, that the more children there are, the more secure a marriage would be, which would prevent a husband from divorcing his wife or taking a second wife. Since traditionally daughters were not expected to contribute to their parents' upkeep, there remained a strong preference for having sons, though women loved their daughters, who were seen as lifelong allies.

Sexuality and sexual desire were viewed by both men and women as

25. This view of circumcision is perhaps more true for Western culture than for the Middle East. In the nineteenth and early twentieth centuries clitoridectomy was practiced in North America to curb women's sexual desire (Lightfoot-Klein 1989).

26. This belief is so strong that young men who seem to be uninterested in women and sexually less inclined are said to be better off marrying uncircumcised women, who are assumed to be less interested in men.

a God-given pleasure, and it was believed that its healthy expression would lead to a happy family life. Sexual desire was seen as an important reason for male and female interdependence and the creation of human society and morality. Women freely discussed their sex lives and their sexual problems with their friends, and if they were not happy, they often sought advice from more experienced and knowledgeable women. Young women took pains to prove to their neighbors and friends that they had healthy sexual relations with their husbands and that their marriage was flourishing. Older women with grown-up children and women who were near menopause tried to withdraw from sexual relations with their husbands. This move was often resisted by their husbands, at least superficially, since healthy men are expected to remain virile all their lives.

As a way of enhancing healthy sexual desire and fertility in their children, both male and female children were circumcised. Contrary to the general assumption, female circumcision was viewed as enhancing girls' sexual desire and receptivity to men and improving their fertility. In this way, families assumed that they were improving their daughters' chances of successful marriage and of having many children. It was believed that uncircumcised women grow sexually cold. The decision and the arrangements for the circumcision of daughters were the mother's domain; fathers played a minimal role in the process. In fact, in a few cases in which fathers had tried to resist the operation on their daughters, they were ostracized by their wives and had to give in.

CHAPTER 10

Conclusion

The impact of Egyptian economic, political, and social policies at the national level has been the subject of considerable scholarly scrutiny, while little attention has been paid to the way in which these policies have been translated into everyday life for ordinary men and women. However, despite their formal powerlessness at the state level, as was discussed in the course of this work and borne out by research findings elsewhere (Scott 1985; Singerman 1995), people and their households do influence the structure of their society. They do so by exercising control over their own resources, such as their labor power and fertility. By privileging one alternative over another, they do resist, influence, shape, and reshape the wider society and economy, at times in ways very different from what the authorities had intended.

In this study, I have focused on the way low-income households and their individual members respond to macro changes. I explored first the economic and social strategies that low-income households adopt to protect and promote their own interests in the face of rapid economic changes in Egypt and the consequences of structural adjustment policies. The process of assessing and adopting economic strategies takes place within a social and cultural context where class and gender inequalities, among others, are a given. Therefore, although the central concern of the study has been material well-being, I departed from conventional economic approaches by integrating the way in which cultural context and ideological factors, particularly gender and family ideology, played a significant role in the articulation of the strategies people employed. Moreover, by defining economic contribution as all those activities that satisfy human material needs through the production of goods and services, I have tried to capture a more encompassing picture of the different survival strategies households adopt without neglecting the role of ideology and gender dynamics that are at work.

In Egypt, as in most other developing nations, the insertion of individuals into the wider society is mediated by their position within their household (Beneria and Roldan 1987; Gonzalez de la Rocha 1994; Safa 1995; Singerman 1995). A household, however, with its marked gender divisions, actual and ideological, is not an egalitarian unit; and in the process of assessing and adopting economic and social strategies to cope with increasingly commercialized urban life, many existing gender inequalities may be reproduced or intensified while others become less pronounced. Yet new forms of inequalities are created where they did not exist. This does not detract from the reality that a household is also a site of different kinds of resistance and conflict. It is an arena in which its members struggle to enhance their own positions of power and access to resources. Structural gender inequalities, conflicting interests of different members, and collective social and economic interest make the household a "cooperative-conflictive" unit (Sen 1990). This perspective allows us to see the agency of different household members in negotiating their positions within the household as a collective; for instance, reinterpreting or giving nuances to a particular set of traditions and religious beliefs to reformulate the institution of household/family to better accommodate their self-interest. Family and gender ideology (including "legitimized" psychological and physical violence), patterns of labor market participation, and strategies adopted by conjugal partners in renegotiating their position within the household are integral parts of survival strategies.

In Egypt, households are formed on the basis of blood and marriage kinship. While blood relations are a given, marriages are subject to choice, and thus individuals and their families have much room to deploy strategies that enhance their economic well-being and fulfill emotional needs. Hence premarital negotiation has gained unprecedented prominence in these economically changing times. Tradition and ideology of parenthood continue to hold parents responsible for facilitating good and stable marriages for both male and female children. However, due to meager economic resources, many parents in the neighborhoods had withdrawn or reduced their role in the marriage of their sons; the marriage of daughters remained a constant preoccupation. This transformation of custom gave men even more freedom in choosing their marriage partner than traditional ideology had accorded them. Given the social context, however, few women viewed the change as furthering inequality between them and their male counterparts. They recognized that the institution of marriage prescribed asymmetric, if complementary, rights and responsibilities for husbands and wives which were justified by tradition and religious beliefs. Aware of the legal and ideological inequality that rendered them more vulnerable both within marriage and society, women increasingly favored the involvement and consent of their parents in their marriages, at times despite their fascination with love marriages. They stressed the important role parents played in negotiating on their behalf for more agreeable terms. They felt this compensated for some of the legal and social inequalities they faced in marriage. In other words, social and economic modernization has encouraged women, whose interests are rarely high on the agenda of politicians and social policy makers, to revive those aspects of traditions that offer them some protection in the face of rapid social change and commercialization of the economy. So among poor women arranged marriages have been modified to accommodate women's preferences but have not been replaced by purely individual choices. This, at the cost of losing some individual liberty, has placed the women of the working poor in Cairo in a relatively strong position vis-à-vis their husbands when compared with the poor Mexican women described in similar studies (Beneria and Roldan 1987; Chant 1991; Gonzalez de la Rocha 1994).

Among other new developments in recent decades is the increased prominence of the religious and social institution of mahr, a gift that according to Islam a husband must pledge to give to the bride at the time of marriage. In the past this gift, at least among the poor, was a often a nominal amount, much of which would remain a promise. However, during the last two decades many women and their families have manipulated the mahr to demand substantial household items that, though used for setting up the new household, remained the wife's property. This strategy forced grooms to devote a few more years of hard work to financing the mahr and setting up the new household. At the same time, these financial demands deterred low-income men from employing their virtually unilateral right to divorce. Neither could they easily enter into polygynous marriages, since normally they would be expected to provide mahr for a new bride. Consequently, marriages have become more secure for women. Economically, this strategy has made it possible for the younger generation to marry at a higher material level than their parents had done. Furthermore, delaying marriage has increased the average age at marriage, an outcome that the national government with its interest in population control approves. Many associate the higher age of marriage for women with improved health and welfare because older brides tend to be more self-confident and better able to promote their own interests. On the negative side, the deployment of such strategies also has made most women in these neighborhoods disinterested in the periodically fervent national debates over the liberalization of the personal status law, which regulates marriage. Nor did they take much notice of the demands of Islamic groups, whose political platform advocates a more conservative Muslim marriage institution in which women's role would be limited to nurturing the family.

Marriage negotiations, however, might include a wide range of issues, including financial and residential arrangements and even the use of contraception. What is significant in this process is the manipulation and transformation of familiar components of marriage practice, such as mahr and parental involvement, to reshape the marriage institution and to safeguard the interests of women in the changing socioeconomic conditions. These strategies are corrective action, but they do not question or reject the existing inequalities of gender ideology or the institution of marriage. This practical approach stands in sharp contrast to the demands of many elite and middle-class Egyptian women who promoted secular debates based on equity and civil justice for reforming marriage and the personal status law (Abdel-Kader 1988; Badran 1995).

There are other strategies that men and women have adopted to ensure a less conflictual and more secure marriage. According to traditional (and modern) family ideology and the law, men are the designated heads of their households, and in marriage women have to accept their husbands' leadership. Viewing themselves as equals, and at times wiser than their male counterparts and aware of their lack of power to challenge the ideological supremacy of husbands within marriage, many women have consciously opted to marry older men with more education and generally higher social credentials, thus making it logical to look up to their husbands and accept their judgment. Men, in contrast, have tended to prefer to marry women with lower social and economic credentials so as to eliminate the possibility that their power within marriage will be questioned. Although this strategy has yielded some economic benefit for women in addition to helping them resolve the conflicts they face between their own perception of and belief in the equality of men and women and the unequal position that they are subjected to, it nevertheless has meant that they also participate in the reproduction of asymmetric gender relations and gender ideology within marriage.

The old Muslim and Egyptian convention reinforced by the new ideology of "man the breadwinner" designates men as the primary cash contributors in their households. This gender ideology has not only affected the way in which government allocates its resources, for instance, in providing technical training mostly for men, but also has had a profound influence on household allocation of resources in training and preparing male and female children for their adult lives. The household's allocations are decided with a high degree of flexibility and alertness to changing market conditions. Thus the liberalization of the Egyptian economy that resulted in a restructuring of the labor market has had a profound effect on the resource allocation strategies of the low-income strata. Until the early 1980s, households invested their meager resources in educating their sons to qualify for relatively well-paying jobs in the public sector. However, as the salaries of these jobs failed to keep up with the astronomical inflation rates of the late seventies and eighties, many households are taking their sons out of school after primary and secondary school and arranging for them to go through apprenticeship training for traditional and modern technical jobs, whose salaries are now considerably higher than those in the public sector. Ironically, this situation has released resources for daughters to continue their education, in turn enhancing chances of a suitable marriage. It also qualified them for public sector employment, which, despite its low pay, is still considered best for women because it has made several legal provisions that accommodate women's dual role as employees and mothers/homemakers. Inadequate salaries are not considered an obstacle for women since ideologically they are not viewed as the breadwinners of the household. However, this situation means that despite women's participation in the formal labor market, they remain economically dependent on their husbands.

Inadequate wages in the public sector have also encouraged male white-collar employees to take on second jobs in the informal and manual sectors despite their lower prestige. This situation created considerable anxiety for those who had, through years of studying and hardship, strived to improve their social and economic position. Engaging in manual jobs in their and their own community's eyes represents a descent below the threshold of lower-middle-class status, already tenuous at best. Thus public sector employees, who as a social group had formed the most solid supporters of the state in the 1960s and 1970s, tend now to be the most serious critics of government policies and, ironically, the most sympathetic to organized political opposition, including Islamic groups.

The constant threat of unemployment and the absence of any social security and unemployment benefit system had a profound impact on the income-generating strategies of unskilled and semiskilled men. To secure a flow of cash to their households, most unskilled and semiskilled men in the neighborhoods, particularly those past their youth, adopted a combination of several cash-generating activities. While these multiple strategies were indispensable for the survival of many households, they were open only to men, who had access to their wives' and children's labor power. Nationally these strategies have meant that the pool of semiskilled and unskilled workers is very elastic and can easily adapt to new market conditions without much cost to the government, although it has often meant more working hours for women and children.

Migration has opened up a new option for raising cash, and many Egyptians have taken advantage of jobs in the oil-rich countries. Massive male migration, though generally short term, has affected not only the migrants but the Egyptian economy as a whole. The removal of a great many unskilled and semiskilled workers from the Egyptian labor market enabled those who remained behind to renegotiate higher wages. Many previously economically underprivileged groups thus enjoyed a series of wage increases that upgraded their standard of living, a goal that many government policies—even during the golden years of Nasser's socialism—had largely failed to achieve. While this situation has blurred the relationship between status and the economic reward of many jobs, it has acted as a buffer against the economic shock of structural adjustments and liberal market policies in Egypt, in particular, the substantial reduction in subsidies and the deterioration of such social amenities as public health care and schooling. In fact, one could argue that the massive migration initiative on the part of many poor households has been translated into increased political stability for Egypt during the 1980s since it relieved some of the economic pain of structural adjustment.

The primary role of women as homemakers and mothers has had a profound influence on women's cash-earning strategies and labor market participation as they search for jobs that can accommodate their diverse responsibilities. Women with less formal education have preferred locally based trading and other forms of self-employment in the informal sector if they felt that cash-generating activities were essential. This preference did not stem from traditionalism but rather was the outcome of economically rational calculations, since the cost of blue-collar jobs to women and their households outstripped their financial benefits. Despite low rewards, flexible working conditions and nearby informal economic activities allowed women to accommodate domestic responsibilities, as well as stretch cash resources through efficient shopping and access to public goods and services, advantages offered by few formal, especially blue-collar, jobs.

The relatively low rate of female labor market participation in Egypt and many other Middle Eastern countries is often taken as a negative indicator of women's position and is frequently blamed on Islamic ideology and conservatism. The revival of religious and Islamic tendencies in Egypt has reinforced some of these assumptions. However, my examination of women's lives and choices in the social context of the neighborhoods revealed a different picture. All women with a high school education were engaged in the formal labor market as white-collar workers, and they preferred to work for the state. This is an indication that when women had access to better pay and job conditions, Islamic ideology was not an obstacle to labor market participation. On the contrary, adherence to Islam and tradition not only provided emotional and spiritual satisfaction but also enabled them to prevent erosion of the privileges offered by Islam and tradition, such as complete control over their own incomes.

Apart from control over their own wages and property, the most important privilege that Muslim women have is the unquestioned right to economic support from their husbands, regardless of their own financial resources. In these times of economic hardship and changing society and morality, women in the neighborhoods had a vested interest in reminding their husbands of the "words of God" that made them economically responsible for their families. Moreover, not only did women not view religion as an obstacle to the realization of their social and economic goals, quite to the contrary, many felt that demonstrating religious observance, particularly the wearing of the veil, removed some of the social obstacles that they would otherwise face in their interaction with the wider society and the labor market (see also Hoodfar 1991). As the veil has been adopted more widely, however, the privileges it once offered to women are rapidly disappearing.

That the majority of women who had young daughters indicated their desire to have them educated so they could obtain good jobs signified they were aware that entitlement to a right is not necessarily the same as having it. They wanted their daughters to have some financial independence and security and not be totally dependent financially on their husbands. They were aware that the commercialization of daily life had upset the equilibrium of interdependence between husbands and wives in favor of men and hence wished to protect their daughters, who would face a life that was even more commercialized.

Islamic ideology and tradition dissuaded men from laying direct claim on women's cash, thus allowing women to invest their wages as they saw fit. However, many men, torn between familial responsibilities and personal interests, tended to limit their material family obligation to the most narrow Qur'anic definition, while women held a much broader conception of the responsibilities of husbands and fathers. These conflicting perspectives have become a major source of marital problems. Although based on the research accounts (Beneria and Roldan 1987; Gonzalez de la Rocha 1994) it appears that poor Egyptian women are far less subject to physical violence than many of their counterparts in Latin America; mostly thanks to the low consumption of alcohol, men frequently use psychological violence to silence their wives. Husbands threaten that if women complain too much they will be divorced and lose their children, or they will marry a second wife to get away from the nagging. Every woman fears these prospects.

Still worse, some men had resolved their contradictory desires to spend their often limited income on themselves and to have a family and authority over it, by deliberately marrying women with cash income and little family support. Once married, these men refused to pay housekeeping costs to their wives, as if they were permanent guests in their own households. This forced wives to spend their own income on daily basics. The situation was resented by the wives who felt, with the agreement of their neighbors, that their employment had led to their exploitation rather than the better married life they had hoped for based on pledges of "modernization" that they had once believed. Wives would commonly spend their income on the daily basics if their husbands were unemployed through no fault of their own. Otherwise they would invest their income in buying household or other items that were considered outside the husbands' responsibilities. These investments brought women power and prestige because even though husbands are given authority and power over their wives socially, ideologically, and legally, nonetheless power is a process of negotiation and renegotiation in which personal and ideological resources are the bargaining medium. Thus any reversal of the pattern of budgeting whereby women became primary providers, whether due to migration or other factors, was unsatisfactory for women because "bread and beans" were ephemeral resources. Thus women often developed strategies, though not always successful, to reestablish their husbands' financial responsibility to the family. Nonetheless, given the consequences of divorce for women, many felt compelled to remain in their marriages, even though unhappy with their husbands' lack of financial commitment, a fact their husbands were well aware of.

A sexual division of labor was viewed as natural, hence not subject to change, and the basis for the interdependence of the sexes. Domestic and child care responsibilities were commonly viewed as women's instinctive domain, and women themselves were strong defenders of such a division, actively discouraging the participation of men in these respects. Women's resistance stemmed from their understanding that the division of labor justified financial dependence on their husbands. As more services and subsistence activities traditionally provided by women for their households moved either totally or partially to the cash market, women jealously guarded or tried to salvage what the market had not yet claimed. Although women compensated for losses of contribution in that domain by investing time and energy in funneling public goods and services such as free health care and subsidized goods to their households, these contributions often went unrecognized by the households, the wider society, and even the women themselves and thus did not translate into increased power.

For social human beings, earning a livelihood is only part of the survival equation; consumption strategies are the other significant, if often neglected, aspect of daily life. In fact, consumption is an important channel through which individuals and their household participate in the life of their actual community or the one they aspire to. Where income is limited and unpredictable, consumption strategies assume an even more significant role as people have to strike a balance between their physiological and social needs—which may not always coincide. Furthermore, consumption is a domain where social hierarchy is formed and re-formed. Modes of consumption are primarily social markers that indicate the social position of an individual or a household. Low-income households, like all other social groups, strive to redefine their social position positively, and since their income is unpredictable and limited, consumption strategies assume an even more crucial role in a household's economic and social concerns. Moreover, the inclusion of consumption and distribution of material rewards within a household provides a window through which we can observe the intersection of economic contribution and allocation of resources and the influence of gender ideology.

Different socioeconomic conditions encourage different consumption strategies. The spirit of sharing and communal life that prevents people from holding back their resources from the needy members of their network, on the one hand, and the desire to increase economic security and combat the high rate of inflation during the 1980s, on the other, encouraged and reinforced the tendency to promote the consumption of modern household goods by cutting costs for other, seemingly more basic, expenses. Many households spent not just their savings but also their forecasted cash earnings on the accumulation of durable household items. In other words, they deliberately put themselves in a constant state of financial indebtedness such that no one could turn to them with cash requests. Sharing the use of these items with their neighbors and friends brought the household status and created an indebtedness on the part of others, enabling them to redefine their social position. These assets also provided a real and perceived source of security because they could always be sold in times of need, often at no loss thanks to inflation. The consumption of these items was the most efficient form of accumulating assets, both materially and socially. In the national context, consumption of these modern items is a means through which a nation, particularly its low-income groups, who are usually excluded from the formal power structure, expresses its acceptance or rejection of new goods that are introduced into their "modernizing" economies. Adoption and integration of many novel items is an indicator not only of approval of the rapidly changing culture and society but also of a desire to be a part of it.

Besides the efficient use of material resources, the survival and economic improvement of low-income households also hinged on the innovative and effective use of social resources. Hence preserving and creating both horizontal and vertical networks to which one could turn for assistance in times of economic crisis was an important preoccupation of all adults, but especially women, whose social networks were often multipurpose and incorporated all members of their households. In contrast, men's nonkin networks were usually personal. In forming and re-forming their networks, individuals and families were very attentive to preserving contacts that yielded support but limited their financial responsibilities. For instance, in contrast to conventional ideology and Islamic tenets, which accord special value to paternal kin relations, many households interacted more intensely with women's and maternal kin networks. At least in part such developments were a result of the unaffordability of men's traditional and religious material obligation to their natal families. By virtue of their sex, women were exempted from economic obligation. Hence they could easily set the terms and the extent as well as the kind of reciprocal relationship that suited them best. This delicate nuance in kin interaction had a positive impact on women's sense of security, if not always on the extent of their power, in their marriage.

In the process of social change, some traditional customs were neglected, but others, notably the traditional rotating credit associations or saving clubs, gained prominence and played a major role in the lives of most households. These associations, which formed an alternative banking system, compensated for the exclusion of low-income groups from formal financial institutions. In these saving clubs, people traded on their reputation and face-to-face relationships to find access to funds while supporting one another. As the gamᶜiyat were usually locally based, keeping a good reputation in the neighborhood and among the women who organized and managed the clubs was essential. In effect, the saving clubs have conferred on the local communities the power to exert social pressure, particularly on men, who carry the major burden of providing for the cash needs of their households. This has to some extent compensated for the newfound freedom enjoyed by men as a result of new job opportunities outside the residential areas in the anonymity of greater Cairo.

Fertility and sexuality are another neglected domain in studies of survival and economic strategies. Sexual desire and procreation were seen as an important reason for male and female interdependence, and women often viewed a healthy sexual relationship as an important pillar of a secure marriage, one that a clever woman could manipulate to her advantage. Hence parents, in the hope of ensuring fertility and a healthy sexual life for their children, particularly their daughters, arranged for their circumcision. While circumcision of boys confirmed their membership in the community of Muslims, female circumcision was done primarily to ensure their fertility and enhance their sexuality. Popular opinion, confirmed by national statistics, holds that the birth of several children shortly after the consummation of marriage is the best strategy to counter marital breakdown. Moreover, many women see their fertility as the ultimate tool for dealing with economic insecurity and widowhood and try to have many sons, who would be expected to support their mother. This has hindered the state's considerable efforts to control Egypt's rapidly growing population, and today Egypt faces a considerable challenge to provide basic education, minimum health care, and job opportunities for its growing and youthful population.

To sum up, the low-income group in urban Egypt, despite their lack of formal power, has been resourceful in responding to and coping with economic and social change, especially the imposition of structural adjustment policies. By diversifying their economic activities and adjusting to labor market opportunities, they have managed to influence the urban wage structure to their advantage. They have turned the traditional saving clubs into a means of promoting their consumption pattern while preventing the skyrocketing inflation rate from carving further into their standard of living. By manipulating the old gender ideology and religious beliefs and through introducing nuances in translating these to everyday practice, both men and women have been able to promote their own interests in marriage and in the marketplace. In this process, however, they have also reproduced some of the social inequalities that lie at the root of gender inequalities.

References

Abdalla, Ahmed. 1988. "Child Labour in Egypt: Leather Tanning in Cairo." In *Combatting Child Labour*, ed. Assefa Bequiele and Jo Boyden. Geneva: International Labour Office.

Abdalla, Raqiya. 1982. *Sisters in Affliction: Circumcision and Infibulation of Women in Africa*. London: Zed Press.

Abdel-Fadil, Mahmoud. 1975. *Development in Income Distribution and Social Changes in Rural Egypt, 1952–1972*. University of Cambridge Department of Applied Economics Occasional Papers, no. 45. Cambridge: Cambridge University Press.

———. 1980. *The Political Economy of Nasserism: A Study of Employment and Income Distribution Policies in Urban Egypt, 1952–1972*. Cambridge: Cambridge University Press.

———. 1982. "Educational Expansion and Income Distribution in Egypt." In *The Political Economy of Income Distribution in Egypt*, ed. Gouda Abdel-Khalek and Robert Tignor. New York: Holmes and Meier.

———. 1983. "Informal Sector Employment in Egypt." In *Cairo Papers in Social Science* 6(2): 55–89.

Abdel-Kader, Soha. 1988. *Egyptian Women in a Changing Society, 1899–1987*. Boulder, Colo.: Lynne Rienner.

Abdel-Khalek, Gouda. 1983. "The Open Door Policy in Egypt: A Search for Meaning and Implication." *Cairo Papers in Social Science* 2(3): 73–100.

Abu-Lughod, Janet. 1961. "Migrant Adjustment to City Life: The Egyptian Case." *American Journal of Sociology* 47: 22–32.

———. 1971. *Cairo: 1001 Years of the City Victorious*. Princeton: Princeton University Press.

Abu-Lughod, Lila. 1986. *Veiled Sentiments: Honor and Poetry in a Bedouin Society*. Berkeley, Los Angeles, and London: University of California Press.

Ahlander, Nancy Rollins, and Kathleen Slaugh. 1995. "Beyond Drudgery, Power and Equity: Toward an Expanded Discourse on the Moral Dimensions of Housework in Families." *Journal of Marriage and Family* 57: 54–68.

Ahwany, N. al-. 1984. "The Migration of Egyptian Labour to Oil States and Its Relations with Structural Changes in the Egyptian Economy, 1967–80" (Arabic). Ph.D. dissertation, Economics Faculty, Cairo University.

ait-Sabbah, Fatna. 1984. *Women in the Muslim Unconscious.* Translated by Mary Jo Lakeland. New York: Pergamon Press.

Alderman, Harold, and Joachim Von Braun. 1984. *The Effect of the Egyptian Food Ration and Subsidy System on Income Distribution and Consumption.* Egyptian Food Program Study, International Food Policy Research Institute. Washington, D.C.

Alloula, Malek. 1986. *The Colonial Harem.* Minneapolis: University of Minnesota Press.

Altorki, Soraya. 1986. *Women in Saudi Arabia: Ideology and Behavior among the Elite.* New York: Columbia University Press.

Amin, Galal. 1989. "Migration, Inflation, and Social Mobility." In *Egypt under Mubarak,* ed. Charles Tripp and Roger Owen. London: Routledge.

———. 1995. *Egypt's Economic Predicament: A Study in the Interaction of External Pressure, Political Folly, and Social Tension in Egypt, 1960–1990.* Leiden: E. J. Brill.

Amin, Galal, and Elizabeth Awny. 1985. *International Migration of Egyptian Labour: A Review of the State of Art.* Ottawa: International Development Research Center Publications, no. IDRCMR-108e.

Anderson, Michael, Frank Bechhofer, and Jonathan Gershuny, eds. 1994. *The Social and Political Economy of the Household.* New York: Oxford University Press.

Angotti, Thomas. 1993. *Metropolis 2000: Planning, Poverty, and Politics.* London: Routledge.

Anker, Richard. 1983. "Female Labour Force Participation in Developing Countries: A Critique of Current Definitions and Data Collection Methods." *International Labour Review* 122(6): 709–723.

Appadurai, Arjun, ed. 1986. *The Social Life of Things: Commodities in Cultural Perspective.* Cambridge: Cambridge University Press.

Aramaki, Michiko. 1994. "Family, Paesani, and Networks: Politics and Economy of Montreal Italians." Ph.D. dissertation, McGill University.

Asad, Talal. 1986. "The Concept of Cultural Translation in British Social Anthropology." In *Writing Culture: The Poetics and Politics of Ethnography,* ed. James Clifford and George Marcus. Berkeley, Los Angeles, and London: University of California Press.

Assaad, Ragui. 1991. "Structure of Egypt's Construction Labour Market and Its Development Since the Mid-1970s." In *Employment and Structural Adjustment: Egypt in the 1990s,* ed. Heba Handoussa and Gillian Potter. Cairo: American University in Cairo Press.

———. 1993. "Formal and Informal Institutions in the Labor Market, with Applications to the Construction Sector in Egypt." *World Development* 21: 925–939.

Association of African Women for Research and Development (AAWORD).

1983. "A Statement on Genital Mutilation." In *Third World Second Sex: Women's Struggles and National Liberation, Third World Women Speak Out,* ed. Miranda Davies. London: Zed Press.

Aswad, Barbara C. 1974. "Visiting Patterns among Women of the Elite in a Small Turkish City." *Anthropological Quarterly* 47: 9–27.

Ayata, Sencer. 1986. "Entrepreneurship and Social Mobility in the Informal Sector." Paper presented at the conference Informal Sector, Bielefeld University, Tübingen, 18–31 July.

Badran, Margot. 1993. "Independent Women: More than a Century of Feminism in Egypt." In *Arab Women: Old Boundaries, New Frontiers,* ed. Judith E. Tucker. Bloomington: Indiana University Press.

———. 1995. *Feminists, Islam, and Nation: Gender and the Making of Modern Egypt.* Princeton: Princeton University Press.

Baer, Gabriel. 1964. *Population and Society in the Arab East.* New York: Routledge and Kegan Paul.

Balses, D. W. 1982. "The Hidden Economy and the National Accounts." *OECD Observer* 114: 15–17.

Barker, D. M. L., and S. A. Allan, eds. 1976a. *Dependency and Exploitation in Work and Marriage.* London: Tavistock.

———. 1976b. *Sexual Divisions and Society.* London: Tavistock.

Barnett, Steve, and Martin G. Silverman. 1979. *Ideology and Everyday Life: Anthropology, Neo-Marxist Thought, and the Problem of Ideology and the Social Whole.* Ann Arbor: University of Michigan Press.

Bartos, Rena. 1988. *Marketing to Women Around the World.* Boston: Harvard Business School Press.

Baumgartner, M. P. 1993. "Motives for Sexual Coercion." In *Aggression and Violence: Social Interactionist Perspectives,* ed. Richard B. Felson and James T. Tedeschi. Washington, D.C.: American Psychological Association.

Beattie, K. J. 1994. *Egypt During the Nasser Years: Ideology, Politics, and Civil Society.* Boulder, Colo.: Westview Press.

Becker, Gary Stanley. 1981. *A Treatise on the Family.* Cambridge, Mass.: Harvard University Press.

Becker, Lawrence C. 1990. *Reciprocity.* Chicago: University of Chicago Press.

Benedict, Peter. 1974. "The Kabul Gunu: Structured Visiting in an Anatolian Provincial Town." *Anthropological Quarterly* 47: 28–47.

Beneria, Lourdes. 1981. "Conceptualizing the Labour Force: The Underestimation of Women's Economic Activities." *Journal of Developing Area Studies* 17(3): 10–28.

———. 1992. "Accounting for Women's Work: The Progress of Two Decades." *World Development* 20(November): 1547–1560.

Beneria, Lourdes, and Shelley Feldman, eds. 1992. *Unequal Burden: Economic Crises, Persistent Poverty, and Women's Work.* Boulder, Colo.: Westview Press.

Beneria, Lourdes, and Martha Roldan. 1987. *The Crossroad of Class and Gender: Industrial Homework, Subcontracting, and Household Dynamics in Mexico City.* Chicago: University of Chicago Press.

Berk, Sarah Fenstermaker, ed. 1980. *Women and Household Labor.* Beverly Hills, Calif.: Sage Publications.

Beshai, Adel. 1993. "Interpretations and Misinterpretations of the Egyptian Economy." In *Contemporary Egypt: Through Egyptian Eyes,* ed. C. Tripp. London: Routledge.

Betteridge, Anne. 1980. "The Controversial Vows of Urban Muslim Women in Iran." In *Unspoken Worlds: Women's Religious Lives in Non-Western Cultures,* ed. N. A. Falk and R. M. Gross. New York: Harper and Row.

Bloch, Maurice, and Jonathan Parry, eds. 1989. *Money and the Morality of Exchange.* Cambridge: Cambridge University Press.

Boddy, Janice P. 1989. *Wombs and Alien Spirits: Women, Men and the Zar Cult in Northern Sudan.* Madison: University of Wisconsin Press.

Booth, William James. 1993. *Households: On the Moral Architecture of the Economy.* Ithaca, N.Y.: Cornell University Press.

Boserup, Ester. 1970. *Women's Role in Economic Development.* New York: St. Martin's Press.

Botiveau, B. 1993. "Contemporary Reinterpretations of Islamic Law: The Case of Egypt." *Islam and Public Law: Classical and Contemporary Studies,* ed. Chibli Mallat. London: Graham and Trotman.

Bourdieu, Pierre. 1990. *The Logic of Practice.* Cambridge: Polity.

Brink, Judy H. 1991. "The Effect of Emigration of Husbands on the Status of Their Wives: An Egyptian Case." *International Journal of Middle East Studies* 23(2): 201–211.

Brody, W. H. 1975. "The Economic Value of the Housewife." *Research and Statistics Notes* 9.

Butter, David. 1989. "Debt and Egypt's Financial Policies." In *Egypt under Mubarak,* ed. Charles Tripp and Roger Owen. London: Routledge.

Buvinic, Mayra, Margaret A. Lycette, and William P. McGreevey, eds. 1983. *Women and Poverty in the Third World.* Baltimore: Johns Hopkins University Press.

CAPMAS (Central Agency for Public Mobilization and Statistics) and UNICEF (United Nations Children's Fund). 1993. *The State of Egyptian Children and Women.* Cairo: CAPMAS and UNICEF.

Castells, Manuel. 1977. *The Urban Question: A Marxist Approach.* London: E. Arnold.

———. 1989. "The World Underneath: The Origins, Dynamics, and Effects of the Informal Economy." In *The Informal Economy: Studies in Advanced and Less Developed Countries,* ed. Alejandro Portes, Manuel Castells, and Lauren Benton. Baltimore: Johns Hopkins University Press.

Chaianov, Aleksandr Vasil'evich. 1966. *The Theory of Peasant Economy [by] A. V. Chayanov,* ed. Daniel Thorner and Basile Kerblay. Homewood, Ill.: Published for the American Economic Association by R. D. Irwin.

Chamie, M. 1985. "Labour Force Participation of Lebanese Women." In *Women, Employment and Development in the Arab World,* ed. Julinda Abu Nasr et al. Berlin: Mouton.

Chaney, Elsa M., and Mary Garcia Castro, eds. 1989. *Muchachas No More: Household Workers in Latin America and the Caribbean.* Philadelphia: Temple University Press.

Chant, Sylvia H. 1991. *Women and Survival in Mexican Cities: Perspectives on*

Gender, Labour Markets, and Low-Income Households. Manchester: Manchester University Press.

Cigno, Alessandro. 1991. *The Economics of the Family.* Oxford: Clarendon Press.

Cohen, Sheldon, and S. Leonard Syme, eds. 1985. *Social Support and Health.* New York: Academic Press.

Cole, Sally. 1991. *Women of the Praia: Work and Lives in a Portuguese Coastal Community.* Princeton: Princeton University Press.

Collins, Jane L., and Martha Gimenez. 1990. *Work without Wages: Comparative Studies of Domestic Labor and Self-Employment.* Albany: State University of New York Press.

Cooper, Mark Neal. 1982. *The Transformation of Egypt.* Princeton: Princeton University Press.

Cronin, Constance. 1987. "Tehran: The National Elite Family." Paper presented at the Twenty-first Annual Meeting of the Middle East Studies Association of North America, Baltimore, 14–17 November.

Crow, Graham. 1989. "The Use of the Concept of 'Strategy' in Recent Sociological Literature." *Sociology* 23(1): 1–24.

Danielson, Virginia. 1991. "Artists and Entrepreneurs: Singers in Cairo During the 1920s." In *Women in Middle Eastern History: Shifting Boundaries in Sex and Gender,* ed. Nikki R. Keddie and Beth Baron. New Haven: Yale University Press.

Dauber, Roslyn, and Melinda Cain, eds. 1981. *Women and Technological Change in Developing Countries.* Boulder, Colo.: Westview Press.

Davidson, Caroline. 1982. *A Woman's Work Is Never Done: A History of Housework in the British Isles, 1650–1950.* London: Chatto and Windus.

Davis, Angela. 1989. "Women in Egypt: A Personal View." In Davis, *Women, Culture and Politics.* New York: Random House.

De Beauvoir, Simone. 1949. *Le deuxieme sexe.* Paris: Gallimard.

de Certeau, Michel. 1984. *The Practice of Everyday Life.* Berkeley, Los Angeles, and London: University of California Press.

Deere, Carmen Diana. 1990. *Household and Class Relations: Peasants and Landlords in Northern Peru.* Berkeley, Los Angeles, and London: University of California Press.

Delphy, Christine. 1976. *The Main Enemy.* London: Women's Research and Resource Center.

———. 1979. "Sharing the Same Table: Consumption and the Family." In *The Sociology of the Family: New Directions for Britain,* ed. C. Harris. Sociological Review Monograph, no. 28. Staffordshire: University of Keele.

Dessouki, Ali E. H. 1978. "Development of the Migration Policies in the Arab Republic of Egypt." Paper prepared for the Cairo University/MIT Technology Adaptation Program, Cairo.

———. 1991. "The Public Sector in Egypt: Organisation, Evolution, and Strategies for Reform." In *Employment and Structural Adjustment: Egypt in the 1990s,* ed. Heba Handoussa and Gillian Potter. Cairo: American University in Cairo Press.

Dey, Jennie. 1981. "Gambian Women: Unequal Partners in Rice Development Projects?" *Journal of Development Studies* 17(3): 109–122.

Dixon, Ruth. 1982. "Women in Agriculture: Counting the Labour Force in Developing Countries." *Population and Development Review* 8(3): 539–566.

Douglas, Mary, and Baron Isherwood. 1978. *The World of Goods: Towards an Anthropology of Consumption.* London: Penguin Books.

Duque, Joaquin, and Ernesto Pastrana. 1973. "Las estrategias de supervivencia economica de las unidades familiares del sector popular urbano: Una investigacion exploratoria." FLASCO, Santiago. (Mimeograph.)

Dwyer, Daisy H., and Judith Bruce, eds. 1988. *A Home Divided: Women and Income in the Third World.* Stanford: Stanford University Press.

Early, Evelyn A. 1993. *Baladi Women of Cairo: Playing with an Egg and a Stone.* Boulder, Colo.: Lynne Rienner.

Ecevit, Yildiz. 1991. "Shop Floor Control: The Ideological Construction of Turkish Women Factory Workers." In *Working Women: International Perspectives on Labour and Gender Ideology,* ed. Nanneke Redclift and M. Thea Sinclair. London: Routledge.

Eickelman, Christine. 1984. *Women and Community in Oman.* New York: New York University Press.

El-Issawy, Ibrahim. 1985. *Subsidization of Food Products in Egypt.* Food Energy Nexus Programme. United Nations University, Paris.

Esposito, John. 1982. *Women in Muslim Family Law.* Syracuse, N.Y.: Syracuse University Press.

Fergany, Nader. 1987. *The Differentials in Labour Migration by Education Status: Egypt 1974–84.* Occasional Paper no. 4 (CDC/S83/17). Cairo: Cairo Demographic Centre.

Fernea, Elizabeth Warnock. 1975. *A Street in Marrakech.* Garden City, N.Y.: Waveland Press.

———. 1993. "The Veiled Revolution." In *Everyday Life in the Muslim Middle East,* ed. Donna Lee Bowen and Evelyn A. Early. Bloomington: Indiana University Press.

Fiske, Alan Page. 1991. *The Structure of Social Life: The Four Elementary Forms of Human Relations.* New York: Free Press.

Fluehr-Lobban, Carolyn, and Lois Bardsley-Sirois. 1990. "Obedience (Ta'a) in Muslim Marriage: Religion, Interpretation and Applied Law in Egypt." *Journal of Comparative Family Studies* 21(1): 41–54.

Folbre, Nancy. 1984. "Household Production in the Philippines: A Non-Neoclassical Approach." *Economic Development and Cultural Changes* 321(2): 303–330.

———. 1986a. "Cleaning House." *Journal of Development Economics* 22: 5–40.

———. 1986b. "Women's Work and Women's Households: Gender Bias in the U.S. Census." *Social Research* 56: 546–569.

———. 1988. "The Black Four of Hearts: Toward a New Paradigm of Household Economies." In *A Home Divided: Women and Income in the Third World,* ed. Daisy Dwyer and Judith Bruce. Stanford: Stanford University Press.

———. 1991. "The Unproductive Housewife: Her Evolution in Nineteenth-Century Thought." *Signs* 16: 463–484.

———. 1993. "How Does She Know? Feminist Theories of Gender Bias in Economics." *History of Political Economy* 25: 167–184.

Folbre, Nancy, and Barnct Wagman. 1993. "Counting Housework: New Estimates of Real Product in the United States, 1800–1860." *Journal of Economic
History* 53: 275–288.

Fong, M. 1980. "Victims of Old-Fashioned Statistics." *CERES: FAO Review
on Agriculture and Development* 13(3): 29–32.

Freeman, Derek. 1970. *Report on the Iban.* London: Athlone Press.

Gallagher, Nancy. 1990. *Egypt's Other Wars: Epidemics and the Politics of Public
Health.* Syracuse, N.Y.: Syracuse University Press.

Gell, Alfred. 1986. "Newcomers to the World of Goods: Consumption among
the Muria Gonds." In *The Social Life of Things: Commodities in Cultural
Perspective,* ed. Arjun Appuradai. Cambridge: Cambridge University Press.

Gershuny, Jonathan I., and G. S. Thomas. 1984. *Changing Times: Activity Patterns in the U.K., 1937–75.* Oxford: Oxford University Press.

Gerson, Kathleen. 1993. *No Man's Land: Men's Changing Commitments to Family and Work.* New York: HarperCollins.

Gilbert, Alan. 1992. *Cities, Poverty, and Development: Urbanization in the Third
World.* Oxford: Oxford University Press.

Glazer, Nona. 1990. "Servants to Capital: Unpaid Domestic Labor and Paid
Work." In *Work without Wages: Comparative Studies of Domestic Labor and
Self-Employment,* ed. Jane L. Collins and Martha Gimenez. Albany: State
University of New York Press.

Goldschmidt-Clermont, Luisella. 1982. *Unpaid Work in the Household: A Review
of Economic Evaluation Methods.* Women, Work and Development Series, no.
1. Geneva: ILO.

———. 1987. *Economic Evaluations of Unpaid Household Work: Africa, Asia,
Latin America and Oceania.* Women, Work and Development Series, no.
14. Geneva: ILO.

———. 1990. "Economic Measurement of Non-Market Household Activities:
Is It Useful and Feasible?" *International Labour Review* 129: 279–299.

Gonzalez de la Rocha, Mercedes. 1994. *The Resources of Poverty: Women and
Survival in a Mexican City.* Oxford: Blackwell.

Good, M. V. 1987. "Maragheh: Kinship and Limits of the Obligation." Paper
presented at the Twenty-First Annual Meeting of the Middle East Studies
Association of North America, Baltimore, 14–17 November.

Gordon, Daniel. 1992. "Female Circumcision and Genital Operations in Egypt
and Sudan." *Medical Anthropology,* n.s., 5: 3–14.

Gran, Judith. 1977. "Impact of the World Market on Egyptian Women." *Middle East Research and Information Project* 58: 3–7.

Grasmuck, Sherri, and Patricia R. Pessar. 1991. *Between Two Islands: Dominican
International Migration.* Berkeley, Los Angeles, and Oxford: University of
California Press.

Greenhalgh, Susan. 1988. "Families and Networks in Taiwan's Economic Development." In *Contending Approaches to the Political Economy of Taiwan,*
ed. Edwin A. Winckler and Susan Greenhalgh. Armonk, N.Y.: M. E. Sharpe.

———. 1991. *Women in the Informal Enterprise: Empowerment or Exploitation?*
New York: Population Council Working Papers, no. 33.

Grieco, Margaret. 1987. *Keeping It in the Family: Social Networks and Employment Chances.* London: Tavistock.

Gronau, Robert. 1977. "Leisure, Home Production, and Work: The Theory of the Allocation of Time Revisited." *Journal of Political Economy* 85(4): 1099–1124.

Guenena, Nemat. 1986. "The Jihad: An 'Islamic Alternative' in Egypt." *Cairo Papers in Social Science* 9(2).

Guindi, Fadwa el-. 1981. "Veiling Infitah with Muslim Ethic: Egypt's Contemporary Islamic Movement." *Social Problems* 28(4): 465–487.

Gunning, Isabelle R. 1991. "Arrogant Perception, World-Traveling and Multicultural Feminism: The Case of Female Genital Surgeries." *Columbia Human Rights Law Review* 23: 189.

Hall, Alan, and Harry Wellman. 1985. "Social Networks and Social Support: Rediscovering Social Sciences." In *Social Support and Health,* ed. Sheldon Cohen and S. Leonard Syme. New York: Academic Press.

Hamalian, Arpi. 1974. "The Shirkets: Visiting Patterns of Armenians in Lebanon." *Anthropological Quarterly* 47: 71–92.

Hammam, Mona. 1979. "Egypt's Working Women: Textile Workers of Chubra el-Kheima." *Middle East Research and Information Project* 82: 3–7.

Handoussa, Heba. 1991. "Reform Policies for Egypt's Manufacturing Sector." In *Employment and Structural Adjustment: Egypt in the 1990s,* ed. Heba Handoussa and Gillian Potter. Cairo: American University in Cairo Press.

Handoussa, Heba, and Gillian Potter, eds. 1991. *Employment and Structural Adjustment: Egypt in the 1990s.* Cairo: American University in Cairo Press.

Hansen, Bent, and S. Radwan. 1982. *Employment Opportunities and Equity in Egypt.* Geneva: ILO.

Harris, Olivia. 1981. "Households as Natural Units." In *Of Marriage and of the Market: Women's Subordination Internationally and Its Lessons,* ed. Kate Young, Carol Wolkowitz, and Roslyn McCullagh. Boston: Routledge and Kegan Paul.

Hartman, H. 1981. "The Family as Locus of Gender, Class and Political Struggle: The Example of Housework." *Signs* 6: 366–394.

Hassan, Nawal. 1996. "Beyond Western Paradigms of Development: A Pragmatic Response to Popular Housing." In *Development, Change, and Gender in Cairo: A View from the Household,* ed. Diane Singerman and Homa Hoodfar. Bloomington: Indiana University Press.

Hayes, Rose Oldfield. 1975. "Female Genital Mutilation, Fertility Control, Women's Roles and Patrilineage in Modern Sudan: A Functional Analysis." *American Ethnologist* 2: 617–633.

Herrera, Linda. 1992. "Scenes of Schooling: Inside a Girls' School in Cairo." *Cairo Papers in Social Science* 15(1).

Hijab, Nadia. 1988. *Womanpower: The Arab Debate on Women at Work.* Cambridge: Cambridge University Press.

———. 1994. *Women and Work in the Arab World.* Washington, D.C.: MERIP Pamphlet Series.

Hinnebusch, R. A. 1993. "The Politics of Economic Reform in Egypt." *Third World Quarterly* 14: 159–171.

Holy, Ladislav. 1990. *Kinship, Honour, and Solidarity: Cousin Marriage in the Middle East.* Manchester: Manchester University Press.

Homer, M., A. Leonard, and P. Taylor. 1985. "The Burden of Dependency."

In *Marital Violence,* ed. Norman Johnson. London: Routledge and Kegan Paul.

Hoodfar, Homa. 1984. *Hygienic and Health Care Practices in a Poor Urban Neighbourhood in Cairo.* Regional Papers. Cairo: Population Council.

——. 1986. *Childcare and Child Survival in Low-Income Neighbourhoods of Cairo.* Regional Papers. Cairo: Population Council.

——. 1988. "Patterns of Household Budgeting and the Management of Financial Affairs in a Lower-Income Neighbourhood in Cairo." In *A Home Divided: Women and Income in the Third World,* ed. Daisy H. Dwyer and Judith Bruce. Stanford: Stanford University Press.

——. 1989. "Background to the Feminist Movement in Egypt." *Le Bulletin* 9 (2): 18–23.

——. 1990. "Survival Strategies in Low-Income Households in Cairo." *Journal of South Asian and Middle Eastern Studies* 13(4): 22–41.

——. 1991. "Return to the Veil: Personal Strategy and Public Participation in Egypt." In *Working Women: International Perspectives on Labour and Gender Ideology,* ed. Nanneke Redclift and M. Thea Sinclair. London: Routledge.

——. 1994. "Situating the Anthropologist: A Personal Account of Ethnographic Fieldwork in Three Urban Settings, Tehran, Cairo, and Montreal." In *Urban Lives: Fragmentation and Resistance,* ed. Vered Amit-Talai and Henri Lustiger-Thaler. Toronto: McLelland and Stewart.

——. 1995a. "Child Care and Child Health in Low-Income Neighborhoods of Cairo." In *Children in the Muslim Middle East,* ed. Elizabeth Warnock Fernea. Austin: University of Texas Press.

——. 1995b. "The Impact of Male Migration on Domestic Budgeting: Egyptian Women Striving for an Islamic Budgeting Pattern." Unpublished paper.

——. 1996a. "The Impact of Egyptian Male Migration on Urban Families Left Behind: 'Feminization of the Egyptian Family' or a Re-affirmation of Traditional Gender Roles?" In *Development, Change, and Gender in Cairo: A View from the Household,* ed. Diane Singerman and Homa Hoodfar. Bloomington: Indiana University Press. First published, in an earlier form, in *Sociological Bulletin: Journal of the Indian Sociological Society* 42, nos. 1–2 (Fall 1993): 114–135.

——. 1996b. "Women in Cairo's (In)Visible Economy: Linking Local and National Trends." In *Middle Eastern Women in the "Invisible" Economy,* ed. Richard Lobban. Gainesville: University Press of Florida.

Hunt, Pauline. 1978. "Cash Transactions and Household Tasks." *Sociological Review* 26: 555–571.

Ibrahim, Barbara. 1980. "Social Change and Industrial Experience: Women as Factory Workers in Urban Egypt." Ph.D. dissertation, Department of Sociology, Indiana University.

——. 1981. "Family Strategies: A Perspective of Women's Entry to the Labour Force in Egypt." *International Journal of Sociology of the Family* 11: 235–249.

——. 1983. "Strategies of Urban Labour Force Measurement." *Cairo Papers in Social Science* 6(2): 46–54.

Ibrahim, Saad E. 1982. "Oil Migration and the New Arab Social Order." In

Rich and Poor States in the Middle East: Egypt and the New Arab Order, ed. Malcolm Kerr and el-Sayed Yassin. Boulder, Colo.: Westview Press.

Ikram, K. 1980. *Arab Republic of Egypt: Economic Management in a Period of Transition.* Baltimore: Johns Hopkins University Press.

Inhorn, Marcia. 1996. *Quest for Conception: Gender, Infertility, and Egyptian Medical Traditions.* Philadelphia: University of Pennsylvania Press.

International Labour Office (ILO). 1976. *International Recommendation on Labour Statistics.* Geneva: ILO.

———. 1982. *Employment Opportunity and Equity in Egypt.* Geneva: ILO.

———. 1983. "Resolution 1: Resolution concerning Statistics of Economically Active Population, Employment, Unemployment and Underemployment." In *Thirteenth International Conference of Labour Statisticians.* Geneva: ILO.

———. 1984. *Statistical Yearbook.* Geneva: ILO.

———. 1989. *Urban Poverty and the Labour Market: Access to Jobs and Incomes in Asian and Latin American Cities.* Geneva: ILO.

———. 1991. *ILO Yearbook of Labour Statistics, 50th Issue.* Geneva: ILO.

———. 1994. *Statistical Yearbook.* Geneva: ILO.

Ismail, S. D. Abdou, et. al. 1982a. *Utilization Patterns of the Primary Subsidized Food Commodities in Egypt.* Economic Working Paper no. 145. Egypt Ministry of Agriculture/University of California.

———. 1982b. *The Distribution of Consumption of Basic Food: Consumption in Urban and Rural Areas of Egypt.* Economic Working Paper no. 59. Egypt Ministry of Agriculture/University of California.

Jacobs, Jerry. 1988. *The Search for Self: Consumerism, Sexuality and Self among American Women.* Bristol, Ind.: Wyndham Hall Press.

Jayawardena, Kumari. 1992. *Feminism and Nationalism in the Third World.* London: Zed Press.

Jelin, Elizabeth. 1977. "Migration and Labor Force Participation of Latin American Women: The Domestic Servants in the Cities." *Signs* 3: 129–141.

———. 1991. *Family, Household, and Gender Relations in Latin America.* London: Kegan Paul International in association with UNESCO.

Johnson, Norman, ed. 1985. *Marital Violence.* Sociological Review, Monograph 31. London: Routledge and Kegan Paul.

Joseph, Suad. 1983. "Working-Class Women's Networks in a Sectorian State: A Political Paradox." *American Ethnologist* 10(1): 1–22.

———. 1987. "Models of the Arab Family in Anthropological Studies: A Critical Assessment." Paper presented at the Twenty-First Annual Meeting of the Middle East Studies Association of North America, Baltimore, 14–17 November.

———. 1993. "Gender and Relationality among Arab Families in Lebanon." *Feminist Studies* 19: 465–486.

———. 1994. "Brother/Sister Relationships: Connectivity, Love, and Power in the Reproduction of Patriarchy in Lebanon." *American Ethnologist* 21: 50–73.

Kabbani, Rana. 1986. *Europe's Myths of the Orient.* Bloomington: Indiana University Press.

Kagitcibasi, Cigdem. 1982. "Sex Roles, Value of Children and Fertility." In *Sex Roles, Family and Community in Turkey,* ed. Cigdem Kagitcibasi. Bloomington: Indiana University Turkish Studies.

Kamel Rizk, Soad. 1991. "The Structure and Operation of the Informal Sector in Egypt." In *Employment and Structural Adjustment: Egypt in the 1990s,* ed. Heba Handoussa and Gillian Potter. Cairo: American University in Cairo Press.

Kamphoefner, Kathryn R. 1996. "What Is the Use? The Household, Low-Income Women, and Literacy." In *Development, Change, and Gender in Cairo: A View from the Household,* ed. Diane Singerman and Homa Hoodfar. Bloomington: Indiana University Press.

Keddie, Nikki, and Beth Baron, eds. 1991. *Women in Middle Eastern History: Shifting Boundaries in Sex and Gender.* New Haven: Yale University Press.

Kerr, Malcolm, and el-Sayed Yassin, eds. 1982. *Rich and Poor States in the Middle East: Egypt and the New Arab Order.* Boulder, Colo.: Westview Press.

Kessler-Harris, Alice. 1990. *A Woman's Wage, Historical Meaning and Sexual Consequences.* Lexington: University Press of Kentucky.

Khafagy, Fatma. 1984. "Socio-Economic Impact of Temporary Migration from the Village of Qababar." Ph.D. dissertation, University College, London.

Khattab, H., and S. el-Daeif. 1982. *Impact of Male Labour Migration on the Structure of the Family and the Role of Women.* Regional Paper no. 16. Cairo: Population Council.

Khouri-Dagher, Nadia. 1985. "La Survie Quotidienne au Caire." *Maghreb-Machrek Review* 10 (Fall): 53–68.

——. 1986. *Food and Energy in Cairo: Provisioning the Poor.* A report prepared for the United Nations University, Food and Energy Nexus Programme, Cairo.

——. 1996. "Households and the Food Issue in Cairo: The Answers of Civil Society to a Defaulting State." In *Development, Change, and Gender in Cairo: A View from the Household,* ed. Diane Singerman and Homa Hoodfar. Bloomington: Indiana University Press.

el-Korayem, K. 1981. "Women and the International Economic Order in the Arab World." *Cairo Papers in Social Science* 4(4).

——. 1982a. "Estimation of the Disposable Income Distribution in the Urban and Rural Sectors of Egypt." *Cairo Papers in Social Science* 5(2): 1–43.

——. 1982b. "The Impact of the Elimination of Food Subsidies on the Cost of Living of Egypt's Urban Population." *Cairo Papers in Social Science* 5(2): 44–100.

Kressel, Gideon M. 1986. "Prescriptive Patrilateral Parallel Cousin Marriage: The Perspective of the Bride's Father and Brothers." *Ethnology* 25: 163–180.

Kunstadter, Peter. 1984. "Culture, Socioeconomic Change and Household Composition: Karen, Lua', Hmong and Thai in Northwestern Thailand." In *Households: Comparative and Historical Studies of the Domestic Group,* ed. Robert Mac Netting, Richard R. Wilk, and Eric J. Arnould. Berkeley, Los Angeles, and London: University of California Press.

Lazreg, Marnia. 1994. *The Eloquence of Silence: Algerian Women in Question.* New York: Routledge.

Lee, Everett S. 1966. "A Theory of Migration." *Demography* 3(1): 47–57.

Leibenstein, Harvey. 1981. "Economic Decision Theory and Human Fertility Behaviour: A Speculative Essay." *Population and Development Review* 7(3): 381–400.

Leites, Justin. 1991. "Modernist Jurisprudence as a Vehicle for Gender Role Reform in the Islamic World." *Columbia Human Rights Law Review* 22: 251–330.

Lewis, Oscar. 1959. *Five Families: Mexican Case Studies in the Culture of Poverty.* New York: Basic Books.

———. 1961. *The Children of Sanchez: Autobiography of a Mexican Family.* New York: Random House.

———. 1966. *La Vida: A Puerto Rican Family in the Culture of Poverty.* New York: Random House.

Lightfoot-Klein, Hanny. 1989. "A History of Clitoral Excision and Infibulation Process in the Western World." In Lightfoot-Klein, *Prisoners of Ritual: An Odyssey into Female Genital Circumcision in Africa.* New York: Haworth Press.

Lipman-Blumen, Jean. 1984. *Gender Roles and Power.* Englewood Cliffs, N.J.: Prentice-Hall.

Lloyd, Peter. 1979. *Slums of Hope? Shanty Towns of the Third World.* Harmondsworth, Middlesex: Pelican Books.

Lobban, Richard, ed. 1996. *Middle Eastern Women in the "Invisible" Economy.* Gainesville: University Press of Florida.

Lobo, Susan. 1982. *A House of My Own: Social Organization in the Squatter Settlements of Lima, Peru.* Tucson: University of Arizona Press.

Lofgren, H. 1993a. "Economic Policy in Egypt: A Breakdown in Uniform Resistance?" *International Journal of Middle East Studies* 25: 407–421.

———. 1993b. "Egypt's Program for Stabilization and Structural Adjustment: An Assessment." *Cairo Papers in Social Sciences* 16(3): 20–37.

Lomnitz, Larissa Adler de. 1977. *Networks and Marginality: Life in a Mexican Shantytown.* Translated by Cinna Lomnitz. New York: Academic Press.

Lomnitz, Larissa Adler de, and Marisol Perez-Liazur. 1987. *A Mexican Elite Family, 1820–1980: Kinship, Class, and Culture.* Translated by Cinna Lomnitz. Princeton: Princeton University Press.

Mabro, Judy. 1991. *Veiled Half Truths: European Perceptions of Middle Eastern Women.* London: I. B. Taurus.

McCracken, Grant. 1990. *Culture and Consumption: New Approaches to the Symbolic Character of Consumer Goods and Activities.* Bloomington: Indiana University Press.

MacLeod, Arlene Elowe. 1991. *Accommodating Protest: Working Women and the New Veiling in Cairo.* New York: Columbia University Press.

———. 1996. "Transforming Women's Identity: The Intersection of Household and Workplace in Cairo." In *Development, Change, and Gender in Cairo: A View from the Household,* ed. Diane Singerman and Homa Hoodfar. Bloomington: Indiana University Press.

Maher, Vanessa. 1976. "Kin, Clients and Accomplices: Relationships among Women in Morocco." In *Dependency and Exploitation in Work and Marriage,* ed. D. M. L. Barker and S. A. Allan. London: Tavistock.

———. 1981. "Work, Consumption, and Authority Within the Household: A Moroccan Case." In *Of Marriage and of the Market: Women's Subordination Internationally and Its Lessons,* ed. Kate Young, Carol Wolkowitz, and Roslyn McCullagh. Boston: Routledge and Kegan Paul.

Mahfouz, Najib. 1966. *Midaq Alley.* Translated by Trever Le Gassick. Beirut: Khayats.

Mansbridge, Jane. 1990. *Beyond Self-Interest.* Chicago: University of Chicago Press.

March, Kathryn S., and Rachelle L. Taqqu. 1986. *Women's Informal Associations in Developing Countries: Catalysts for Change?* Boulder, Colo.: Westview Press.

Mayhew, Henry. 1965. *Selections from London Labour and the London Poor.* Chosen with and introduction by John S. Bradley. London: Oxford University Press.

Mencher, Joan P. 1988. "Women's Work and Poverty: Women's Contribution to Household Maintenance in South India." In *A Home Divided: Women and Income in the Third World,* ed. Daisy Dwyer and Judith Bruce. Stanford: Stanford University Press.

Mencher, Joan P., and Anne Okongwu. 1993. *Where Did All the Men Go? Female-headed/Female-supported Households in Cross-Cultural Perspective.* Boulder, Colo.: Westview Press.

Meskoub, Mahmood. 1992. "Deprivation and Structural Adjustment." In *Development Policy and Public Action,* ed. Marc Wuyts, Maureen MacKintosh, and Tom Hewitt. Oxford: Open University Press in association with Oxford University Press.

Messiri, Sawsan el-. 1978a. *Ibn al-Balad: The Concept of Egyptian Identity.* Leiden: E. J. Brill.

———. 1978b. "Self-Images of Traditional Urban Women in Cairo." In *Women in the Muslim World,* ed. Lois Beck and Nikki Keddie. Cambridge, Mass.: Harvard University Press.

Meyer, Gunter. 1987. "Socio-Economic Structure and Development of Small-Scale Manufacturing in Old Quarters of Cairo." Paper presented at the Twenty-First Annual Meeting of the Middle East Studies Association of North America, Baltimore, 14–17 November.

Mies, Maria. 1982. *The Lace-Makers of Narsapur: Indian Housewives Produce for the World Market.* London: Zed Press.

Mingione, Enzo. 1994. "Life Strategies and Social Economies in the Post-Fordist Age." *International Journal of Urban Regional Research* 18: 24–45.

Mohanty, Chandra. 1988. "Under Western Eyes: Feminist Scholarship and Colonial Discourses." *Feminist Review* 30 (Autumn): 61–88.

Mohanty, Chandra, et al. 1991. *Third World Women and the Politics of Feminism.* Bloomington: Indiana University Press.

Mohie El-Din, A. 1982. "The Development of the State of Agricultural Wage Labour in the National Income of Egypt." In *The Political Economy of Income Distribution in Egypt,* ed. Gouda Abdel Khalek and Robert Tignor. New York: Holmes and Meier.

Mohsen, M. 1985. "Women and the Veil." In *Women and the Family in the Mid-*

dle East: New Voices of Change, ed. E. W. Fernea. Austin: University of Texas Press.

Molyneux, Maxine. 1979. "Beyond the Domestic Labour Debate." *New Left Review* 116: 3–27.

———. 1985. "The Role of Women in the Revolution." In *Nicaragua: The First Five Years,* ed. T. Walker. New York: Praeger.

Morris, L. 1984. "Redundancy and Patterns of Household Finance." *Sociological Review* 33(3): 492–523.

———. 1987. "Constraints on Gender: The Family Wage, Social Security and the Labour Market." *Work, Employment and Society* 1(1): 85–106.

Morsy, Soheir A. 1978. "Sex Differences and Folk Illness in an Egyptian Village." In *Women in the Muslim World,* ed. Lois Beck and Nikki Keddie. Cambridge, Mass.: Harvard University Press.

Moser, Caroline. 1981. "Surviving in the Suburbs." In *Women in the Informal Sector,* ed. Caroline Moser and Kate Young. Sussex: IDS Bulletin 12(3).

Moser, Caroline, and Kate Young, eds. 1981. *Women in the Informal Sector.* Sussex: IDS Bulletin 12(3).

Murata, Sachiko. 1992. *The Tao of Islam: A Sourcebook on Gender Relationships in Islamic Thought.* Albany: State University of New York Press.

Murray, Allison J. 1991. *No Money No Honey: A Study of Street Traders and Prostitutes in Jakarta.* Singapore and New York: Oxford University Press.

Musallam, B. F. 1983. *Sex and Society in Islam: Birth Control Before the Nineteenth Century.* Cambridge: Cambridge University Press.

Nada, Atef Hanna. 1991. "The Impact of Temporary International Migration on Rural Egypt." *Cairo Papers in Social Science* 14(3): 1–75.

Nadim, Assad. 1980. "Living Without Water." *Cairo Papers in Social Science* 3(3).

Nadim el-Messiri, Nawal. 1975. "The Relationships Between the Sexes in a Harah of Cairo." Ph.D. dissertation, Indiana University.

———. 1977. "Family Relations in a Harah in Old Cairo." In *Arab Society: Social Science Perspectives,* ed. Nicholas S. Hopkins and Saad Ibrahim. Cairo: American University in Cairo Press.

Nelson, Cynthia. 1991. "Biography and Women's History: On Interpreting Doria Shafik." In *Women in Middle Eastern History: Shifting Boundaries in Sex and Gender,* ed. Nikki Keddie and Beth Baron. New Haven: Yale University Press.

Netting, Robert Mac, Richard R. Wilk, and Eric J. Arnould, eds. 1984. *Households: Comparative and Historical Studies of the Domestic Group.* Berkeley, Los Angeles, and London: University of California Press.

Newland, Kathleen. 1979. *The Sisterhood of Man.* New York: W. W. Norton.

Oakley, Ann. 1974a. *The Sociology of Housework.* Oxford: Martin & Robinson.

———. 1974b. *Housewife: High Value Low Cost.* London: Allen Lane.

Obermeyer, Carla Makhlouf. 1994. "Reproductive Choice in Islam: Gender and State in Iran and Tunisia." *Studies in Family Planning* 25: 41–51.

Oldham, Linda. 1984. *Safia and Her Family: A Family Profile.* Cairo: Population Council (Mimeographed.)

Oldham, Linda, Haguer el-Hadidi, and Hussein Tamaa. 1987. "Informal Communities in Cairo: The Basis of a Typology." *Cairo Papers in Social Sciences* 10(4): 1–110.

Omran, Abdel Rahim. 1992. *Family Planning and the Legacy of Islam*. London: Routledge.

Pahl, Jan. 1989. *Money and Marriage*. London: Macmillan Press.

Pahl, R. E. 1984. *Divisions of Labour*. Oxford: Basil Blackwell.

———. 1988. "Some Remarks on Informal Work, Social Polarization, and the Social Structure." *International Journal of Urban and Regional Research* 12(2): 247–267.

Papanek, Hanna. 1990. "To Each Less than She Needs, from Each More than She Can Do: Allocation, Entitlements and Value." In *Persistent Inequalities: Women and World Development*, ed. Irene Tinker. Oxford: Oxford University Press.

Papanek, Hanna, and Barbara Ibrahim. 1982. *Economic Participation of Egyptian Women: Implications for Labour Force Creation and Industrial Policy*. Cairo: USAID.

Parfitt, Trevor. 1993. "The Politics of Structural Adjustment with Special Reference to Egypt." *Cairo Papers in Social Sciences* 16(3): 4–19.

Patel, Tulsi. 1994. *Fertility Behaviour: Population and Society in a Rajasthan Village*. Delhi and New York: Oxford University Press.

Perlman, Janice E. 1976. *The Myth of Marginality: Urban Poverty and Politics in Rio de Janeiro*. Berkeley, Los Angeles, and London: University of California Press.

Pfeifer, K. 1993. "Does Food Security Make a Difference? Algeria, Egypt, and Turkey in Comparative Perspective." In *The Many Faces of National Security in the Arab World*, ed. Baghat Korany, P. Noble, and R. Brynen. Basingstoke: Macmillan.

Pinchbeck, I. 1981. *Women Workers and the Industrial Revolution, 1750–1850*. London: Virago Press.

Portes, Alejandro, Manuel Castells, and Lauren Benton, eds. 1989. *The Informal Economy: Studies in Advanced and Less Developed Countries*. Baltimore: Johns Hopkins University Press.

Recchini de Lattes, Z., and C. H. Wainerman. 1986. "Unreliable Account of Women's Work: Evidence from Latin American Census Statistics." *Signs* 11: 740–750.

Redclift, Nanneke, and Enzo Mingione, eds. 1985. *Beyond Employment: Household, Gender and Subsistence*. Oxford: Basil Blackwell.

Redclift, Nanneke, and M. Thea Sinclair, eds. 1991. *Working Women: International Perspectives on Labour and Gender Ideology*. London: Routledge.

Reid, M. G. 1934. *Economics of Household Production*. New York: John Wiley and Sons.

Richards, Alan, and John Waterbury. 1990. *A Political Economy of the Middle East: State, Class, and Economic Development*. Boulder, Colo.: Westview Press.

Rogers, Barbara. 1980. *The Domestication of Women: Discrimination in Developing Societies*. London: Tavistock.

Roldan, Martha. 1985. "Industrial Outworking: Struggles for Reproduction of Working-Class Families and Gender Subordination." In *Beyond Employ-ment: Household, Gender and Subsistence,* ed. Nanneke Redclift and Enzo Mingione. Oxford: Basil Blackwell.

———. 1988. "Renegotiating the Marital Contract: Intrahousehold Patterns of Money Allocation and Women's Subordination among Domestic Out-workers in Mexico City." In *A Home Divided: Women and Income in the Third World,* ed. Daisy Dwyer and Judith Bruce. Stanford: Stanford University Press.

Rosenfeld, H. 1960. "Non-Hierarchical, Hierarchical and Masked Reciprocity in an Aran Village." *Anthropological Quarterly* 47: 139–166.

Rowntree, D. S. 1902. *Poverty.* London: Macmillan.

Roy, Delwin A. 1992. "The Hidden Economy of Egypt." *Middle Eastern Studies* 28: 689–711.

Rugh, Andrea. 1979. "Coping with Poverty in a Cairo Community." *Cairo Papers in Social Science* 2(1): 1–100.

———. 1984. *Family in Contemporary Egypt.* Syracuse, N.Y.: Syracuse University Press.

———. 1986. *Reveal and Conceal: Dress in Contemporary Egypt.* Syracuse, N.Y.: Syracuse University Press.

Sa'dawi, Nawal el-. 1980. *The Hidden Face of Eve: Women in the Arab World.* London: Zed Press.

Saad el-Din, I., and M. Abdel-Fadil. 1983. *Arab Labour Movements: Problems, Effects and Policies.* Beirut: Center for Arab Unity Studies. (Arabic.)

Safa, Helen I. 1995. *The Myth of the Male Breadwinner: Women and Industrialization in the Caribbean.* Boulder, Colo.: Westview Press.

Sahlins, Marshall. 1972. *Stone Age Economics.* Chicago: Aldine-Atherton.

———. 1976. *Culture and Practical Reason.* Chicago: University of Chicago Press.

Said, Edward W. 1978. *Orientalism.* London: Penguin.

Sayed Said, Mohamed el-. 1990. *The Political Economy of Migration in Egypt: 1974–1989.* West Asia and North Africa Regional Papers, no. 36. Cairo: Population Council.

Sayigh, R. 1981. "Roles and Functions of Arab Women: A Reappraisal." *Arab Studies Quarterly* 3(3): 258–274.

Sayyid Marsot, Afaf Lutfi el-. 1978. "The Revolutionary Gentlewomen in Egypt." In *Women in the Muslim World,* ed. Lois Beck and Nikki Keddie. Cambridge, Mass.: Harvard University Press.

Schmink, Marianne. 1982. *Women in an Urban Economy in Latin America: Women, Low-Income Households and Urban Services,* Working Paper no. 1. New York: Population Council.

———. 1984. "Household Economic Strategies: Review and Research Agenda." *Latin American Research Review* 19(3): 87–101.

Scott, Alison M. 1986. "Women and Industrialization: Examining the 'Female Marginality' Thesis." *Journal of Development Studies* 22(4): 643–680.

Scott, James. 1985. *The Weapons of the Weak.* New Haven: Yale University Press.

Sen, Amartya K. 1990. "Gender and Cooperative Conflicts." In *Persistent In-*

equalities: Women and World Development, ed. Irene Tinker. Oxford: Oxford University Press.

Sha'rawi, Huda. 1986. *Harem Years: The Memoirs of an Egyptian Feminist, 1879–1924.* Translated and introduction by Margot Badran. London: Virago Press.

el-Sharkawi, Ahmed. 1993. "Economic Reforms in Egypt: Selected Aspects." *Economic Papers* 26: 5–18.

Sharma, Ursula. 1986. *Women's Work, Class, and the Urban Household: A Study of Shimala, North India.* London: Tavistock.

Sholkamy, Hania. 1994. "The Quest for Fertility." Paper presented at the Annual Meeting of the American Anthropological Association, Atlanta.

Shorter, Frederic C. 1985. "Preliminary Analysis of Manshiet Nasser Study." Unpublished report. Cairo: Population Council.

———. 1989. "Cairo's Leap Forward: People, Households, and Dwelling Space." *Cairo Papers in Social Science* 12(1).

Shorter, Frederic C., and Huda C. Zurayk. 1988. *The Social Composition of Households in Arab Cities: Cairo, Beirut, Amman.* Regional Papers no. 31. Cairo: Population Council.

Singerman, Diane. 1987. "Individual, Household, Family and the State: The Politics of Resource Mobilization." Paper presented at the Twenty-First Annual Meeting of the Middle East Studies Association of North America, Baltimore, 14–17 November.

———. 1990. "Politics at the Household Level in a Popular Quarter of Cairo." *Journal of South Asian and Middle Eastern Studies* 12(4): 3–21.

———. 1994. "Where Has All the Power Gone? Women and Politics in Popular Quarters of Cairo." In *Reconstructing Gender in the Middle East: Tradition, Identity, and Power,* ed. Fatma Muge Gocek and Shiva Balaghi. New York: Columbia University Press.

———. 1995. *Avenues of Participation: Family, Politics and Networks in Urban Quarters of Cairo.* Princeton: Princeton University Press.

———. 1996a. "The Family and Community as Politics: The Popular Sector in Cairo." In *Development, Change, and Gender in Cairo: A View from the Household,* ed. Diane Singerman and Homa Hoodfar. Bloomington: Indiana University Press.

———. 1996b. "Engaging Informality: Women, Work and Politics in Cairo." In *Middle Eastern Women in the "Invisible" Economy,* ed. Richard Lobban. Gainesville: University Press of Florida.

Singerman, Diane, and Homa Hoodfar, eds. 1996. *Development, Change, and Gender in Cairo: A View from the Household.* Bloomington: Indiana University Press.

Smith, Joan. 1984. "Nonwage Labour and Subsistence." In *Households and the World Economy,* ed. Joan Smith, Immanuel Wallerstein, and Hans-Dieter Evers. Beverly Hills, Calif.: Sage Publications.

———. 1990. "All Crises Are Not the Same: Households in the United States during Two Crises." In *Work Without Wages: Comparative Studies of Domestic Labor and Self-Employment,* ed. Jane L. Collins and Martha Gimenez. Albany: State University of New York Press.

Smith, M. Estellie. 1976. "Networks and Migration Resettlement: Cherchez la Femme." *Anthropological Quarterly* 49(1): 20–27.

———. 1989. "Informal Economy." In *Economic Anthropology,* ed. Stuart Plattner. Stanford: Stanford University Press.

Sokkari, Myrette Ahmed el-. 1984. "Basic Needs: Inflation and the Poor of Egypt." *Cairo Papers in Social Science* 7(2).

Springberg, Robert. 1991. "State-Society Relations in Egypt: The Debate Over Owner-Tenant Relations." *Middle East Journal* 45(2): 232–249.

Stack, Carol. 1974. *All Our Kin: Strategies for Survival in a Black Community.* New York: Harper and Row.

Standing, Hilary. 1984. "The Control and Disposal of Women's Wages in the Urban Bengali Family." Mimeograph.

———. 1989. *Sexual Behaviour in Sub-Saharan Africa: A Review and Annotated Bibliography.* London: Overseas Development Administration.

———. 1991. *Dependence and Autonomy: Women's Employment and the Family in Calcutta.* New York: Routledge.

Stauth, Georg. 1991. "Gamaliyya: Informal Economy and Social Life in a Popular Quarter of Cairo." *Cairo Papers in Social Science* 14(4): 78–103.

Stirling, Paul. 1965. *Turkish Village.* London: Weidenfeld and Nicholson.

Stirratt, Jonathan. 1989. "Atittudes to Money among Catholic Fishing Communities in Sri Lanka." In *Money and the Morality of Exchange,* ed. Maurice Bloch and Jonathan Parry. Cambridge: Cambridge University Press.

Stolcke, Verena. 1988. *Coffee Planters, Workers, and Wives: Class Conflict and Gender Relations on São Paulo Plantations, 1850–1980.* Basingstoke: Macmillan in association with St. Anthony's College, Oxford.

Sullivan, Denis J. 1992. "Extra State Actors and Privatization in Egypt." In *Privatization and Liberalization in the Middle East,* ed. Iliya Harik and Denis J. Sullivan. Bloomington: Indiana University Press.

———. 1994. *Private and Voluntary Organization in Egypt: Islamic Development, Private Industries, State Control.* Gainesville: University Press of Florida.

Sullivan, Earl L. 1981. "Women and Work in Egypt." *Cairo Papers in Social Science* 4(1).

Tadros, Helmi R., Mohamed Feteeha, and Allan Hibbard. 1990. "Squatter Markets in Cairo." *Cairo Papers in Social Science* 13(1): iii–74.

Taylor, Elizabeth. 1984. "Egyptian Migration and Peasant Wives." *Middle East Research and Information Project* 124 (June).

Tekçe, Belgin, Linda Oldham, and Frederic C. Shorter. 1994. *A Place to Live: Families and Child Health in a Cairo Neighbourhood.* Cairo: American University in Cairo Press.

Thomas, Duncan. 1991. *Gender Differences in Household Resource Allocations.* Washington, D.C.: World Bank.

Thomas, Susan L. 1994. *Gender and Poverty.* New York: Garland.

Thomas-Emeagwali, Gloria, ed. 1995. *Women Pay the Price: Structural Adjustment in Africa and the Caribbean.* Trenton, N.J.: Africa World Press.

Thompson, T. 1987. "Popeli: Village, Marriage, and Kinship." Paper presented at the Twenty-First Annual Meeting of the Middle East Studies Association of North America, Baltimore, 14–17 November.

Thorbek, Susanne. 1994. *Gender and Slum Culture in Urban Asia*. London: Zed Press.

Tillion, Germaine. [1966] 1983. *The Republic of Cousins: Women's Oppression in Mediterranean Society*. Translated by Quintin Hoare. London: Al Saqi Books.

Tinker, Irene. 1987. "Street Foods: Testing Assumptions about Informal Sector Activity by Men and Women." *Current Sociology* 35: 1–110.

Tinker, Irene, ed. 1990. *Persistent Inequalities: Women and World Development*. Oxford: Oxford University Press.

Toch, Hans. 1993. "Violence Against Women, Violent Networks: The Origin and Management of Domestic Conflict." In *Aggression and Violence: Social Interactionist Perspectives*, ed. Richard B. Felson and James T. Tedeschi. Washington, D.C.: American Psychological Association.

Toubia, Nahid. 1985. "The Social and the Political Implications of Female Circumcision: The Case of the Sudan." In *Women and the Family in the Middle East*, ed. Elizabeth Warnock Fernea. Austin: University of Texas Press.

———. 1988. *Women of the Arab World: The Coming Challenge*. London: Zed Press.

———. 1993. *Female Genital Mutilation: A Call for Global Action*. New York: Women Ink.

———. 1995. *Female Genital Mutilation*. New York: Rainbo.

Tripp, Mani Aili. 1991. "Economic Liberalization and the Urban Informal Economy in Tanzania." Paper presented at the XVth World Congress of the International Political Science Association, Buenos Aires, 21–25 July.

Tucker, Judith E. 1976. "Egyptian Women in the Workforce: A Historical Survey." *Middle East Research and Information Project* 50.

———. 1985. *Women in Nineteenth-Century Egypt*. Cambridge: Cambridge University Press.

———. 1993a. *Arab Women: Old Boundaries, New Frontiers*. Bloomington: Indiana University Press.

———. 1993b. "Decline of the Family Economy in Mid-Nineteenth-Century Egypt." *The Modern Middle East: A Reader*, ed. A. Hourani, P. S. Khoury, and M. C. Wilson. London: Tauris.

United Nations (UN). 1971. *Demographic Yearbook*. New York: United Nations.

———. 1992. *Demographic Yearbook*. New York: United Nations.

Vaneck, Joann. 1974. "Time Spent on Housework." *Scientific American* 233(5): 116–120.

Velez-Ibañez, Carlos. 1983. *Bonds of Mutual Trust; The Cultural Systems of Rotating Credit Associations among Urban Mexicans and Chicanos*. New Brunswick, N.J.: Rutgers University Press.

Viano, Emilio C., ed. 1992. *Intimate Violence: Interdisciplinary Perspectives*. Washington, D.C.: Hemisphere.

Vickers, Jeanne. 1990. *Women and the World Economic Crisis*. London: Zed Press.

Wallerstein, Immanuel. 1984. "Household Structures and Labour-Force Formation in the Capitalist World Economy." In *Households and the World Economy*, ed. Joan Smith, Immanuel Wallerstein, and Hans-Dieter Evers. Beverly Hills, Calif.: Sage Publications.

Warde, Alan. 1994. "Consumption, Identity-Formation, and Uncertainty." *Sociology* 28: 877–898.

Waring, Marilyn. 1988. *If Women Counted: A New Feminist Economics.* San Francisco: Harper and Row.

Waterbury, John. 1978. *Egypt: Burdens of the Past, Options for the Future.* Bloomington: Indiana University Press.

———. 1983. *The Egypt of Nasser and Sadat: The Political Economy of Two Regimes.* Princeton: Princeton University Press.

Watson, Helen. 1992. *Women in the City of the Dead.* Trenton, N.J.: Africa World Press.

Wellman, Barry, and Scot Wortley. 1989. *Different Strokes from Different Folks: Which Type of Ties Provide What Kind of Social Support?* Toronto: Centre for Urban and Community Studies, University of Toronto.

Werlhof, Claudia von. 1980. "Notes on the Relation between Sexuality and Economy." *Review: Journal of the Fernand Braudel Centre for the Study of Economies, Historical Systems and Civilizations* 4: 32–42.

———. 1984. "The Proletarian Is Dead: Long Live the Housewife?" In *Households and the World Economy,* ed. Joan Smith, Immanuel Wallerstein, and Hans-Dieter Evers. Beverly Hills, Calif.: Sage Publications.

Weyland, P. 1993. *Inside the Third World Village.* London: Routledge.

White, Jenny B. 1994. *Money Makes Us Relatives: Women's Labor in Urban Turkey.* Austin: University of Texas Press.

Whitehead, Ann. 1981. "I'm Hungry, Mum: The Politics of Domestic Budgeting." In *Of Marriage and of the Market: Women's Subordination Internationally and Its Lessons,* ed. Kate Young, Carol Wolkowitz, and Roslyn McCullagh. Boston: Routledge and Kegan Paul.

Wikan, Unni. 1980. *Life Among the Poor in Cairo.* Translated by Ann Henning. New York: Tavistock.

———. 1985. "Living Conditions Among Cairo's Poor: A View from Below." *Middle East Journal* 39(1): 7–26.

Wilk, Richard R. 1984. "Household in the Process: Agricultural Changes and Domestic Transformation Among the Kekchi Maya of Belize." In *Households: Comparative and Historical Studies of the Domestic Group,* ed. Robert Mac Netting, Richard R. Wilk, and Eric J. Arnould. Berkeley, Los Angeles, and London: University of California Press.

Williamson, Bill. 1987. *Education and Social Change in Egypt and Turkey: A Study in Historical Sociology.* Basingstoke: Macmillan.

Wilson, Gail. 1987. *Money in the Family: Financial Organization and Women's Responsibility.* Sydney: Avenbury Press.

Wilson, Rodney. 1993. "Whither the Egyptian Economy?" *British Journal of Middle East Studies* 20: 204–213.

Wood, Charles. 1981. "Structural Changes and Household Strategies: A Conceptual Framework for the Study of Rural Migration." *Human Organization* 40(4): 338–344.

World Bank. 1991. *Gender and Poverty in India.* Washington, D.C.: World Bank.

———. 1993. *World Tables.* Baltimore: Johns Hopkins University Press.

Yalman, Galip L. 1991. "The State and the 'Informal Sector' in Contemporary Turkey." Paper presented at the XVth World Congress of the International Political Science Association, Buenos Aires, 21–25 July.

Young, Kate, Carol Wolkowitz, and Roslyn McCullagh, eds. 1981. *Of Marriage and of the Market: Women's Subordination Internationally and Its Lessons.* Boston: Routledge and Kegan Paul.

Youssef, Nadia. 1976. "Women in Development: Urban Life and Labour." In *Women and World Development,* ed. Irene Tinker, Michelle Bo Bramsen, and Mayra Buvinic. London: Praeger.

Youssef, Nadia, and Carol Hetler. 1983. *Rural Households Headed by Women: A Priority Concern for Development.* Geneva: ILO World Employment Program Working Papers.

Zuhur, Sherifa. 1992. *Revealing Reveiling: Islamic Gender Ideology in Contemporary Egypt.* Albany: State University of New York Press.

Zurayk, Huda. 1985. "Women's Economic Participation." In *Population Factors in Development Planning in the Middle East,* ed. Frederic C. Shorter and Huda C. Zurayk. New York and Cairo: Population Council.

Index

Abortion, 245, 249
Accumulation of assets: decision making, 211–215; as investment, 150, 190, 191, 204–209, 273
Agriculture, 45n.31; women's participation in, 109
Alcohol, 161
Apprenticeship, 101

Backgammon approach, 16–17
Bread, 46, 179, 194–195

Cairo, 23–24
Cash: dependence on male income earner for, 115, 168, 192; increasing need for, 80
Cash-saving labor, 181–184. *See also* Non-monetary contributions
Chaianov, Aleksandr Vasil'evich, 9n.9
Child care, 70, 172–175
Children: cash contributions to household, 100–101, 137; desire for, 159; employment of, 100–101; unmarried women as, 159. *See also* Daughters; Sons
Circumcision, 256–262, 263; female, 241–242, 257–262; male, 257; marriage and, 258–261; opposition to, 241–242, 259, 260–261, 262; and sexuality, 258–259
Clothing, 196–199; men's, 161, 198, 199; modern Islamic, 196–197; neighborhood, 197; status and, 198. *See also* Veil
Consumption, 20–21, 188–216; individual, 159–161; social aspects of, 20–21,

188–189, 204, 208–209, 272–273. *See also* Accumulation of assets
Contraception, 66, 244–245; men's involvement in, 244, 245
Copts, 41, 52n.1
Cost-benefit calculcations, 1–3, 9, 14, 20, 74, 116–119, 124–125, 134–135, 178, 269–270
Cross-cousin marriage, 55–56
Custody, 53

Daughters, 198–199; family honor and, 2, 223n.7, 265; preference for, 245–248, 262
Davidson, Caroline, 164
Divorce, 53–54, 70, 76, 107, 235
Domestic servants, 113–114, 130–131; male, 130
Domestic violence, 55, 234–235, 271; and altruism theory of domestic economy, 11
Domestic work, 163–172, 272; attitudes toward, 30–31, 60–61, 165–166, 167; employment and, 106–107, 139, 169–171; informal sector work and, 122–123; men's participation in, 167–171; as proportion of national economy, 12–13, 164–165; state's devaluation of, 106–107. *See also* Child care; Food; Washing
Dower. *See* Mahr
Dowry. *See* Trousseau
Durable goods. *See* Household goods

299

Economic activity: definition of, 12–
13; and honor, 2, 72, 112; measuring,
13; among women informants, 112–113;
women's reluctance to report, 14–15,
112; women's unpaid, 110–112, 127–128.
See also Formal sector employment;
Home production; Informal sector employment; Labor force; Production of
utility
Education: expenses, 200–202; free universal, 43; girls', 84, 268; as household-
level strategy, 57n.12, 84, 200–202,
268; among informants, 36–37; and
marriage, 56–58; and public sector jobs,
137; quality of, 47, 199; and social mobility, 43; technical, 83–84; tutoring,
47, 199–200. *See also* Apprenticeship
Electricity, 42
Engagement, 67, 69, 74. *See also* Marriage; Negotiations (marriage)

Family, 18. *See also* Household; Kinship
Female circumcision. *See* Circumcision
Female labor market participation, 20,
103, 104–105, 108–112, 137–140, 269–
270
Fertility, 241–250, 262; social aspects of,
243, 245
Fictive kinship, 25, 225–226
Fieldwork, 16, 22–35. *See also* Interviewing; Methodology
Financial obligations, 19, 52, 54, 60, 70–
71, 80–81, 101, 115, 138–139, 142–143,
162, 270
Folbre, Nancy, 10n.10, 11n.11, 13
Food, 151, 160, 166–167, 168, 175–181,
182, 193–196; convenience or modern,
194–196. *See also* Bread; Home production; Meat; Subsidies (food)
Formal sector employment, 1–3, 9, 14,
20, 44, 52, 74, 81, 83, 113–119, 124–
125, 134–139, 174, 178, 269–270; guaranteed jobs for high school graduates,
43n.27, 114; and mobility, 52; private
sector, 82, 113; public sector, 43–44,
47, 50, 53, 74, 80–87, 137, 268; and
status, 82, 113–114. *See also* Moonlighting; Pensions
Friendships, 77, 224–226

Gallabiya, 197–198. *See also* Clothing
Gam'iyat. *See* Saving clubs

Garbage collection, 42
Gender division of labor. *See* Sexual divi-
sion of labor
Gender ideology, 51, 78–79, 115, 140, 275.
See also Marriage; Sexual division of
labor
Gendered space, 40, 87–88, 105, 223–
224, 225
Gift exchanges, 18, 28–29, 203, 222–223.
See also Reciprocity
Goldschmidt-Clermont, Luisella, 12–13
Government employment. *See* Formal
sector employment
Gronau, Robert, 13–14n.18
Guest husband, 152–154

Health care, 43, 47, 203
Hijab. *See* Veil
Home production, 2; chicken, pigeon,
and rabbit, 129–130, 182; eggs, 193
Honor, 2, 223n.7, 265
Hospitality, 25–29, 30. *See also* Networks;
Reciprocity
Household, 7–12, 15, 17, 19, 20, 51, 68,
70, 100, 222, 265; definition of, 9n.9,
18; single-person, 8, 51, 159
Household goods, 204–214
Housekeeping allowances. *See* Money
management
Housewives (sittat al bayt), 110; status
of, 112, 115, 165–166. *See also* Domestic
work
Housework. *See* Domestic work
Housing, 24, 37–39, 203; and informal
neighborhoods, 39; key money, 68;
renovation, 24, 38, 183, 203; shortage
of, 41; and status, 37–38; unsafe, 38, 39;
and young families, 41, 202–203
Hunt, Pauline, 158

Illiteracy, 36–37
Income, 15, 18. *See* Money management
Infibulation. *See* Circumcision
Infitah, 46–47
Informal sector employment, 7, 89, 91,
93, 126–130; casual workers and, 92–
93; definition of, 88–89; and domestic
responsibilities, 174, 178–179, 269–270;
men's, 89–93; older workers and, 91–
92; overlapping with formal sector, 89–
90, 102, 115; and status, 84–85, 87, 113–
114; wages in, 89–91; women's, 113,

— Bring Hunter S. Thompson books
→ The Electric Kool-Aid Acid tests
— Planet Earth DVD
— Kenya books
— big maps of the world